To Pat:-
with appreciation
[signature]
Aug. '7[?]

The Honorable Mr. Marigold

Books by Norma Lee Browning

THE HONORABLE MR. MARIGOLD
THE PSYCHIC WORLD OF PETER HURKOS
THE OTHER SIDE OF THE MIND (with W. Clement Stone)
JOE MADDY OF INTERLOCHEN
CITY GIRL IN THE COUNTRY

The Honorable Mr. Marigold

My Life with Everett Dirksen
by Louella Dirksen
with Norma Lee Browning

Doubleday & Company, Inc., Garden City, New York, 1972

GRATEFUL ACKNOWLEDGMENT IS GIVEN TO THE FOLLOWING FOR PERMISSION
TO REPRINT:

Excerpt from an article appearing in June 9, 1951, edition of the Washington
Post by Jack Anderson. Used by permission of Jack Anderson.

Danny Boy by F. E. Weatherly. Copyright 1913 by Boosey and Company.
Renewed 1944. Used by permission of Boosey and Hawkes.

Gallant Men, words by Charles Wood and music by John Cacavas. Copyright © 1965 and 1966 by Chappel & Co., Inc. Used by permission of Chappel & Co., Inc.

"Dirksen's Look Back at 40 Happy Wedded Years," December 4, 1967. Reprinted, courtesy of the Chicago Tribune.

"I Nominate the Marigold" by Everett M. Dirksen. Copyright 1968 by The
National Wildlife Federation. Reprinted from December-January issue of
National Wildlife magazine.

From the book The Complete Bean Cookbook by Victor Bennett. Copyright
© 1967 by Victor Bennett. Published by Prentice-Hall, Inc., Englewood
Cliffs, New Jersey.

"What a Joy to Spend One Hour With Ev," January 1968, by Rick Du
Brow and "A Man of Wavering Loyalty?" September 17, 1967, by Dick
West. Reprinted by permission of United Press International.

FOR DAREK DIRKSEN BAKER
and
CYNTHIA BAKER
Everett's favorite little marigolds

PREFACE

This is a book of memories, my memories of 45 years with Everett Dirksen. It is a love story and at the same time, a personal look at the myriad important political events which took place during my husband's long and colorful career, which spanned the administrations of six Presidents.

This book is not intended as an analysis of Everett Dirksen's position as a legislator and statesman. I leave that to future political historians.

At the risk of seeming immodest, I must say that no one else could have written this book. I am proud to share these personal memories and hope that readers of all ages will find some inspiration—as I did—in the deeds, philosophy, and words of the senator. I have deliberately included and leaned heavily on Everett's own words because it would have been presumptuous to think I could ever express certain thoughts better than he. I have also borrowed from eulogies to him and articles about him to present a spectrum of opinions on Everett Dirksen as a man and as a politician.

Here then, in these pages, is the way I remember my husband.

ACKNOWLEDGMENTS

Many people have contributed richly to the writing of this book and we wish to thank them for their collective generosity. But we would like to single out some whose valuable information, advice, and encouragement made this book possible.

First and foremost is the senator's mother-in-law, Mrs. Lillie Carver, who in her ninety-sixth year astonished us with her total recall of certain early events in Everett's life. We are especially indebted to W. Clement Stone and Dr. and Mrs. Ralph Kunstadter, the senator's long-time friends and supporters, who initiated the whole enterprise by bringing us together and giving us the inspiration to write this book.

We wish to acknowledge our debt to Glee Gomien, the senator's secretary, and to Harold Rainville, the senator's campaign manager, whose personal recollections of political campaigns and of events in Washington proved invaluable. And for the stimulus in helping the senator's wife recall events outside the political sphere, special thanks to Mrs. W. C. Naegel, who gave most generously of her time.

We are grateful to Professor Keith Berwick, Department of History, the Claremont Colleges, who read the entire manuscript and offered many helpful suggestions. For research on many specific facts and for help in preparation of the manuscript, we wish to thank Vera Servi, Pam Gallagher, and Jean Lewis. Also thanks to Patti White for her secretarial assistance. And last but not least, our thanks to Patrick Wilson, Chicago *Tribune* Library, and Romeo Carraro, Los Angeles Times Library, who were never too busy to check facts and dates for accuracy; and to Roy Preston who writes the "Old Timer" column for the Pekin *Times* and who provided us with valuable dates and facts regarding the settling of Pekin and the Centennial.

CONTENTS

The Honorable Mr. Marigold

PART I

MY MARIGOLD MAN

The marigold will flourish on soil not blessed with fertility. It marches through spring, summer, and autumn until the frost of early winter takes its toll . . . robust, rugged, bright, stately, single-colored, and multicolored, somehow able to resist the onslaughts of insects . . . What a flower the marigold is . . . It is as sprightly as the daffodil, as colorful as the rose, as resolute as the zinnia, as delicate as the carnation, as haughty as the chrysanthemum, as aggressive as the petunia, as ubiquitous as the violet, as stately as the snapdragon. It beguiles the senses and ennobles the spirit of man . . .

Everett McKinley Dirksen
(From a speech on the Senate floor)

A SENATOR'S NOTEBOOK

(By Everett McKinley Dirksen)

Long ago, the poet Shelley wrote, "O, Wind, if Winter comes, can Spring be far behind?"

It takes a careless spirit to write that, and today, in all the turmoil of our world, we would do well to take some moments to dream of careless things—like spring and marigolds and other flowers that soon will come.

It is March. I look out the window and it is snowing, a wet kind of snow that clings to the branches like cotton and magnifies the appearance of winter. But I don't care, because on the desk before me is a chart of my garden and beside it are some seed catalogs—a feast for the eyes and the soul, too.

I wouldn't care at all about the bluster and cold of winter if I could only get results in my garden that would be something like the beauties painted by the seed catalog artist.

Now I begin to think about my garden to come as I turn the pages of the catalog. First, I look out to a shady spot that gets little sun. It's a place for blue ageratum and impatiens because they do so well in full shade, and what a color combination they will be.

The humble nasturtium grows almost anywhere with half a chance—now a showy creation, but as cut flowers nasturtiums are a comfort indeed.

Now to the tulips, those dark red, stately soldiers of the garden who defy the elements and come nosing out of the soil almost as soon as nature relents with the balmy breezes and the warm sun. How good it is that tulips come so early.

The daffodil and narcissus are not far behind. They can pop

their gorgeous yellows before I expect it, and they are a joyous note in early spring.

Now I must leave the catalogs for a few moments to think of some other things in the garden. It's time to prune back the tea roses, cut away the dead wood and make ready for the grandeur of the roses in all their colors. Is there anything more beautiful than the rose?

Where do we put the snapdragons that will stand like gorgeous sentinels against the roughest of weather and the bugs? The garden closest to the roadway is best, where every passer-by can enjoy them. And snapdragons are exquisite as cut flowers for all occasions.

The zinnias must have full sun. Somehow, more than any other flower, the zinnias seem to drink the bright sunlight and the heat and then are transformed into deep, majestic colors—peach, salmon, deep red, yellow, ivory—with huge, many-petaled heads. But the zinnias should have some edging. The petunia is just the dish—singles and doubles, plain blue, white, crimson, peppermint-stick, candy-stripe in vast variety. How hardy they are and how determined not to be outdone.

Now a momentary detour to look at the climbing roses. They wintered well, but they must be tied up. What a rare diversion that will be after a day that has tried the soul and tired the mind.

Now here are the clematis, both regular and hybrid. How dead they seem. But wait a little while and suddenly they'll be there in the warming days in their red, white, and blue. All this and much more with the resurrection of spring.

Could the Resurrection have come in any season but spring? It makes me think of the question that Job in all his misery propounded to his friends: "If a man die, shall he live again?" He will, surely, for the earth becomes vital all over again with spring.

Most important of all, I must not forget the marigold. For ten years I have sought to persuade the Congress to adopt the marigold as our national floral emblem. Some prefer the rose (a shrub) or the carnation or the petunia, violet, daffodil, or some other bloom. But the marigold is native to this hemisphere and grows in every one of the fifty states, evidence of a robustness against the elements or insects that is unequaled in performance by any other flower.

Let kings and emperors, Presidents and senators suffer highly important matters to furrow their brows. There must be a little time to draw back and think just about the noblest creations from the hand of a generous Creator—the endless variety of flowers.

Was it not the Galilean who said, "Consider the lilies of the field, how they grow; they toil not, neither do they spin; And yet I say unto you, that even Solomon in all his glory was not arrayed like one of these?"

And the flowers are there—for every man, woman, and child, —for the asking.

(From the Congressional Record, March 26, 1969 . . . Only six months before the senator's death on September 7, 1969)

Chapter 1

Flower Child

How do I find words to tell the story of forty-two years with the man I married?

Especially when that man's name was Everett McKinley Dirksen.

My sun rose and set in him.

He was *sui generis*, one of a kind, and there were times, the lonely times, when I lived only in his shadow, when he seemed to belong more to everyone else than to me. But there were the sweet times, too. Looking back now, I would say it was a sweet life, even in the rough times.

I was his sounding board. He was my idol.

Ours was an old-fashioned love story, for my husband was basically an old-fashioned man who awakened me every morning of our married life—when he was not off somewhere campaigning —by gently rubbing a warm wet washcloth across my face. That was his way of telling me it was time to get up and prepare his breakfast. And there would always be a flower, one flower only, on the breakfast table, a single rosebud, or a petunia, or a marigold . . .

This man belongs to history. But for a little while part of him also belonged to me.

Now that he is gone and that part of my life I shared with him is empty, now that I find time to remember the joys, the sorrows, and the sweetness of our life together—what do I say?

What is there left to say about a man named Everett McKinley Dirksen?

Others have already said it: "One of the great ones is gone."

How do I remember him? That is like Elizabeth Barrett Browning asking, "How do I love thee? Let me count the ways."

Some will remember my husband as the tousle-haired, homespun Senior Senator from Illinois, a man of remarkable oratorical ability and innate showmanship. Many will remember him as one of the greatest patriots of his time, who placed his country second only to God. I believe anyone who knew my husband well would readily attest that he loved his God first, next his country, and then his family and the Republican party. The ranking position of those last two was frequently in doubt.

I specifically recall, for example, an important dinner party I gave but which the senator missed because he was detained by a very important and high-ranking Democrat—*not* a Republican— namely none other than President Lyndon B. Johnson. My husband had known Lyndon Johnson from their earliest years together in Washington, and their friendship continued after Mr. Johnson became President. He often called Everett to come over to the White House to meet with him at the end of his working day. On this particular day, Everett called to tell me that the President wanted him at the White House for "a little session." But he assured me that he would be home in time to greet our dinner guests.

We waited dinner as long as possible, and were halfway through dessert when the phone rang again. This time it was the telephone operator at the White House, calling to say that Everett and the President were still busy but that he would come home as soon as he could. She called back several times later with the same message, and the last time she called, our guests were just leaving to go home.

I must admit I was a bit piqued. I left some food on the table for my husband and went to bed. I did not hear him come in. But I did awaken sometime in the middle of the night, as I often do, and went out to the kitchen. There on the table was a large brown paper bag with an assortment of initialed LBJ trinkets and souvenirs—a watch, a pen, an ashtray and cigarette lighter, an electric shaver, a little paperweight with a bird on it (for Lady

Bird), and a lovely color photograph of the whole family, the President and Lady Bird, Luci and Lynda, autographed by the President especially for me.

The next morning my husband rather sheepishly presented the bag of goodies to me as a domestic peace token from the President for spoiling my dinner party. Everett explained that he had started to leave five or six times but before he could get to the door, the President would have another idea, and he would say, "Now, Ev, just another minute or two . . ." (With his Texas informality, President Johnson was one of the few who called my husband Ev, instead of Everett.) And each time the President asked Everett to stay longer, he would also summon one of his aides and say, "Bring me one of those watches" . . . or "one of those pens" . . . and he would give them to Everett to bring home to me. I still have them in my trophy cabinet. Each one has the initials LBJ imprinted on it somewhere. I suppose that has something to do with ego. President Johnson's fetish for the L.B.J. initials was well known.

Many will remember my husband as the "Mr. Republican" in a predominantly Democratic political era. Many will remember his leadership in troubled times. I believe history will record that it was my husband, Everett Dirksen, who in a sense symbolized what is great about the U. S. Senate, through his total commitment and dedication to his country, and a leadership that rose above partisan politics. I believe history will record that without Everett Dirksen, President John F. Kennedy would not have had the nuclear test ban treaty which is regarded as his tallest monument; and President Johnson would not have had the civil rights legislation which many people consider his greatest contribution to the nation.

But that is all for the history books.

How does a widow convey the charisma of a man like Everett McKinley Dirksen?

—A man whose Ciceronian rhetoric and rumpled hair made him a favorite of political cartoonists . . .

—A man who had a hand in shaping so many important laws that affect our lives today and yet did it with a dash of theatrics unique on the national Capitol scene . . .

—A man who was fiercely patriotic, who had no use for draft card burners or anti-war protesters . . .

—A man who was deeply religious, who found time each day for meditation and prayer . . .

—A man who never became President but whose impact and influence on the nation was greater than that of many Presidents in our history.

I believe my husband would have made a great President, but he was grateful for the position he had achieved from his humble beginnings, for the affection and respect of his fellow senators, and the admiration of the American people.

As the one who knew him better than anyone else, I can say with pride that Everett Dirksen was a great American; and with sorrow, that he died without fulfilling two of his greatest dreams —to have prayer restored in the public schools and to have the marigold made America's national flower.

Somehow, these two things were so closely entwined with our personal life together, the joys and sorrows we shared, our own religious beliefs and faith in God's creations, and my husband's deep and abiding love of nature, that when I remember him now it is always in his garden with his marigolds.

For me, it is almost impossible to remember him otherwise, for even as I write this, I am looking out upon the gardens he created and loved, gardens that are as glorious and eloquent in their beauty as were the words he sometimes used to describe them. On the river side there are the hanging baskets of begonias, the rows of red geraniums and petunias and zinnias and dahlias. Beyond the vast sea of flowers is the vegetable garden, and on down toward the Potomac a sun-dappled forest of incredible beauty which brings back a flood of memories . . .

On the front side of our house is a vast expanse of lawn and gardens stretching out to the road, renamed Marigold Lane, with a long archway of stately locust trees and the lovely weeping willows we planted fifteen years ago—they are now breathtakingly beautiful. And over here is the rose garden he loved, and over there the lily beds and the chrysanthemums . . . the fruit trees and shrubbery we planted . . . and always, everywhere, his beloved marigolds.

In perfect symmetry on our front lawn, on either side of the weeping willows, are two enormous circular marigold beds. In the center of one stands a two-story-high pole with a magnificent white martin house mounted on top, one of the largest of our bird dormitories. In the other marigold bed standing tall and straight toward the sky is another pole, a flagpole with a magnificent red, white, and blue American flag proudly waving from it.

When he was here, my husband and I would go out of a morning to the marigold bed and raise the flag together. Now I do it alone. It is a big flag, the largest one I have seen for a private residence. But my husband was unashamedly proud of it, as am I also.

The marigolds in this bed are very special ones. They were developed by David Burpee especially for my husband, and named for him—the Dirksen Marigold. They grow tall and big and golden yellow. Our gardener Paul Jackson lovingly cares for the flowers and trees and each year the flag marigold garden seems more beautiful.

Let others remember my husband as a great political orator, a leader of men, but if I may be permitted a touch of sentimentality, to me he will always be my marigold man—Mr. Marigold.

He loved America. His patriotism was manifested in many ways, but perhaps no more clearly than in his constant struggle to make the marigold the national flower, and in planting the American flag in his own marigold garden.

The marigold, he told the Senate, has a "rugged humility of character; and, like the American eagle and the American flag, is an exclusively American emblem." This is also, I think, a rather apt description of himself.

My husband spent ten years trying to get a bill passed to make the marigold the national flower. And of course the issue brightened the copy of many a political reporter. Even the staid New York *Times* carried a page one story about a man in Minnesota who ripped out all the marigolds from his garden when he read that my husband had nominated Barry Goldwater as the presidential candidate at the 1964 Republican convention in San Francisco.

I remember my husband on a sunny spring day in Washington when he had been invited to plant the first marigolds in the inner courtyard of the Old Senate Office Building in 1967. It was part of a beautification project, and the planting ceremonies attracted a number of tourists, as well as the press and television cameras to cover the event.

Everett was introduced with the words, "We are happy to have our marigold man with us today." Then "gardener" Dirksen raised his trowel, and declared, "I am in ecstasy over this . . . You can't beat a marigold . . . It has humility, it has pungency, and it is resistant to man and bug and beast . . ." He was enjoying every minute of it. And so was the press, who duly reported that another senator was overheard to say, "I'm a petunia man myself." Senator George Murphy privately told a reporter that "the marigold could never replace the red geranium in California."

I remember my husband on a very special occasion as we rode in a rose-bedecked car in the New Year's Day Rose Bowl Parade in Pasadena, on January 1, 1968. Everett had been invited to serve as Grand Marshal of the 79th Tournament of Roses . . . A Marigold Man leading the Rose Bowl Parade! Heavens! What a marigolden bowl of rosy journalese that inspired. It was all delightfully distilled by Washington UPI columnist Dick West in a column of September 17, 1967 entitled, "A Man of Wavering Loyalty?"

I'm not accusing Senator Everett McKinley Dirksen of perfidy, you understand, yet he gives every appearance of being a man of wavering loyalty. How else can one interpret the fact that Dirksen this very week accepted an invitation to serve as Grand Marshal of the 79th annual Tournament of Roses Parade in Pasadena, California? The news of Dirksen's appointment hit the city like a thunderbolt for he is known throughout this city and in much of the country at large as the marigold's best friend. For as many years as modern man can remember, the marigold has been a candidate for the national flower, and in each of those years it was Dirksen who made the nominating speech. To fully appreciate the exquisite irony of the situation, you must realize that the marigold's chief rival has been the rose. Indeed many public opinion polls show the rose leading the marigold. In the opinion of impartial observers here, only Dirksen's considerable influence as Senate Republican leader has prevented Congress from designating the rose as the official national floral emblem. These observers are now predicting that the Illinois Senator's appearance as honorary leader of the Rose Bowl Parade will be enough to tip the scales in the rose's favor.

Dirksen's action doesn't mean he has turned his back on the marigold. Nevertheless it is obvious that his effectiveness as the marigold's chief spokesman in Congress has been severely compromised. His sonorous senatorial tributes of the marigold are heard by only a few colleagues but millions will see his splendiferous televised ride at the head of the Rose Bowl Parade—and in living color yet. Few deliberately calculated developments could do more to undermine the cause of the marigold. Needless to say, this turn of events has left the marigold lobby badly shaken. One marigold partisan with whom I discussed the matter voices suspicion that Dirksen has been brainwashed with rose water. "This is definitely an escalation of the flower war," he commented bitterly. There is talk that his side might retaliate by sponsoring yet another New Year's Day football game called the Marigold Bowl. Whether Dirksen should be in the Rose Bowl Parade is open to argument, but demands that he withdraw are useless. After all, a commitment is a commitment is a commitment . . .

We were both amused by Dick West's column, but let me amplify on this. My husband took very good care of the marigold at the Rose Bowl Parade—such good care, in fact, that some of the Rose Bowl promoters were not terribly happy about all the attention the marigold received, unexpectedly.

You see, there had been a bit of a cold spell in Southern California that year. The roses had done well but the garden flowers had suffered some, and there were not all that many marigolds to make a float for the parade.

But there were enough of them so that people could make little hand bouquets from the flowers in their gardens, and that is exactly what they did. And as the Rose Parade rolled down the street, hundreds of people rushed out from the crowd clutching and waving their little bunches of marigolds, and tossing them to us in our rose-bedecked car. My husband was so excited and delighted that he stood up in the car, waving the little bouquets of marigolds and tossing them back into the crowd. This flower-throwing generated great hilarity and enthusiasm, and later, the people who ran the Rose Bowl Parade said that Senator Everett Dirksen drew more spontaneous acclaim from the crowd than any Grand Marshal they ever had. But the driver of our car, who was a member of the Tournament of Roses committee, was obviously piqued at all the attention his Grand Marshal was getting with his marigolds. He seemed not quite sure that the rose was holding its own in the Rose Bowl Parade, even though our car was enwrapped in roses. We heard a few rumbles later that the Tournament of Roses committee was somewhat disgruntled because their roses were "sabotaged" by the marigolds. But that was probably only more "journalese."

Behind the lighthearted façade of the marigold issue, and the colorful verbal clashes that sometimes enlivened those dreadfully dull and prolonged Senate sessions, my husband was a very serious and dedicated man in his crusade to get his marigold bill passed. But it created quite a controversy because all the other senators wanted to make their own state flower the national flower.

Margaret Chase Smith, Maine's Republican senator, who always wears a rose in a tiny flask on her lapel, naturally favored the rose as the national flower. Senator Albert Gore of Tennessee wanted the iris. Senator Gordon Allott of Colorado introduced a bill to make the carnation our national flower, because carnations grow profusely in his home state. At one point someone even suggested the dandelion as our national flower, and then there was my husband's Democratic colleague from Illinois, Senator Paul Douglas, who introduced a bill to make the corn tassel our national flower. Corn is native to our state, of course, and is the basis for the livelihood of many families in Illinois. Everett always kept three ears of seed corn displayed like a coat of arms in his Senate office in Washington. Personally, he loved the little brown corn tassels of Illinois—but as a national emblem? Ridiculous, he would argue with great passion. The corn tassel could not compare with the beauty of the marigold.

In debating the merits of the marigold my husband became

quite knowledgeable on the subject. He also became a close personal friend of David Burpee, who was associated with the W. Atlee Burpee Growers Company in Philadelphia.

Mr. Burpee always sent him a big florist's box with a dozen of his biggest marigolds, as the first flowers of spring. Some were as big as soup bowls. And between Mr. Burpee and the encyclopedia, my husband learned a great deal about marigolds, as for instance . . . the American marigold is often called the "Friendship Flower" because it is one of the most popular annuals. It is a native of southwest United States and Mexico. Cortez found it growing in the botanical gardens of the Aztec Indians in 1518.

The Aztecs grew marigolds for their beauty and because they were thought to have medicinal value. Marigold seeds were among the gifts that the Aztec chief, Montezuma, sent to Emperor Charles V of Spain. This was the marigold's introduction into Europe. Its botanical name is *Tagetes erecta*. But according to plant lore, monks and nuns called them "Mary's Gold" when they dedicated the golden flowers to the Virgin Mary. And from this came the common name, "Marigold."

One of my most cherished and vivid memories is of my husband poring over Burpee's seed catalogs. He could not wait for spring. He was so restless and impatient. While the snow was still on the ground he would write to David Burpee and order packets of seeds in great quantities, everything from little green beans, wax beans, and kale, to the most beautiful flowers he could find in the catalog.

Looking back now, I believe one reason his flowers meant so much to him is that they brought happiness and color and contentment into his life. His boyhood was drably devoid of these things.

Many times my husband's secretary, Glee Gomien, would call to say that the senator would be late but he was on his way home. "We've been ordering from the seed catalog," she would say. And we would both laugh about it. There was nothing else we could do. There would still be snow on the ground, but there was my husband all absorbed in the seed catalog, ordering his seeds and plants, some new shrubbery or fruit trees . . . We always knew—if the senator was ordering his seeds, could spring be far behind?

I am sure that ordering from the seed catalog when the snow was on the ground did indeed give my husband the feel that spring was on the way.

But there was more to it than that. Somehow the seed catalog seemed to act as a tranquilizer. He had so little time for any hobby. But when pressures were greatest, he would pull a seed catalog out of a mountain of urgent work and proceed to order from it to his heart's content, and when he finished filling out his order, then he could go on to other work.

I think he must have been the original "flower child." He could make anything grow. He had a loving way with flowers and they reciprocated by blooming big and beautiful for him . . .

In the early years, especially, he liked to do all his own gardening without help from anyone, although occasionally he would grudgingly let me help him with the planting. I remember one spring day when I was trying to help him and he said, "Look, you have to talk to these little plants as you put 'em in." So, just in a fit of humor, I said, "Grow, darn you, grow!"

He was quite indignant, and he scolded me, "That isn't the way you're supposed to talk to plants—any plants. You're supposed to be gentle with them."

My husband was always gentle with them and he would talk softly and tell them they were little works of nature and God, and now would they please grow? And they always did.

Occasionally it might be misconstrued that I played second fiddle to my husband's marigolds and his birds. There was the time a few years ago, for example, when he heard about some threats on his life, and he told police: "Look, I don't want my head blown off. I've got flowers in bloom and they need me. I've got 65 birdhouses now and the birds need me. [Not a word about his wife needing him.] Whoever this creature is [the alleged assassin-to-be] why doesn't he wait until the frost has slashed at the flowers and the birds have gone south? . . ."

Yes, my husband's impassioned plea for the marigold provided a great amount of mirth and laughter during times when these simple ingredients were sorely missing from all our lives. He could describe his gardens with each plant and each flower, making an artist's picture unfold before his listeners' eyes. His mellifluous voice was like a tonic in extolling the virtues of the marigold. It enlivened and brightened the political landscape, which all too often seems to lack a sense of humor. But beneath the bucolic warmth and humor of it all, my husband's gardens were a projection of his religious philosophy based on Job's question, "If a man die, shall he live again?"

My husband very definitely believed in the affirmative, and for him each year his marigold reaffirmed his faith in the living immortality of all that God created.

I was deeply touched when I learned that on the day of the memorial services for my husband in Washington, a single marigold lay on his desk in the Senate chamber. It was put there by Senator Margaret Chase Smith, who had opposed my husband's marigold motion by proposing the rose as our national flower. But she had gone to the chamber and placed that lone flower on his desk, saying, "He loved his marigolds."

Mrs. Smith told me later that she had received many letters urging her to take Everett's place in carrying the banner for the marigold. "I am honored that some would think I could take his place in this crusade," she said. "But I know he would not have me desert the rose any more than I would have him desert the marigold."

How do I remember my husband? Let me count the ways. But I remember him best in his garden, hands clasped, head bowed in quiet meditation at the end of a long day's work, beside a small gray marker engraved with his credo:

> *The kiss of the sun for pardon,*
> *The song of the birds for mirth,*
> *One is nearer God's heart in a garden*
> *Than anywhere else on earth.*

(INTRO FOR PRINCESS OF PEKIN)

Sing Loo: My Cherry Blossom, look you yonder. The sun rises like a fiery ball to bathe the world in splendor. But one rival has he for splendor, and that is my Pan Toy . . . Know you, my Blossom, what the lover calls his love here in America?

Pan Toy: I yearn to know, august and exalted lover.

Sing Loo: They say "sweetheart" . . . And do you know what the lover expects from his love in that golden moment when they are betrothed?

Pan Toy: I do not know.

Sing Loo: Shall I show you?

Pan Toy: Is it dangerous?

From a play, *Chinese Love.*
Written by Everett McKinley Dirksen

Chapter 2

Princess of Pekin

I might as well go back to the beginning.

On the twenty-seventh day of March in Pekin, Illinois, the last year of the century, a baby girl was born to Alfred Dare Carver and Lillie Bruder Carver. There were twenty-seven inches of snow on the gound. It was nine o'clock in the morning when they decided that Alfred should go for the doctor. He put on his hip boots and started sloshing down the street through the drifts of snow. There were no sidewalks or pavement in those days. Alfred returned with the doctor sometime later in the doctor's horse and buggy carriage. They put a little sack of oats around the horse's neck, covered him with a blanket and came into the house. The doctor had received his medical education and training in Germany. He had learned to use forceps, something which our doctors in Pekin knew nothing about. Lillie kept getting weaker and at nine o'clock that night the doctor laid out his instruments and took the baby. He announced that the baby and mother were fine, but there could be no more children in the family.

Only later did my parents learn that the doctor's practical experience with the forceps was limited. He had delivered only two other instrument babies, and both had died. I have always believed it was God's will for me to live so that I would meet Everett McKinley Dirksen.

My parents spent two days trying to decide on a name for me, and finally settled for one inspired by an incident on the Pekin wagon bridge.

They always went for Sunday afternoon walks across the bridge, and on a recent Sunday they had overheard a woman calling to her child, "Louella, don't get too near to the edge of the bridge." I am sure a psychiatrist would find some hidden meaning in that, but my parents always insisted that they just liked the ring of the name Louella, and they did not think it needed a middle name. So the baby's name was Louella Carver.

As a child and in my high school years I never liked the name Louella. I had a fancy to be called Millicent or Constance or Abigail or something more romantic. Strangely enough I think my husband never liked the name either because he never called me Louella. When our Joy was a little girl he usually called me Mother. His favorite pet name for me was Toots—always in private, of course. But to our friends and the public I was always Mrs. D. I was not unhappy with this. It gave me a warm feeling to be called Mrs. D. and I always called him Everett, never Ev. Only those who wanted others to think they knew him that well called him Ev. But those who did know him well knew that he preferred Everett.

I was a shy but happy child. My father brought home a weekly paycheck and mother supplemented it with money she earned from dressmaking. She sewed beautifully and many Pekin ladies were proud to have clothes made by Lillie Carver, including their wedding dresses. There was always enough material left over for her to make something for me, and I had some of the prettiest clothes that any girl could wish for. Mother was always a very serious person and concerned about where our next meal would come from, especially after my father became ill.

We were never really hard pressed for money, though. Money values were different then, and I do not recall that my father ever brought home more than $25 a week, even at the peak of his business. He worked with his uncle in a wholesale cigar store, and carried on the business after his uncle passed away. When my father was no longer able to carry on in the wholesale tobacco company due to his health, he became a bookkeeper in our local drygoods store.

My father was a very happy, delightful man. I like to think I may have inherited some of his happy disposition; and most of my childhood memories are happy ones. I have always been especially happy on holidays because as a child my memories of holidays were always happy, especially at Eastertime and Christmas.

I recall vividly those wonderful Easter mornings. There would be a knock on my bedroom window, and my daddy would say, "The bunny rabbit has been here," and regardless of whether our yard was early spring grass green or still covered with snow, I would find those beautifully colored eggs that Mother and Daddy had sat up late coloring on Saturday night after I had gone to sleep.

My father was an original Mr. Five-by-Five and made an authentic-looking and delightful Santa Claus. It was years before I realized that Santa Claus was a myth because Santa Claus always came to our house and to all the neighbors. One of the reasons I wanted to be married on Christmas Eve was that I had such happy memories of this Holy Day from my childhood. Although both Christmas and Easter were holidays filled with joy for a child, my parents never let me forget that they were Holy Days. My religious upbringing turned out to be a valuable preparation for marriage with Everett McKinley Dirksen.

My father was in and out of the hospital during my high school years but I do not recall his ever being sad. He always kept his happy disposition. We moved in with my grandmother Carver so that she could help Mother take care of Daddy.

I went to Normal University at Normal, Illinois, for two years, planning to be a public school music teacher. But when my father died, I left school and took a job as a comptometer operator.

We were the forerunners of computers, and I became quite adept at operating a comptometer. For a while I was an instructor in a comptometry school. Then I went to work for a wholesale grocery store in Peoria for the magnificent sum of $25 a week —as much as my father had earned—which was quite sufficient to take care of Mother and me, including my expenses for commuting back and forth by train between Pekin and Peoria, a distance of ten miles.

It was about this time that my personality changed, and I have always secretly felt that it was due to a little change in my name which was a slight shock to all of us. For some reason which I cannot now recall I was required to produce a birth certificate. When I went to the County Clerk's office for this vital document, I learned for the first time that my name was spelled Louella—and not Luella, as we had been spelling it.

Well, don't the seers tell you that if you want to change your personality, you must first change your name?

With the addition of only one letter my personality began to change. I started to blossom out, so to speak. I had been dating a boy in Peoria who once a week brought me a box of Dutch black chocolates. I only weighed 105 pounds in those days, and Mother and I thoroughly enjoyed the chocolates.

But then I acquired a new beau, who was to change the course of my life. He was a Pekin boy and his name was Hubert Ropp. He was an artist and he also wrote and directed local plays on the side. But what impressed me most was his automobile. It was a bright red Jordan with white wire wheels. How could he afford such a flashy car? Well, cars were not too expensive in those days (1924). It probably cost all of $350. And Hubert came from a family of wealthy farmers. How proud I was to be met at the Pekin railroad station each night by a handsome young man in a white-wire-wheeled red Jordan! No wonder my personality began changing.

I enrolled in some night courses in music at Bradley University in Peoria and became a member of the chorus. To my delight, I was chosen to play Pitti Sing, one of the Three Little Maids in the famous Gilbert and Sullivan operetta, *The Mikado*. But I learned that it would require some afternoon rehearsals, which would fall during my working hours.

When I asked my boss if I could be relieved for rehearsals, it didn't go over too well with him. "Would you rather sing or hold down a job?" he asked.

My new personality asserted itself, and I replied, "I'd rather sing." Whereupon I picked up my little pocketbook and out of the door I went.

We put on *The Mikado* and it was delightful.

Within a week I had another job in a department store in Peoria. I was head bookkeeper in charge of sales and credits and I thoroughly enjoyed each working day. There was also an extra dividend—we received a discount on all our purchases.

And my beau with the big red Jordan still came to the train to meet me every evening when I came home from work.

Then one wintry evening in February 1924 he brought another young man with him. This one was tall and gawky with a lot of tousled hair that hung down like a mop over his forehead. He was smoking a smelly pipe and he looked a little rumpled in his ill-fitting clothes.

As I descended from the train in grand style, I overheard Hubert saying to him, "There she is . . . She's going to be our Princess."

His friend only had time to ask, "Who is she?" and then Hubert introduced us. His name was Everett McKinley Dirksen. I must say I was terribly unimpressed.

It wasn't that I had any serious feelings toward Hubert. I think I was much more impressed with his car than with him. But he *was* my boyfriend at the time and I don't think anyone could have budged me from that big red Jordan. Certainly not Everett McKinley Dirksen.

We piled into Hubert's car and they filled me in on the details. It turned out that this gangling, bushy-haired boy with the big name was Hubert's best friend and sort of a home-town hero from the First World War, having served seventeen months overseas.

They told me they were planning to put on a play celebrating the Pekin Centennial on July 2, 1924. The name of the play was A *Thousand Years Ago* and the setting was Peking, China.

It required a Prince and a Princess.

The Prince was to be that bushy-haired boy. They asked me if I would like to be his Princess.

I was almost twenty-four years old, an adult, but I replied, "I'll have to ask my mother."

The Dirksen name had suddenly rung a bell. In a flashback of memory I could hear my mother, always a prim and proper lady, complaining about "those Dirksen boys" in a tone that clearly implied heaven forbid she would ever have one of them in her house. I was vaguely aware that "those Dirksen boys" during my childhood were looked on—at least by my mother— as neighborhood rowdies, and that they lived in a section of town which was called "Beantown" because it was inhabited mainly by immigrant families who grew beans, instead of flowers.

In all fairness, I think I should clarify here that in spite of my wonderful mother's little prejudice against "those Dirksen boys," that description of "neighborhood rowdies" didn't really fit Everett Dirksen, as I was to learn later. The Dirksen boys were part of a gang that gathered under the street lamp after the supper dishes were done. Everett wasn't usually a part of the gang but when they wanted some devious trick mapped out they would call on him for help. On Halloween they would remove gates and tip over outhouses. In the summertime they would steal farmers' watermelons. If they were caught, Everett was always home studying. But the gang would tell how he had planned their attack.

"Those Dirksen boys" were older than I and ahead of me in school, and so I do not recall knowing any of them when I was a child, although my now ninety-six-year-old mother, whose memory is better than mine, tells me that Everett Dirksen was once a guest in our house. He came with a friend to a Valentine party when I was fifteen years old. She remembers it because she noticed that he was wearing only shoes, no socks, and his hair was not combed.

He must have made about the same impact on my mother as he did on me that fateful day in 1924 when he came with Hubert to the train station to meet me.

Frankly, it was hard to know Everett McKinley Dirksen when I first met him. He was shy. He was an introvert. He was not the least bit interested in girls. He was not very sociable. He was always expounding his ideas and quoting from the classics and flinging around those big words. His senior class album called it "Bigworditis." He always smoked that smelly pipe, and he always looked a little rumpled. I remember how Ben, his older brother, used to fuss about Everett borrowing his clothes. He would come home and grab up anything—Ben's coat or trousers—and away he would go. He cared so little about clothes. Even in later years he did not change this casual attitude about his appearance.

But now as I sat between Hubert and Everett in the big red Jordan, listening to their plans for the big Pekin Centennial, I was torn with indecision. It was indeed an honor for me to be chosen as the leading lady in a play that was to climax the

Pekin Centennial. But why had Hubert picked this man as the male lead? I did not know then that Everett Dirksen was a budding actor and that he and Hubert had written several plays together, most of them with Chinese themes. When Everett was young he was interested in the theater. From the time I met him, all his free time was devoted to some aspect of the theater. He and Hubert had begun collaborating on playwriting while they were in high school, and after Everett returned from service, they resumed where they had left off before the war. A *Thousand Years Ago* was not one of theirs. It was written by Percy MacKaye. But it did have the Chinese theme that they favored. The reason for this was that Pekin, Illinois, got its name from Peking, China.

The origin of the name and the town of Pekin, I think, is a rather fascinating one. Historical reference books generally give the date 1829 as the year when Pekin, Illinois, was founded. It is true that this was the year the town was named Pekin. But the first settlers moved into the area in 1824, and for lack of a better name they called the place simply Townsite. The Indians were kind to them and helped them build their houses on the banks of the Illinois River. The first log cabin was built by Jonathan Tharp in 1824, and this was the beginning of the small settlement of Townsite which started out with only five families.

But relatives and friends continued to join them and by 1829 there were enough settlers in the community that they decided they should have a more attractive name than Townsite for their little settlement.

There was an Army fort a few miles from Townsite, and the Army officers had become friendly with the early settlers. The commanding officer was a major by the name of Nathan Cromwell who had a very attractive wife with some knowledge of the world. So when the Townsite settlers could not agree on a new name for their town, they asked the major's beautiful wife to make the choice.

There are different versions of how she did it. One is that she took a map and traced her finger along between the 40th and 41st Parallels until she came to a name she liked. It was Peking, China. The other is that she stuck a hatpin through a world globe and it came out at Peking. In any case, the settlers liked the name. They decided to drop the "g" and call the town Pekin. They laid out the streets and sold lots—for twenty-eight cents apiece. They named the north-south streets numerically. First Street was the first one east of the Illinois River, then Second, Third, and so on.

The east-west streets were named for the wives and daughters of the first settlers. Consequently, Pekin has streets named Mary, Elizabeth, Anna, Eliza, Margaret, Catherine, and so on. The first settlers were English. The big influx of German immigrants started after the Civil War.

The townspeople of Pekin have always regarded the year 1824 as the date it was actually settled, with its original name of Townsite, and 1829 as the year of its change of name. That is why our Centennial was held in 1924, and not in 1929.

From the time it was named Pekin, it has called itself "the Celestial City," and though it was to become predominantly a German community in the heartland of America, it has always leaned heavily on Chinese themes in most of our community affairs. All of our parades always featured Chinese dragons and our high school football team was called the "Chinks."

During the preparation of this book I was told that "Chinks" is a word derogatory to the Chinese. It certainly was not so in Pekin, Illinois. I have asked several old-timers about the name "Chinks" and they were a bit startled to think it might be considered derogatory. We always used it as an affectionate fun-name, and each of our games was preceded by a big parade, the highlight of which was a long slinky dragon filled with a dozen or so little kids wiggling along inside a highly painted heavy cloth that formed the body and the tail of the dragon. It was the goal of every youngster in town to be chosen as one of the wigglers in the dragon in any Pekin parade. And the bystanders would shout with glee when the mouth of the dragon would spout fire.

Pekin is fond and proud of its Chinese heritage and its "Chinks." The "Chinks" have always been a great team and won many championships. Everett Dirksen had played center for the "Chinks" when he was in school . . . And we were about to play Prince and Princess in a play set in Peking, China . . .

My boyfriend Hubert felt that Everett Dirksen had a natural talent for the stage, and although I did not notice anything especially unusual about his voice then, Hubert assured me that his friend had a wonderful way of "projecting" his voice to an audience. He seemed overjoyed at the prospect of directing us together in the play.

He also seemed pleased with himself at choosing Everett for the Prince, the more so because of Everett's overseas war service. He had been a second lieutenant. The local boy just home from the wars is always a hero . . . at least he used to be.

The whole town was caught up in the fever and excitement of the big fair—the biggest ever—that Pekin was planning for its Centennial celebration.

My mother and I talked it over and in the end we agreed that my participation in the Pekin Centennial was far more important than any lingering first impression of "those Dirksen boys."

So arrangements were made for Louella Carver to be the Princess of Pekin. Everett McKinley Dirksen was the Prince.

And that is how it all began . . .

Almost immediately we went into rehearsal for the play. I was still working in Peoria and commuting by train. Hubert still came to meet me in his big red Jordan, and now more often than not Everett came with him. We rehearsed in the evening, two or three evenings a week. The play had quite a large cast, all local talent, and our rehearsals went on for a period of about two months to get everything right.

It used to be the custom in most small towns, after any social evening out, for a young man and his girlfriend to stop by the local ice-cream parlor. In Pekin, the place to stop in was Johannes's. At first it was Hubert and I who would stop at Johannes's, often taking Everett in with us. Then as the big day drew near and we speeded up our rehearsals—three evenings a week plus weekends—it was Everett who would ask me to stop at Johannes's with him and Hubert who more or less tagged along. Hubert had no role in the play, but he was our director. So there was always plenty of reason for the three of us to be together, plenty of details for us to discuss about the play.

But eventually it became just the two of us, Everett and Louella . . . We were drifting into a courtship . . .

Unlike our first meeting at the station, by now I had become quite smitten with Everett Dirksen. Not head over heels, mind you. But I was surprisingly impressed with his performance during rehearsals, although in no way was he ever trying deliberately to impress me. I began to find him much more attractive than I had thought he was when I first met him.

Paradoxical as it may seem now, in his youth Everett Dirksen was genuinely shy around girls. Many years later he was to become known as "the kissing senator," but he once publicly admitted that as a boy "I was frightened to death to even ask a girl for a date. I had to walk around the block a couple of times to get up the nerve."

Our romance developed during those summertime rehearsals and over the banana splits we had at Johannes's ice-cream parlor in Pekin.

In those days I was thin enough so that I could eat banana splits and chocolate sundaes and sodas with rare enjoyment.

The Big Day, July 2, 1924, finally came. Our Centennial was a great success. Every citizen who was able took part in it. In our parade we had the biggest dragon ever, spouting more fire than ever. And in the early evening we produced our play, A Thousand Years Ago, with its huge local cast. The setting was a natural bowl in the Pekin Park, with the audience sitting around on the hillside.

The theme song for our play was that hauntingly lovely old one, Song of Songs. It soon became our personal theme song and remained our theme song throughout our life together. That and Everett's beloved Danny Boy . . .

I must immodestly admit that Everett and I were a real hit as the Prince and Princess in A Thousand Years Ago. He played the role of a romantic lover panting after the charms of the Princess. He won her, of course—and little did anyone know then, lo those many years ago, that his "princess" would become his real-life bride on Christmas Eve of 1927.

Hubert Ropp and his white-wire-wheeled red Jordan gradually

faded out of my life, at least romantically. We have remained
friends through the years. He became a well-known artist and
in later years, until his retirement, he was curator of the
Chicago Art Institute. He is best known for his murals; among
the most beautiful are those in the railroad station in Cincinnati.

I cannot help but note the twist of fate and touch of irony
in the fact that it was Hubert Ropp, my first steady beau and
closest friend of Everett's during their boyhood in Pekin,
who many years later was commissioned to paint an official
portrait of my husband, which was presented to me in Chicago
soon after his death at a meeting of the Board of Directors of
the Everett McKinley Dirksen Research Center, now being
erected in Pekin. This portrait will hang in the foyer of the
research center. Hubert Ropp has painted into it his love for
Everett Dirksen.

Sometimes, after our banana splits and sodas, Everett and I
would walk from the ice-cream parlor over to my house singing
our *Song of Songs* together and then we would sit in the big
long old-fashioned wooden swing that hung from a maple tree
in our yard, and just talk. He was a very serious young man.
I recall how concerned he was about his future and I remember
his telling me so many times that the only thing he really
wanted to do, next to acting, was to "represent the people"—
in government. That was how he always put it—he wanted to
"represent the people."

I was quite at sea about the whole thing, I knew so little
about politics. But I would sit there and listen to him expound
by the hour because I could not help myself.

Even if I did not understand what he was talking about, his
voice seemed to mesmerize me. He was in such dead earnest
about wanting to "represent the people" that I found myself
wishing I could help him, whatever he wanted to do.

I think I was falling in love.

And he didn't even own an automobile, much less a white-
wheeled red Jordan!

DANNY BOY

(First verse)

Oh, Danny Boy,
the pipes, the pipes are calling
From Glen to Glen,
and down the mountain side,
The summer's gone,
and all the roses falling,
It's you, it's you must go and I must bide.
But come ye back
when summer's in the meadow,
Or when the valley's hushed and white with snow,
It's I'll be here
In sunshine or in shadow,
Oh, Danny Boy, oh Danny Boy, I love you so!

(Everett Dirksen's favorite song)

Chapter 3

Our Song of Songs

The other evening I took some friends to dinner at the Marriott Inn at Dulles Airport. The hostess seated us at a table near the piano, and the pianist, Jack White, smiled at me and remembered.

He began playing *Danny Boy*, the song which during all our years in Washington became almost synonymous with the Senior Senator from Illinois, Everett McKinley Dirksen. It was my husband's favorite song, and he sang it very well before his emphysema became so bad.

Any time we entered a room where a band or orchestra was playing, the conductor would immediately strike up *Danny Boy* for Everett. And he was never bashful about singing along with them. The truth is he always thoroughly enjoyed singing with an orchestra. On the Washington party circuit it is customary to engage small orchestras for the guests' entertainment, and all the orchestra leaders loved having us at these parties. They could always depend on Senator Everett Dirksen as one of their vocalists, perhaps sometimes to the embarrassment of a dignified host or hostess. But everyone else seemed to enjoy it.

Although Everett and I were never great partygoers, there were certain functions that we did attend and enjoyed. I liked the White House parties especially because the U. S. Marine Corps Orchestra in their handsome red uniforms usually played for them, and my husband was a great favorite with this orchestra.

No matter how formal the occasion, the conductor would always step down from the platform to shake hands with Everett and to lend him his baton.

And Everett would step up and direct a few bars, usually singing along at the same time, much to the delight and amazement of guests waiting in line to be introduced to the President and First Lady.

If the orchestra was near the end of a song, they would do a fade-out and then start *Danny Boy* for Everett.

I suppose nearly everyone in Washington knew that this was the senator's favorite song, but no one knew that it all started back there in Pekin, in our early courting years.

Our courtship was a rather prolonged one. We could not afford to get married. We went together nearly three years, and we had a regular Saturday night ritual. Instead of going out, he would come to our house for dinner—or supper as we called it in those days. His favorite Saturday-night supper was fried eggs and bacon. As soon as we finished supper we would repair to the living room, where we had a big pot-bellied stove and a beautiful black rosewood piano that my daddy had bought for me as a child. We spent our Saturday evenings together at the piano, singing. I would play the piano, and the two of us would sing. We sang all the old-time favorites and religious hymns and the patriotic songs that we found in old songbooks. We sang our romantic theme song, *Song of Songs* from *A Thousand Years Ago*, the play that had brought us together. And we sang Irish songs because Everett Dirksen, who was pure-bred German without a drop of Irish blood in his veins, loved Irish songs the best.

Everett would have made a fine Irishman and a great Irish tenor, or should I say an Irish basso profundo? He had a beautiful singing voice and could have become an opera singer if he had wished to do so.

We spent many happy times together at the piano, and we never said our goodbyes on Saturday night until after we had sung *Danny Boy*.

And then on Sunday morning he would sing in the Presbyterian church choir with me.

Throughout all our married life there was always a piano or

an organ in our home, and we always found time to use it and sing the songs we still carried in our hearts from Pekin.

Our courtship developed during a crucial period in Everett's life, when he was trying to tear himself away from his deep-down yearnings for the theater and chart a different course for his future.

I think I was good for him. I was blessed with a rather sunny disposition and a listening ear, so even then I was a good sounding board for him. I remember those treasured moments when we sat in the big wooden swing in my yard, and he talked—mostly about his future and what he must now do to earn a living.

It was only in little bits and pieces that he talked about his childhood, his youth.

His parents were old-country German immigrants who had settled in Pekin soon after the Civil War, in the growing colony of Deutschlanders. His mother, Antje Conrady, who spoke no English, had landed in this country in 1874 with a tag around her neck and instructions that she be sent to Pekin where she would be met by a brother, a farmer. She had married soon after her arrival here, but her first husband met an untimely death. She had two children from her first marriage, both now deceased.

Everett's father was Johann Frederick Dirksen, born in Jannailt, Ostfriesland, Germany, on February 9, 1842. He came to America in 1866, and became a fancy painter—or a wagon "striper," to use the colloquialism of the period. He worked for the Pekin Wagon Company and his job was to paint those fancy freehand stripes and curlicues on buggy wheels and on the sides of the carriages.

Both Antje and Johann Frederick Dirksen were devout church members, and in fact had met in church in Pekin. They discovered that they were from the same part of Germany, Jannailt, Ostfriesland, as was Antje's first husband, whose name, Ailts, was derived from his birthplace.

Everett's father was a scholar and a historian, a very learned man, and although I never knew him, I have always felt that he would have been very influential in the lives of his sons if he could have lived longer, or if he could have had his children when he was younger. He was fifty-four and Antje was forty-two when their twin boys, Everett and Tom, were born in 1896. Their first-born, Ben, was fourteen months older.

Everett's father had studied political philosophy and knew a great deal about American politics. He believed in being active in local and community affairs. He had been a member of the Pekin School Board.

More importantly, perhaps, from the standpoint of his influence on at least one of his sons, he had been an adamantly staunch Republican.

It was Everett's father, not his mother, who named their three sons for the three most prominent Republicans on the scene at that time:

Benjamin Harrison Dirksen, born November 16, 1894, named for the 23rd President, Benjamin Harrison (1889–93); the twins, Everett McKinley Dirksen and Thomas Reed Dirksen, born January 4, 1896. Everett was named for William McKinley, who was elected President in 1896, re-elected in 1900, and assassinated in 1901. (Vice-President Theodore Roosevelt succeeded him as President.)

The other twin was named for Thomas Reed, the Maine Republican, a long-time and perhaps the most powerful Speaker of the House in American history. He had been a member of Congress from 1877 to 1899, was chosen Speaker of the House in 1889 and again in 1895.

There is a story that Everett's father waited almost a year to name the twins—probably because they were born in January of an important election year, and he wanted to wait and see who won in November. William McKinley's Democratic opponent in 1896 was the great political orator William Jennings Bryan, who turned out to be a three-time loser in presidential races (1896, 1900, 1908) but paradoxically one of Everett's early idols as an orator.

It is interesting to speculate how all three Dirksen boys might have turned out if their father had lived longer. But he suffered a stroke and was confined to a wheelchair almost totally paralyzed for several years until he died on April 15, 1905. He was sixty-three years old. Ben was eleven, the twins nine.

They learned very early about the realities of life in "Bean-town"—or "Bohnchefiddle," to use the proper German name. The boys had to pitch in to help their mother keep the wolf from the door.

Antje Dirksen was apparently a very self-sufficient woman who made ends meet by using every inch of the acre and a half of ground around the family house as a vegetable garden.

They had several cows, chickens, and fifteen stands of bees. The bees were Everett's. They belonged to him, and they were his pride and joy. He told me on many occasions that he had read everything he could get his hands on about raising bees and cultivating honey, and he felt that he had some of the best honey anywhere in the area. People would come from some distance to buy the honey from his collection of bees.

Even as a youngster still in grade school Everett had to work hard. He arose at dawn to milk the cows. Then he traveled the neighborhood with his milk pails suspended from a notched broomstick over his shoulder, and earned a few cents from each quart he sold before going to school. He spent his evenings working the vegetable crops and hoeing the weeds. From those early days, he developed a fetish about weeds. He felt there was a place for wild flowers and wild plants, but when he planted a garden there was no room for wild grasses. I have often seen him stoop when we were passing someone's home and pull a weed from their garden.

Everett's mother made the boys' clothes from cast-offs the neighbors gave her.

They grew most of their food in the garden. Once a year Mrs. Dirksen would manage to buy a small pig and raise it and butcher it with the help of the neighbors, so that they would have meat in one form or another for the rest of the year.

There was always church on Sunday, followed by Sunday school, and then a meeting of the Young People's Christian Endeavor, a Bible group that elected Everett president year after year.

Mrs. Dirksen was a religious woman. She taught Sunday school. She had helped build with her own hands the Dutch Reformed Church in Pekin, and the family spent many hours in this church. At Christmastime, Everett told me, they would spend the whole day at church and their only gifts were a sack of candy with an orange in it from the church, and either a pair of mittens or a pair of stockings which Mother knitted for the boys.

There was also the Big Book on the parlor table at home. And in those days you opened the Big Book. And read it.

Growing up, Everett spent his free time reading everything he could get his hands on, and his constant companion was the Bible. He had read it from cover to cover three times, he told me, and after he went to Washington he always carried a copy of the Bible in his briefcase.

His earliest experience in the art of extemporaneous oratory came from practice-preaching to one of the favorite Dirksen cows, named Bossy.

While other boys were out playing "run, sheep, run" or climbing trees for fun, Everett was usually climbing his own little platform in the barn, and orating by the hour to Bossy the cow about affairs of the world, or preaching sermons from the Bible.

His idea of fun really came when it rained, for then he could practice projecting his voice above the noise of the rain as it pelted the barn. In later years he often recalled that his boyhood preaching to Bossy the cow was an excellent foundation for his oratorical techniques.

When the kids on the corner got into arguments, Everett would use his amateur powers of persuasion—which were later developed to a fine point—with words that had the other boys shaking their heads.

I still treasure a slim and well-worn little blue-gray volume held together with a blue-green tassle, and titled *The Pekinian* . . . Class of 1913. Inside, is a photograph of the Pekin High School, and then the senior class photos. Under Everett's picture is this accolade:

"Dirk, the man of many words, is that type of fellow with whom one must be intimately acquainted before he is fully appreciated. He merits the high regard in which he is held and is one of the ablest fellows of the class. He has all those sterling qualities that win the friendship of those with whom he is thrown in contact, and is truly a man's man."

Under an amusing section titled "Senior Diseases":

Patient	Disease	Remedy	Remarks
Everett Dirksen	Big Worditis	Primary Reader	Absolutely Hopeless

And under "Senior Class Will" is this gem:

The gentleman from Bohnchefiddle, Everett Dirksen, gives to all ye ambitious the double negative. N.B.—This must be exercised daily in English. (Everett also spoke German fluently.)

Personally, I think the Class of 1913 in Pekin was most astute if not clairvoyant in pinpointing some of the qualities that would be so closely identified with Everett Dirksen more than half a century later . . .

Sometimes those kids on the street corners would tell him, "You don't even know what those big words mean." But he did. He had ambitions from a youngster on.

His brothers Tom and Ben had quit school. But Everett went on to finish high school, and when he graduated, Class of 1913, he was class treasurer and vice-president, on the football, track and debating teams, and business manager of *The Pekinian*.

All the part-time jobs he had held, from milking cows to working in a corn-refining plant, had left him precious little study time for school. But he still graduated as valedictorian of his class.

As a graduation gift a half brother in Minneapolis sent him the fare for a week's trip to that city.

This was a turning point in his life, for it was here he decided that by hook or crook he would attend the University of Minnesota. He did, with the help of a little nest egg his frugal mother had saved, as well as an all-night job (11 P.M. until 5 A.M.) at the Minneapolis *Tribune*.

It was during his college years that Everett's interest in politics blossomed, possibly from the seeds sown by his father but nourished also by his introduction to two men prominent on the political scene in those years. One was Senator Ernest Lundeen of Minnesota, whom he admired because of his conservative Republican politics. The other was none other than William Jennings Bryan, the thrice-defeated Democratic presidential candidate, who had ironically lost twice to Everett's namesake, William McKinley, and was Secretary of State in the cabinet of President Woodrow Wilson when Everett met him.

He had gone to hear the great orator speak, and he deliberately sat far back in the auditorium to see how well Mr. Bryan's voice would project. He was surprised that he could hear it so distinctly from where he sat.

He was thrilled and captivated and emboldened to go up to William Jennings Bryan next morning at breakfast and say, "Mr. Bryan, how are you able, with such a large audience as you had last night, to make everyone hear your message?"

Mr. Bryan looked at him and said, "Young man, if you are serious about public speaking, let me tell you a secret. Always look at the last person in the last row and direct your speaking to him. If he indicates that he's hearing you, you're safe."

In spite of the fact that Everett Dirksen didn't care much for three-time losers, as he so dramatically indicated at the 1952 Republican Convention in Chicago, he had great admiration for the one he met back in 1914—and a Democrat at that! He never hesitated to acknowledge William Jennings Bryan's influence on the oratorical aspect of his political career. But don't ask me what his father would have said about it!

A few ardent Republicans formed a Republican Club at the University of Minnesota and Everett was one of them—because of his admiration for Senator Lundeen. This was his first excursion into politics. He did a great deal of speaking at various political meetings held in the Twin Cities. One morning as he was crossing the campus, a political advertisement mentioning one of his speeches fell from his book and into the path of his history professor. The professor admonished him before his whole class, asking, "Dirksen, do you want to be a history student or a politician?"

Everett Dirksen replied grandly, with a fine sampling of his

incurable "bigworditis," "Since you inquire, sir, I would not
deem it a transgression of educational propriety to be both."

Fortunately, the history teacher did not flunk him, nor did
he dim Everett's ardor for Senator Lundeen, which continued
until the senator's tragic death in a plane accident in Virginia
on August 31, 1940.

Everett's college funds didn't stretch too far, so during sum-
mers he took a job with the Home Remedy Book Company.
As a salesman he was assigned to South Dakota.

Throughout the hot summer months he trudged through the
Dakota farmlands selling home-remedy books to farmers in order
to earn his tuition money for the next term. The books, which
sold for $10 each, contained remedies which supposedly cured
everything from housemaid's knee to lump jaw and scabies in
cattle, or spavin and stringhalt in horses.

There were times when he became frightfully discouraged but
by the end of each summer he had accumulated enough money
to return to school for another year, as well as enough knowledge
of the Dakota farmlands and its people to come in handy on
many an occasion after he went to Washington.

Everett was in his third year at the university when America
entered the war (April 1917). He joined the ROTC on the
University of Minnesota campus, in hopes of being able to
finish college. But he learned that back in Pekin his mother
was being intimidated by patriotic, anti-German citizens who
objected to a picture of Kaiser Wilhelm which she had hanging
on her wall. This was one of the few possessions she had brought
with her from Germany. Many old-country immigrants still clung
to that loyalty to their own country's "king" or leader, long
after they had settled in their new "free world." They may
have been subjected to various forms of servitude in the old
country, but they brought with them to the new country a
special kind of patriotism, which I believe is one reason that
foreign-born are so often more loyal to America than many
native-born Americans.

Many who are reading this I am sure will recall that my
husband, a Republican, was sometimes severely criticized by his
party's colleagues for supporting certain policies of Democratic

administrations, especially those of Presidents Kennedy and Johnson.

I can say unequivocally that he never supported anything against his conscience.

At the same time, he did have an inborn loyalty to his leader, inherited from his parents, and an instinctive respect for the man in office, whoever he might be.

If our memories are not too short, many will recall that during World War I, we in America became quite heated in our patriotism, and so anti-German that there were some people who would not even eat hamburgers because they had been named for Hamburg, Germany, according to popular wartime mythology.

It was in this fervor that a few of Mrs. Dirksen's neighbors, in patriotic overreaction, forced her to remove the Kaiser's picture by threatening to burn her house down. They also demanded that her son Everett enlist and fight for the United States. Tom by now was married, and Ben had been given an honorable discharge because of an ailment. So Everett quit college and joined the Army in 1917, shipped to France in May 1918, and was sent to artillery school. After a short time he became a second lieutenant and was put in charge of manning a tethered balloon 3500 feet above the lines in the Balloon Corps Division, spotting artillery targets and sweating out German fighters. He was discharged in 1919 and immediately offered an enticing post with the Army of Occupation in Germany because of his fluent knowledge of the language.

But he was homesick for Pekin and his mother and he was tired of war and killing.

So he came home to Pekin, where his old school friend and my beau, Hubert Ropp, persuaded him to go into the washing-machine business with him. The two of them had invented a new type of rotary and had great hopes of starting a big factory. It was an ill-fated venture from the beginning, for basically Hubert was an artist and Everett a poet-playwright-actor with budding ambitions.

Their washing-machine business flopped. Hubert and Everett were both out of jobs. They fiddled around at other projects for a while. And then the Pekin Centennial Committee offered them the opportunity to put on the play at the Centennial.

At the time I met Everett, he had collaborated on many plays with Hubert Ropp, both during his school years and after he returned from the service. He had acted in perhaps half a dozen local plays. But his mother disapproved of each one of them. She had passed away on December 7, 1923, only a few months before Everett and I began rehearsing our play for the Centennial, and I am sure she would have disapproved of that, too.

She regarded acting as "sinful." It was Mrs. Dirksen's devotion to the church that led her to oppose vigorously her son's theatrical ambitions—although she could never crush them completely—and to exact a promise from him that he would not go on the stage professionally. But he never totally recovered from his youthful yearning.

Between his mother's religious fervor and the early influence of his artistic, scholarly, politically oriented father—later bulwarked by his college years—it is not surprising that he chose to tread the boards of that much bigger stage on Capitol Hill.

Everett had promised his mother to give up acting professionally. It was a definite promise, a firm commitment. He could not go back on his word.

There was another, even more binding promise she had extracted from him on her deathbed—that Everett would look after his two brothers and take care of them. She had always leaned more heavily on Everett than on the other two boys, and had often told him that he was the strongest of the three, even though Ben was older. Everett was the only one who had an education. So, on her deathbed she reminded him of this and asked him to look after his brothers. As it turned out, they managed quite well on their own in their adult years, but Everett never lost that sense of responsibility to them because of his promise to his mother.

At the time I met him, he and his brother Ben were living alone in the big old Dirksen house in "Beantown."

He did not return to finish college after his service in the Army in World War I, for the simple reason that he preferred to stay in Pekin.

And apart from his playwriting collaborations with Hubert, the jobs he took to earn a living were pure and simple drudgery. Soon after he finished working with Hubert in the Centennial he went to work with a dredging company that had two barges on the Illinois River, and a contract to build a dam in Chautauqua, Illinois.

Everett knew very little about the dredging business, but he did know how to handle a crew of men. Some were illiterate. All they looked forward to was getting their paycheck at the end of the week and spending it in the nearest saloon. But he did get work out of them. They dredged. They pulled up earth and built a dam. They dredged far into the cold winter months. Everett stayed in a little clapboard hotel in Henry, Illinois, during the week, and he would come home for the weekends, cold and wet and tired. Mother and I would fill him with a good dinner, and then we would repair to the living room where the heat from the pot-bellied stove would warm his chilled bones. Sometimes he would fall asleep in his chair.

Those barging days were quite miserable. I remember once on a wintry night we heard a knock on the door at two o'clock in the morning, and there was Everett, soaked and shivering in the cold. He had been returning to shore from the barge in his little motorboat when the motor gave out. He tried to repair it and slipped and fell into the cold waters of the Illinois River. He waded to shore and then had to walk five miles down the highway to his parked car.

By now Everett did have a car. It was an old Maxwell with a quite generous running board. I remember many a time when I felt that I did not have enough of a visit with him and I would jump on the running board as he was leaving, and hold onto the window and ride for blocks that way. When we got up to the middle of town, to that corner we all called Five Points, he would stop the car and tell me to get off. When I wouldn't, then he would push me off, and away he would go with his foot on the gas pedal, and I would walk home alone.

I remember one very special night when he had promised to come home early because we were going to a dance, a most unusual event for us. Everett didn't like to dance, did not know how to dance very well, and we went out dancing only on rare occasions. This occasion was an alumni dance at the high school. My mother had made a very pretty blue silk dress for me to wear, and I was upstairs dressing and primping while Everett, all dressed and waiting, dozed downstairs in his favorite chair beside our pot-bellied stove. It was one of those chilly autumn days and he had been out sloshing around in the water with his dredge boat all day, and so off to sleep he went.

I tried once to awaken him, but I tried only gently because ... well, I suppose I knew how tired he must be and so I just felt that his sleep was more important to him than going to a dance.

I waited ... and waited ... The dance was to begin at nine o'clock ... I sat until ten ... I sat until eleven ... And finally I went upstairs and took off my pretty new dress and went to bed and shed a few tears ...

Everett must have awakened some time in the night and went sneaking home. But the next night he was most apologetic.

And as we sang our *Song of Songs* that night we were closer than we had ever been before.

It was one evening not long after this, a week before Christmas, that he came in jingling a little money in his pocket, and he said, "What would you like for Christmas? Would you like a ring or a radio?"

This was 1926, the year when the first crystal set radios came out.

All my willing little ears could hear was the word "ring." But I had to be sure.

"If I say a ring, will it mean more than a ring?" I asked. With some hesitation, he said, "If you would want it to." I hurriedly said I did. And that was his proposal.

I received my engagement ring for Christmas—and a crystal radio set also. But we waited another year to be married.

Out of life's experiences, we made up our minds to make marriage work. Maybe that's the first rock of failure in a marriage. You've got to make up your mind that it must work. We did that, firmly.

In pursuance of that determination we quickly established a rule in the household that voices must not be lifted in anger and especially not at breakfast, lunch, or dinner.

We developed a complete understanding that if anyone was moved by anger and wanted to raise his voice above the normal conversational level, he or she was to leave the table and come back, according to their conscience, when they cooled off.

Everett McKinley Dirksen

(From an interview in the Chicago *Tribune*,
December 4, 1967, "Dirksen's Look Back
at 40 Happy Wedded Years")

Chapter 4

We Are Married

Ours was a small wedding. We had neither very much money nor family. I had only my mother and Everett had only his two brothers.

We were married in my mother's house with a simple ceremony at 6 P.M. on Christmas Eve of 1927. A friend of mine from Peoria was my maid of honor and Everett's twin brother Tom was his best man.

The ceremony was followed by refreshments—my mother's homemade cake and ice cream.

We heard later that our next-door neighbors had peeked in the window and watched the wedding and thought it was lovely.

I wore a blue velvet wedding dress and a hat made of little silver discs that fitted over my head like a soup bowl. I was still working in the department store in Peoria, so I was able to purchase my dress with my employee discount. It cost $35 and was in the high-fashion style of those days with the waistline down around the hips and the skirt just a touch below the knee. (The Grace Coolidge type.)

Everett had given up his job with the dredging company, thank goodness, and only recently had gone into the bakery business with his two brothers. It was started on a shoestring and barely struggling along, so there was not much money for a honeymoon.

But one of the first things Everett had asked me when we

were planning our wedding was whether I would like to spend our honeymoon in Chicago. Would I! I had never been to Chicago. But then, he needn't have asked. I would have gone anywhere with him, even on a sloppy dredge boat.

He had warned me ahead of time that we would have only three days for our honeymoon. That was all he could afford. He had to get back to the bakery.

So, as soon as the cake and ice cream were served at our wedding, we left for the railway station to take the midnight Rock Island train to Chicago. It was an overnight trip from Pekin, and we sat up all night in the coach. There was not enough money for both a berth *and* the honeymoon.

Our train chugged into Chicago at 7 A.M. on Christmas Day.

We stayed at the Morrison Hotel in the heart of the Loop. We could walk to almost any place downtown from there, and walk we did.

We wanted to see as much as possible in the few days we were there, so we walked, walked, walked everywhere. Window shopping on Michigan Avenue. Skyscraper-gazing in the Loop. (There are much taller ones now.) Treating ourselves to a play at the old Illinois Theatre. (I'll never forget it. It was called *The Clinging Vine*.) And to our first real steak dinner at our first real night club. Oh, it was scandalous, about as scandalous as a Christian Endeavor meeting.

I don't really remember too much about our honeymoon except that I had a new pair of shoes and we walked so much that my heels were always blistered and sore. I had a hard time keeping up with Everett and those big strides of his. But we would go back to our hotel and I would soak my feet and put on more bandages and then we would start off again. Looking back now, I think I can safely say that I was in training for the life of a senator's wife from the time of our honeymoon.

And when the honeymoon was over, he said, "Toots, it's time to go home. I've got to go to work."

It was not only the Dirksen Bakery calling my bridegroom back to work. He was savoring his first sweet smell of success in political office, as a city commissioner in Pekin.

When he had told me that he was going to run for city

commissioner, I really did not know what he was talking about. All I knew was that this man had a big dream that one day would take him far beyond Pekin.

It should not have surprised me but it did—and I suppose it surprised a few other people, also—when the former Prince of *A Thousand Years Ago*, erstwhile actor-playwright, washing-machine vendor, dredge-boat deckhand, and baker boy, announced that he was going to run for city commissioner in Pekin.

He did run and he won. It was a non-partisan election. The city of Pekin elected a mayor and four city commissioners. And Everett Dirksen was one of them. Commissioner of Finance was his title. The year was 1926, just a year before we were married. He was elected to a four-year term, but to me the nice thing about it was that he earned $75 a month. Perhaps not a grand salary for a Commissioner of Finance but it certainly helped our meager budget.

This is what we had to live on when we were married, his commissioner's salary and his small earnings from the bakery, which barely supported us and his brothers in groceries. Although I did not realize it at the time, I know now that Everett regarded the Dirksen Bakery as only an interim means of support while trying to climb the political ladder.

He still had some savings which he had accumulated from his war service and for a while he had debated about whether to return to college and get his degree. He had been taking a pre-law course, and he knew that if he were to return it would still be a long uphill struggle.

There was the added factor that after nearly five years away from home, three in college and seventeen months overseas, he was really homesick for Pekin, and when he came back from the war he could not bring himself to leave again soon. He was enjoying himself too much in those community theatrical projects with his friend Hubert Ropp. And then I came into the picture. So he had decided to remain in Pekin, in the place of his birth, and reach for his stars from there. He never regretted this decision.

But from the moment of his decision he had set his sights on Washington, D.C., which he considered the center of the universe, the place where he had to be if he were going to "represent the people and help run the country." He had no interest in the Illinois State Legislature. He was going straight from Pekin to Washington, D.C., one of these days. He had made up his mind and everything else was merely laying the groundwork.

The reason he gave up his job with the dredging company, after having worked up to general manager, was that he was becoming more and more in demand for speaking engagements. He had been elected commander of the 16th District Post of the American Legion and was being invited to speak at civic clubs all over Tazewell County. He did not wish to miss a single opportunity at public speaking, and he felt that he would be too tied down if he stayed on with the dredging company.

So when his brothers proposed that he go into a wholesale bakery business with them, he decided to do so, using the savings he still had from his war service for his share of the venture.

The Dirksen Bakery was a three-man operation. Ben was the mechanic, Tom the baker, and Everett the salesman. He would get up at five o'clock every morning, go down and help his brothers pull the bread out of the oven, load the loaves onto his truck, and then start off to the grocery stores.

If It's Made of Dough, We Make It, was the slogan printed on the letterheads of Dirksen Bros. Bakers.

It was hard work and long hours, but since the bakery was a family enterprise, Everett could always take time off for his speaking engagements. As an American Legion commander, his speech-making, of course, was usually fervently patriotic—and it was to remain so throughout his lifetime.

Soon after we returned from our honeymoon, we established one of our little hard and fast rules that I believe helped make our marriage successful.

And if I may say so, I think it may have had something to do with helping my husband to be successful in his political career, also. They say that behind every successful man is a woman. This might be translated to read that behind Senator Everett McKinley Dirksen was his personal and devoted book-keeper, Mrs. D., who kept a tight grip on the purse strings.

Should anyone ever raise a question about Senator Everett Dirksen's campaign funds or financial affairs, they will have me to contend with.

For I was the one who handled his campaign ledger as well as our personal and business financial affairs and investments.

I took over the family exchequer long before I knew what a political campaign was, much less a campaign fund. But I was about to learn!

And I really learned the hard way—figuring out how many loaves of bread we would have to sell in order to pay for a carload of flour.

It was Everett who started it all when he brought home his first paycheck, somberly turned it over to his new bride, and said, "Now, I'll bring you the money and I'll spend as little as I need, and you spend what you need. If you can manage to save some of it, then eventually we might be able to have a little nest egg. *But*, if you're not going to save it, then I'll help you spend it. It's up to you."

I knew he meant it, he was so earnest about it.

Everett had a great respect for money but he simply did not like the little details of being bothered with it personally. He preferred to have someone else keep track of it for him.

Not that he couldn't if he had to. Paradoxically, his very first job in public office, as I have said, was as city finance commissioner in Pekin, and throughout his thirty-seven years in Washington he was to serve on many banking, currency, finance, and appropriations committees which dealt with mind-boggling figures.

But Everett preferred to have me take care of the $75 a month he earned as Pekin's Commissioner of Finance and the pittance he brought home from the Dirksen Bakery.

It was an enormous responsibility for me.

I had worked as a bookkeeper in the department store in Peoria. But this was scarcely the kind of training to prepare me for dealing in carloads of sugar and flour for the bakery, and the 10 percent discount we would get if we paid the bills within ten days. It hurt me not to be able to do so always, but it did take a lot of nickel loaves of bread to pay for one carload of flour.

The little bakery, of course, had to support three families, and this gave me some concern at first. But whenever I would mention it to Everett his reaction was always the same: Whatever was needed would always some way be provided. He would work hard and it *would* be provided, he reassured me. I soon developed a simple, childlike faith in my husband's ability to provide for us. That faith never wavered. And it helped me apply myself diligently to the one task that I knew my husband really wanted me to do—to spend his money carefully and save some if I could for our little nest egg.

From childhood he had known the meaning of thrift. He believed it was possible to have happiness without too much in worldly goods.

This was the dowry my husband brought to our marriage.

One of my cherished memories of our first years together was our afternoon tea with the leftovers that he would bring home from the bakery. Afternoon tea is not only a British custom, it is a Low-German ritual as well, or at least it was among the "Bohnchefiddle" colony in Pekin. So after we were married, Everett would take a little break about three o'clock in the afternoon and come home for tea—with cookies or sweet rolls or doughnuts or anything he had left over from the day's deliveries. Then he would go back to the shop.

We happily survived on a great many "leftovers" in our bakery days but I must say that as soon as we had achieved a certain state of solvency, my husband could not stand the sight of a leftover loaf of bread around the house.

I learned to manage the Dirksen Bakery accounts as well as our personal budget, and I was to learn to manage a political campaign fund much sooner than I had expected.

Men in political office are always sitting ducks for critics who like to accuse them of any kind of financial skulduggery —from misuse of taxpayers' money to filching campaign funds for their personal use.

Looking back now I am certain that Everett had another and deeper motive for turning his money over to me. He wanted to be completely free and unfettered of anything that would give his opponents cause to question his campaign funds or personal bank accounts.

He knew that if he turned his money over to me, I would take good care of it and would not misuse it.

First of all, Everett Dirksen was a very devout man, and a very honest man. But he was also a very wise man and he knew some of the risks that went along with a career in politics. He was willing to take these risks and make personal sacrifices. But he believed in eliminating the risks whenever possible; and by divesting himself of all but pocket money he was at least cutting down on one risk even if he could not eliminate it completely.

I seriously question whether that is possible in this business that is sometimes known as "the dirty game of politics."

Even after my husband's death, when we were having some problems in settling his estate, I read that a certain Democratic congressman had complained, "How do we know that Senator Dirksen doesn't have trunkloads of money stashed away somewhere?"

For the record let me intersperse a word here. All the money that was contributed to Everett Dirksen's campaigns through the years went into one account. And I was the treasurer.

I kept complete and accurate records of all such contributions, and I was always meticulously careful so that there could never be a question about any of the items. The moment a campaign contribution was received, I would immediately record the name of the contributor, the amount, and the date.

I kept the same careful check on any expenditures of the money.

There was simply no way that one single dime of Everett Dirksen's campaign funds could be spent for anything else as long as Louella Dirksen did the bookkeeping.

And when the campaign ended, all the bills were paid. There were never any expenses left unpaid.

Those lean years in the bakery business had taught me to be frugal and not to spend more than we earned. In fact, from the beginning I saw to it that we did just the opposite. I made up my mind right at the start that if I had to be in charge of the family exchequer, I was going to learn to be good at it. And I was. We may have dined on a lot of leftovers but when the bills were all paid there were always leftovers in cold cash for the credit columns in my bookkeeping books. My books always balanced.

The same was true in my handling of Everett's campaign funds. I was very careful about expenses, and if we did not have enough money to pay for ten billboards, then we would have fewer billboards.

As soon as possible, following each Election Day, I would balance the books and close them, and there was always a little money left over to start Everett's next election campaign.

On the next blank page in my books, I would always write —"Everett McKinley Dirksen Campaign Account for . . ."— whatever the next election year might be. When he was a congressman, the date was every two years, and of course as a senator it was every six years.

After Everett was re-elected to the Senate in 1968, I immediately started the campaign account for 1974 with a leftover credit of some $52,000. After his death in 1969 (September 7), this fund, which consisted of contributions from individual donors, was used to help establish the Everett McKinley Dirksen Research Center in Pekin. (See Chapter 22).

Oh, what a gift my husband gave me when he brought home that first paycheck.

I listened and learned and sharpened my mind like a calculating machine.

And today I am the only woman member of the Board of Directors of the First National Bank of DeBary, Florida. I understand there are not too many lady members on the Board of Directors of many banks in this country.

But then I suppose there were not too many brides keeping an eye on the bread in the bakery business, either.

I am the master of my fate,
I am the captain of my soul . . .

From W. E. Henley's *Invictus*
(One of Everett Dirksen's favorite poems)

Chapter 5

My Husband, the Congressman from Illinois

Anyone old enough to remember that far back will remember 1929 as the year of the stock market crash.

I remember it as the year of our first personal crisis, our Year of Decision when Everett Dirksen announced his entry on the national political scene. I remember it as the year of our first political campaign, and one that led to my husband's first and only political defeat. And of course I remember it as the year that our first and only child was born.

Everett's venture into politics on a local level had brought him some recognition—both good and bad. As city finance commissioner he was responsible for some of the early reforms in our local government. But not everyone approved of them.

I remember the uproar he caused among his own German compatriots when he led the city's crusade to pave the whole north side of Pekin, including Beantown. Even though he had grown up there, some of the older and frugal German families were quite disgruntled with him. They were opposed to spending money on city improvements, such as paving. Others opposed him in his recommendations for zoning plans.

I was only vaguely aware of his responsibilities as a city commissioner.

I had my own responsibilities trying to make ends meet after balancing the books of the Dirksen Bakery.

I was becoming more and more aware that Everett's heart really was not in that bakery, and although I trusted him somehow to provide for us, as he always assured me he would, I now had a new concern. We were going to have a baby.

We both reacted rather matter-of-factly when we learned that I was expecting. It was not terribly startling news to us. We more or less took it for granted. In those days, you got married and the good Lord willing, you had babies.

We were both pleased to have a baby on the way, but sometimes I secretly fretted because Everett was spending less and less time at the bakery and more time out of town making speeches.

Even though the Dirksen Bakery was still a struggling enterprise, I felt that I had learned my end of it well enough to help pull us through the lean times ahead of us.

But I had absolutely no comprehension of politics. I could be of no use to my husband in that area. In spite of Everett's reassurances, politics to me in those days wore no halo of security at all.

The day came, as I had feared it would, when Everett told me he had made an important decision. He was going to run for Congress—the United States Congress. He was going to be a member of the House of Representatives, where he could "represent the people," which is what he really wanted to do. He didn't want to be in the bakery business. He wanted to be a congressman.

At the time he broke the news to me that he was actually going to run for Congress, I had never met a congressman or a senator. I scarcely knew what a congressman was.

What I did know was that if my husband became a congressman we would have to move to Washington. The thought of leaving Pekin frightened me. I reminded him that our baby was due in a few weeks. He patiently explained that we had over a year to work things out, as he could not run until the April 1930 primaries.

On the night of February 9, 1929, I was taken to the hospital in Pekin to have our baby. My husband was in Peoria making a speech.

I was feeling a little sorry for myself. I didn't understand

what my husband's speech-making was all about nor why it
would be more important than having a baby. I was just a small-
town girl who knew nothing about politics and at that point
didn't care. All I knew was that I was about to have a baby
and the baby's father was not there.

Finally he came and everything was all right again. Our baby
girl was born at 1:10 in the morning of February 10. Everett
stayed with me most of the night, leaving only in time to be at
the bakery at 5 A.M.

At ten o'clock that morning he had an appointment to have
his first political campaign picture taken. The picture was to be
used on cards officially announcing his candidacy for Congress
from the 16th District of Illinois in the April 1930 primaries.
Once his mind was made up, he could hardly wait to get going.
His very first decisive step toward the national political scene was
having his campaign picture made that morning—on the birth
date of our child, February 10, 1929. He was what you might
call an early starter.

That afternoon Everett came back to see his new baby.

We had made an earlier agreement about the name. If our
baby was a boy, I was to name it, and if a girl, he would name
it. He chose the name Danice Joy. The name Danice appealed
to him because of its French sound, and it reminded him
of his days in France during the war. He chose Joy as a name
to remind us of the joy we shared in our early courtship days,
when we were in the Chinese play together.

But she soon lost the name Danice because my Grandfather
Bruder could not pronounce it. Each time he came to see the
baby, we would repeat her name, Danice Joy, over and over for
him, but he spoke broken English and it was difficult for him
to understand. Finally in some desperation, Everett said, "Her
name is Joy." Grandfather's face lighted up and he said, "Choy.
Oh, Choy. Das ist a pretty name." And from then on she was
Joy.

Everett began mapping out his campaign for next year's
primaries. His opponent was Peoria's incumbent Republican
Congressman, William Edgar Hull, a millionaire who owned
the Jefferson Hotel in Peoria, was a very large stockholder in

the Hiram Walker Distillery, and lived at the Wardman Park Hotel in Washington, which very few congressmen were able to do.

Many of Everett's friends tried to dissuade him from running against Ed Hull, as his followers called him. They knew that Everett's chances of beating him were slim. They felt also that Everett would stand a far better chance in running for the state legislature first, rather than the U. S. House of Representatives. But my husband knew what he wanted. And if he didn't get it the first time out, he was willing to try again.

Congressman Hull was much older and far more experienced than my husband, and he capitalized on this by constantly referring to Everett as "that boy" or "that baker boy from Pekin."

This did not ruffle Everett. He peddled his bread by day and made speeches every night, covering the entire 16th District, from Spring Valley to the north to Delavan on the south. But he especially concentrated in the Peoria area where his opponent lived.

My indoctrination into the rigors of campaigning and the name-calling that goes with it was only a mild foretaste of things to come in the years ahead, but I remember how shocked I was during that first campaign to hear the widely circulated rumors that Everett was a "wife beater" and that he "neglected" his child.

On second thought I must admit there was one time during the campaign when he became so immersed in what he was doing that he not only "neglected" both his wife and his child, he completely forgot about them. How well I remember! But I can look back on it with amusement now.

It happened this way. Occasionally, when I felt that the baby and I had not seen enough of our daddy, he would tell me to put the baby in her basket and he would let us ride along with him to Peoria, where we would stay with our friends, Kathleen and Lou Stacey. Or, the baby and I would stay with Kathleen while our husbands went off to political meetings. One night we waited . . . and waited . . . and waited . . . until ten o'clock, 10:30, eleven o'clock. The baby, of course, was sound asleep, and I almost was also.

Eventually Lou came home, but no Everett. Lou told us that he and Everett had separated and gone to different meetings. We were all puzzled, and I was a little worried. No political meeting could last so long. (Ah, innocence!) This was not like Everett. He never stayed out late without calling me. Finally it came, the telephone call, and I'll never forget how apologetic and sheepish he sounded on the phone as he confessed the incredible truth. He had simply forgotten about us. He had driven all the way home to Pekin and was actually in the house and surprised that I was not there waiting for him. Then he realized that he had left us in Peoria. This world of politics was all new and strange to me, but if I did not realize before how much it meant to my husband, I certainly did now. The baby and I bedded down at the Staceys for the night.

For me, with a new baby to look after and a husband away from home so much of the time, that 1929 campaign seemed to go on forever . . . But February 1930 came and went and Joy was now a year old, and the campaign went into its final frantic weeks.

By the time that first Election Day arrived, April 8, 1930, I had become emotionally involved enough to experience the panicky feeling which I am sure every wife of every political candidate always has had and always will.

Roberta Day, who was my closest friend at the time, came to be with me for the day. We spent most of the morning worrying, fussing, and generally wasting time, which we finally realized was doing neither of us any good and nothing constructive to help Everett. So we decided to do a little campaigning of our own. We took a handful of Everett's campaign cards, jumped into Roberta's big Cadillac car, and headed for the river front, to a place known as Shag Point.

We decided—and don't ask me why or how—that perhaps not too many people had been campaigning there. It was an area along the river where at floodtime the waters would wash through the houses, and the families would evacuate and hunt higher ground. When the river receded, the people would come back, scrape the mud out of their homes, and begin living on Shag Point again.

I knocked on each door, introduced myself, asked them to go and vote for Everett Dirksen, and then I left his card.

I could hardly wait to tell Everett that we had been out drumming up votes for him. When we broke the news to him, he grinned and asked where we had been.

We told him. His eyebrows shot up, and he gave us a wry little smile. "Shag Point? In a Cadillac? Perhaps it would be well if you girls left the campaigning to me, until you know a little bit more about it."

Toward evening our house filled with friends to await the election returns. The coffee urn was on the table, along with a big platter of Dirksen doughnuts from our bakery. The returns were nearly all in by one o'clock in the morning and to some of us it seemed almost certain that Everett was winning. But he cautioned us not to be too elated.

"Spring Valley isn't in, yet," he reminded us. Spring Valley was a great hideout for the Chicago bootleggers.

A little later he said, "The feel just isn't there." This was a term he was to use often through the years on various political matters, but never again with reference to his own election.

Early the next morning we heard that the Chicago bootleggers had indeed come down to Spring Valley and flooded the city with money, and the returns had come in favoring Congressman Hull.

That 1930 election was the only one Everett ever lost but he took it in stride. The very next day he was out buttonholing voters as though nothing had happened, and announcing that he was going to try again two years later.

I still have the little one-page campaign bulletin he had printed for his second campaign in the 1932 primaries. On one side is his picture with the caption above it, "A Young Business Man and Student of Affairs," and below it a brief list of his qualifications as a candidate for the Republican nomination for Congress. But I particularly like his presentation on the other side:

In the Primary election on April 8th, 1930, of a total Republican vote of 54,739, Dirksen received 26,612 votes and was defeated by ONLY 1,155 votes.

This is followed by a black outlined box with an excerpt from an editorial in the Peoria *Star* of April 9, 1930:

Hull was opposed by a remarkable young man. The district has never experienced anything just like him. Without newspaper support, with the business interests of the district arrayed against him, he waged one of the most astonishing campaigns this district has ever witnessed. That he came so close to victory is a tribute to his ABILITY as an orator, his GOOD NATURE and his UNBOUNDED ENERGY. He has arrived. (The capitalized words were Everett's idea, in reprinting the excerpt.)

This was followed by his campaign pitch:

The Economic Crisis, the Social Unrest and Discontent, the Industrial Distress, the Futile Efforts of Those Now in Office to Cope With the Present Problems Are Eloquent of the Fact That We Need a Change.
VOTE FOR DIRKSEN.

By 1932 "that baker boy from Pekin" was ready. Again he was pitted against millionaire incumbent Hull, in the April primaries, and this time he won. In the national election in November he became the fair-haired boy of the GOP by winning big in a Democratic landslide.

By now the country was in a real depression. Businesses were going bankrupt and banks were failing. President Herbert Hoover had been campaigning throughout the country promising a chicken in every pot.

But a new name had come on the horizon, Franklin Delano Roosevelt.

When President Hoover campaigned in Illinois, Everett had proudly campaigned with him, but he came home and confided to me, "The feel just isn't there." He seemed to know that Hoover was finished.

Election Day came and the night wore off into morning.

By the time the final count was in Everett McKinley Dirksen had carried his 16th District by a majority of 23,147—which was 1000 more votes than FDR's lead in the same district.

But Franklin Delano Roosevelt was our new President.

In my political naïveté, it seemed to me at the time that nearly everyone who won in that election was a Democrat except my husband. And we were going to have to leave Pekin and move to Washington—in that nest of Democrats?

But Everett was elated.

He could hardly wait to get to Washington and see what it was like. Neither Everett nor I had ever been to that city. He was anxious to see his new office, find a place to live, familiarize himself with the Capitol, and get to work.

We decided that he would go first. The baby and I would come later.

Soon after the election in November, Everett and one of his American Legion buddies, George Chiames, set out for Washington in George's car. George had never been there, either.

According to the report I got from Everett later, it must have been quite a trip, topped off when they rolled into the city, began looking for the Capitol Building, spotted a gold-painted dome in the distance, and headed toward it. It turned out to be a large open-air market beneath a dome-like structure, all right, but not the Capitol dome!

They had to ask someone for directions to the Capitol, and when they finally found it they were overwhelmed with its beauty. Only then did they realize the full humor or embarrassment of mistaking anything less stately for the Capitol dome.

Congress was in session then, but this was the last Lame Duck Congress, so-called because nothing of importance ever happened in the Congress between the November election and the March inauguration. When my husband was first elected, in 1932, the President and congressmen took office in March of the following year, but after FDR was sworn in the inaugurations were moved up to January.

Everett had plenty of time to get ready for the inauguration and the opening session. He rented a room in a small hotel close to the Capitol and went to work. Luckily he hired an assistant, Wendell Cable, who had worked for another congressman and who knew his way around Washington and the congressional cloakroom. He helped familiarize Everett with so many little details that he needed to know about before the opening session.

Everett came home for the Christmas holidays and to celebrate our fifth wedding anniversary. It was a time of great rejoicing and exhilaration—especially for him. He was on his way—straight from Pekin to Washington, just as he wanted it. I was so proud of him. But during that special holiday time of 1932, and as we ushered in the new year, I had very mixed emotions. I did not, of course, realize that my husband was about to begin such an important role on the political stage.

I am older and wiser now. I know that during the thirty-seven years Everett was in politics—years that spanned the Roosevelt, Truman, Eisenhower, Kennedy, Johnson, and Nixon administrations—there were many changes in our government. I think historians may record that the year 1932 was an historical turning point, ushering in some of the most dramatic and drastic changes in our government since the Constitution.

But in 1932, I was happy just being Everett Dirksen's "Princess of Pekin," with our daughter, Joy. Then suddenly my "prince" had turned into the Congressman from Illinois, and from then on everything would be different. I was bewildered. I envisioned life in Washington as dull and gloomy and unexciting, a terrible cross to bear, especially for a Republican among the Democrats. And innocent that I was, I was assuming that this Christmas-anniversary of 1932 was to be our last one in Pekin.

Everett reassured me about this by explaining words like "adjournment" and "constituents." Of course a congressman has to keep his roots at home, in his own district, he told me. Otherwise how can he "represent the people"? And when Congress "adjourned" after each working session, he explained, we would always come back to Pekin.

How could we afford to live in two places?

That was a problem we would have to work out together, he said. But his new job did not change mine as the head of the family exchequer. It was up to me to figure out how to manage two homes!

There were many decisions to be made. Everett's brothers felt they could not keep up the bakery alone. So Everett turned over his one-third interest to them and advised them to sell it.

Joy was about to be four years old, and she would soon be starting to school. My mother had helped take care of her from the time she was a baby, but both Everett and I felt that I should not be away from her for prolonged periods of time. Should we put her in school in Washington or Pekin?

A congressman is elected for only a two-year term, and there was no assurance that Everett would be elected for a second term—although I am sure there was never any doubt of this in his own mind.

But in the end we finally decided that Joy and I would stay in Pekin, that I would "commute" to Washington when I could, and that Everett would go to law school at night. This last was at my insistence, and I have since regretted it and often said to myself, "Oh, ye of little faith." For it was nothing but my own insecurity that made me urge him to go back to school and finish his law degree. In spite of his confidence, the thought kept nagging me, what if he *should* lose the next election? What would he do? I did not realize until in later years how difficult it must have been for him to go to law school at night and take care of the duties of his new job during the day.

It must have been rather trying for him although he never complained. Nor was it ever necessary to fall back on his law degree after working so hard for it because he never lost another election. His legal training, however, of course helped in his political career.

I went to Washington with Everett to watch him take the oath of office on March 4, 1933, the same day that Franklin Delano Roosevelt was sworn in as President.

It was a historic occasion and a memorable day for me. I have only a vague recollection of my first glimpse of FDR up there on the platform in a wheelchair, with Mrs. Roosevelt beside him.

I remember the overpowering feeling of loneliness that engulfed me as I listened to talk that I did not understand, and plans for inaugural festivities that did not include us. We did not participate in any of the parties or celebrations that go along with a presidential inauguration because we were of the "opposition party," a phrase with which I was soon to become quite familiar even if I was not on that day of March 4, 1933. From a practical standpoint it was just as well that we were not included in the inaugural party festivities, for we had neither the money nor the clothes for such fancy affairs.

Most important for me was just being there with my husband to watch him be sworn in as a member of the House of Representatives of the United States of America, from the 16th District of the State of Illinois.

My pride for him was nearly unbearable. What a sense of accomplishment it was for both of us, for I felt that I had given him some help along the way. And no one realized as much as we did the sacrifices he had made and the obstacles he had to overcome to win his first election.

It had been a four-year effort to get over that first hurdle, but he made it. He had reached the goal for which he was striving.

My husband was a Congressman from Illinois.

But my pride was mixed with a heavy feeling of numbness as he kissed me goodbye and I started the long drive back to Pekin alone.

In President Nixon's eulogy to my husband on September 9, 1969, he reminded us of something that had been said when Daniel Webster died more than a century ago:

Our great men are the common property of the country.

I had a premonition a long time ago that this was exactly what was happening to my husband. On a windy March day in 1933, as I drove homeward across the Illinois prairies, I knew that I now would have to share him with something bigger than I was.

There were many times during Everett's first term in office when my heart ached for him. Being so new and naïve in the game of national politics, I was shocked, appalled, and hurt at the vilifications my husband received for not going along with President Roosevelt's sweeping New Deal program.

That new President and the new Congress no sooner took over than they instituted vast changes in our government. Reform and Recovery were the slogans, Welfare the magic word, and a whole new bowl of alphabetical soup was brewed by FDR with his NRA, WPA, OPA, and so on.

One of the first measures passed under the Roosevelt administration was the National Recovery Act (NRA), symbolically represented by the Blue Eagle, with its wings spread wide. The emblem was displayed everywhere, in grocery stores, post offices, and all factories. The bill was intended to provide relief for people who were without work and desperate for money.

Everett studied this bill very carefully—with the same intensity that he was to give every measure presented during his thirty-six years in Washington—and he proceeded to vote against it. This brought down the wrath of the whole 16th District upon his head, and seemingly of the entire state and country as well.

It may be remembered that emotions ran high back in those early Roosevelt years. The majority of the people fervently loved FDR and looked upon him as the saviour of our country. Anyone who disagreed with him was branded as a traitor to the country, or at least to the cause of economic recovery, and was subjected to the most vicious kind of criticism.

It wasn't that Everett was against helping the people. But he could see the far-reaching implications of the NRA. And he felt that for the good of his country and its people he must vote against it. I think many who criticized him then would agree today that he was right.

But back in 1933 I was horrified to hear and read all the fire-breathing epithets hurled at my husband. Those "wife beating," "child neglect" charges during our local primary election campaigns were nothing compared to the mailbags of abuse he received over the NRA issue . . . "You traitor to your country . . . Betrayor to your President . . . Upstart representative from southern Illinois with the unmitigated gall to try to stop our President from saving the country . . . One-term congressman . . . We'll get you at the polls in two years . . ."

Even some of his close friends wrote him letters criticizing his action and calling him a "one-term congressman."

Such critical judgment from friends and strangers saddened Everett. He did not get angry but it hurt him to think that people believed he did not want to help them. He made it a point to answer every letter and to try to make the people understand the reasons for his vote. Once the heat of such a bill was over, and realizing that he had taken time to answer their letters, many of these early critics turned into boosters and would write to Everett asking him to use his influence for or against certain measures.

I especially remember his mail when the President tried to

pack the Supreme Court to seat eleven men instead of the nine, because he wanted some of his friends on the bench. Everett received thousands of letters pleading, "Do not let them pack the Supreme Court." Some only one page: "Dont let them pak the Cort."

There is a popular expression, "Politics makes strange bed-fellows." I think it applies to no one more than to Everett and one of President Roosevelt's top braintrusters, Tommy Corcoran. While Everett opposed much of Roosevelt's reforms, he often called Tommy to explain or clarify certain proposals that mystified him. Thus began a friendship that lasted throughout Everett's lifetime. I feel sure that if Tommy Corcoran had ever had an opportunity to vote for Everett Dirksen, party politics would not have been a barrier.

Everett was grateful for Tommy's advice and I especially have always been grateful for Tommy's friendship through the years for somehow it seemed to soften the sting of those barbs over the NRA issue. In time I would learn to toughen my hide for such onslaughts and accept the fact that this was how the political game is played.

But during those first years, when Everett was fighting his battle alone in Washington, and I was the lonely "commuter" from Pekin, there were times when I wondered whether it was worth it.

I was distressed when people criticized him so violently, and I told him so. He tried to reassure me. Was it worth staying in politics? I asked him. Was it true what they said about his being a one-term congressman? Another campaign would be expensive, and there would always be another . . . and another . . . And all those constituents to please . . . And all the terrible things people would say about him if he didn't vote the way they felt he should . . . How could anything possibly be worth suffering through all that?

I might as well have saved myself all the fretting. Everett's mind was made up and there was no turning back. I doubt if Everett Dirksen ever even considered the possibility of losing an election after winning that first one.

EARLY YEARS IN WASHINGTON

ON ABRAHAM LINCOLN

In the American tradition, shining majestically, there are the Pilgrims and the pioneers, Valley Forge and Gettysburg, the Declaration of Independence and the Constitution. In it, looming large, are William Penn and Daniel Boone, Washington and Paine, Zenger and Marshall, Jefferson and Jackson. In it are faith and hope, tears and laughter. And high in our tradition stands Abraham Lincoln. Can he be explained in any other way than that he was an instrument of divine destiny? History is but the enfoldment of a divine pattern . . . If not this, it can only be materialistic drift. If there be a creative hand behind this universe, there must be a creative hand in its unfoldment and direction. Everything in it—sun, moon, stars, planets, their distances, the calibration so that people will neither freeze nor scorch to death, the procession of the seasons, man's subsistence—all rise to testify to the amazing adjustments in the universe to preserve life. And surely the creative force would not provide it all in such meticulous detail and then ignore its ultimate destiny.

Everett McKinley Dirksen

(From a speech on the Senate floor)

AT LINCOLN'S TOMB

On the night of Good Friday, 1865, he left us to join a blessed procession, in neither doubt nor fear, but his soul does indeed go marching on. For this was the Bible-reading lad come out of wilderness, following a prairie star, filled with wonder at the world and its Maker, who all his life, boy and man, not only knew the Twenty-third Psalm, but more importantly, knew the Shepherd.

Now it seems possible that we shall never see his like again. This is a sobering thought, but it should be a kindling one, for upon us now, as a people and a party, has been laid perhaps the greatest responsibility any nation was ever asked to shoulder, yet certainly not greater than we can bear.

Our days are no longer than were Lincoln's, our nights are no darker, and if there is any difference between his time and this it lies in the tremendous advantage that is ours, that he stood so tall before us. In such a time and at such a moment we surely can say then, from hopeful, brimful hearts:

We are standing, Father Abraham, devoted millions strong, firm in the faith that was yours and is ours, secure in the conviction bequeathed by you to us that right does make might and that if we but dare to do our duty as we understand it, we shall not only survive—we shall prevail.

Everett McKinley Dirksen

from Our American Heritage—Harper & Row

Chapter 6

Land of Lincoln

My husband belongs to history. And to understand him, future historians will have to take a close look at his birthplace, his heritage, and his own fine sense and appreciation of history.

He believed there was no such thing as death of thought or of energy. I have often heard him say that the will and vision which motivated our Republic's Founding Fathers have not disappeared; they have moved on, alive and strong to other episodes of our history.

I also often heard him say, "Why do historians always use that phrase, 'Time marches on'? Time does not march. Time stands still. We are the people who march through time, and we create or destroy as we march."

Everett was a product of America's heartland, and in many ways his life epitomized the essence of America: a free land where opportunity is open to all and where there are no limits to the goals which an individual can achieve. He was a living example of what can be accomplished by hard work and individual initiative in this great country of ours.

But he never for a moment forgot his humble beginnings. He never forgot, nor did he let anyone else forget that he was born of immigrant parents who had faith in man's abilities through Divine guidance and perseverance. He experienced through his immigrant parents the appreciation of a land where possibilities were unlimited.

He knew first hand the "melting pot" America, its diversity and hardship, the brilliance of its people going about the business of forging a magnificent nation, and he loved them.

He never missed an opportunity to let anyone know that in shaping our country's future, we must know where the present came from, and not lose sight of our heritage.

He often quoted those lines from another famous son of Illinois, Carl Sandburg: "For we know that when a nation goes down and never comes back, when a society or a civilization perishes, one condition can always be found. They forgot from whence they came. They lost sight of what brought them along."

One of the qualities that endeared my husband to so many Americans was his great patriotism. He had no hesitation about showing his love for his country. During a time when so many sophisticates looked on patriotism as old-fashioned, he continued to talk about the flag and freedom in every part of this country. His was a different kind of freedom from those we were hearing about in the Roosevelt years. FDR became famous for his Four Freedoms. But Everett was very distressed about Roosevelt's "freedom from want" and "freedom from fear" philosophy. Everett believed in a more positive and constructive kind of freedom, not freedom *from* something but freedom *for*—freedom for the opportunity to work, for example, freedom for the right to earn a living as one saw fit, freedom for the right to succeed or fail depending upon the individual effort put forth.

Someone once described my husband as a kind of bridge to the American past, or to the Middle West of the nineteenth century, and essentially motivated by a need to preserve and employ the values of a more "sanguine" day.

If by that is meant the values of a harder, harsher, more rugged and competitive life of our pioneer forefathers, it is a correct description of my husband.

Part of his patriotism, I am sure, sprang from his place of birth as well as the circumstances.

For, while his parents came from the old country, Everett McKinley Dirksen came from the Land of Lincoln, and this, too, he never let anyone forget.

I think that a great deal of my husband's proud love of his country, his deeper sense of identification with history than some of his colleagues on Capitol Hill, started with the moment of his birth in Pekin, Tazewell County, Illinois, in the heart of Lincoln country.

Illinois *is* the "Land of Lincoln." It is even stamped on our automobile license plates. But it is also stamped into the hearts of children in early school days, and Everett was no exception. He grew up on the legends of Abraham Lincoln, the awkward, simple farm boy who became one of the greatest men in the history of our country.

Everett felt a certain kinship with the Great Emancipator who also had sprung from humble beginnings. Lincoln was his type of man—a simple homespun man of the people, devoted to his country and the cause of freedom. I believe that Everett Dirksen was truly a man of the people, by the people, and for the people in the same sense that Lincoln was.

But let me hasten to emphasize that this comparison is my own. It was not my husband's. He cherished Lincoln, but with a humility that rejected any thought of comparison. I am sure he read everything Lincoln ever wrote—more than once probably —as well as nearly everything written about him. He was always quoting Lincoln and he tried to follow the concepts of the Lincoln legacy.

I hope I will not be accused of blasphemy if I say that next to God my husband worshiped Lincoln most.

From the time he first went to Washington, he made a ritual of walking from his hotel all the way up to the Lincoln Memorial, and standing there at Lincoln's feet with his head bowed in meditation. In later years as Senate Leader, when he was squired around in a chauffeured limousine, he would regularly ask to be driven to the Lincoln Memorial, and then the chauffeur would wait while the Senator from Illinois communed with that kindred spirit from the Land of Lincoln.

Many who knew my husband will remember his special tributes to Lincoln, but among my favorites is this one:

"I have often said that, in my judgment, there is a quiet brooding destiny that looks after the affairs of men and nations. I have puzzled hundreds of times how one could account for the fact that Abraham Lincoln came on the American scene when he did and made his exit when he did, if it were not the unfolding of the Divine pattern of history."

I hope I will not seem immodest if I say that those words might also have been said *about* my husband, instead of by him.

When Lincoln was a young man, he lived in New Salem, only fifty miles from Pekin. He had campaigned in Pekin, as my husband had, and there were still some of the older townspeople who remembered seeing him. He had even tried a few lawsuits in the Tazewell County Courthouse.

The old courthouse had been torn down in 1914 and rebuilt in 1916.

And how well I remember Everett's excitement when he learned that the very desk Lincoln had once used was still stored in the courthouse basement along with a lot of other old furniture. After a great deal of bartering, he was able to purchase that desk for only $10. And with what great reverence he placed his Lincoln desk in our upstairs bedroom. It was his pride and joy. When he was at home in Pekin, instead of Washington, he would take his work upstairs to his Lincoln desk every evening after supper, rather than working in his downstairs study.

The desk is now in the Smithsonian Institution, with a little placard that says this was the desk that was once used by Abraham Lincoln and later belonged to Everett Dirksen.

I sometimes wondered what it was about Pekin that drew us together in the first place, and kept drawing us back, and made it so hard for me to leave. It was more than family ties. Was it Pekin's link with the past, with the American Midwestern tradition of the simple life? Was it that sense of identification with history? With a man who stood tall, tall, tall on the pages of history enriching our lives?

I am no psychoanalyst. All I know is that it was very difficult for me to pull up roots and follow my husband to Washington.

And I know that throughout his lifetime, each time we returned to Pekin we felt an inner peace and strength and a closer bond with each other and with our home ties.

At the time Everett was born, back in 1896, Pekin was a thriving little farm-belt community of 5000 inhabitants. It was a community of churches and shade trees and show boats on the river plying their trade with the likes of *East Lynne* and *Thorns and Oranges* and *Oliver Twist*.

Everett sometimes sneaked off to watch the glittering show boats, but his saintly mother did not approve of such sinful goings-on and kept her boys pretty much under her saintful watching eye.

They went to church on Sundays. Then they made their mother's dinner, and after that they read The Book.

"Life had a rugged quality in those days," Everett used to say.

To the people of Pekin and to Everett also, as a boy, the outside world was a long, long way from the cornfields of Illinois.

Our family home in Pekin—the Carver family home—is a 140-year-old, two-story, wooden clapboard house painted white, with a porch across the front.

This was my mother's home but she insisted that we live with her after we were married. Then, when Everett got into politics, we divided the house into two sections. To the right, after you entered the front door, was his waiting room with a study just behind. To the left of the entrance, our living room, dining room, kitchen, and bath. Upstairs were five bedrooms and bath.

Mother had a very comfortable room upstairs where she generally stayed when she was not helping me run our side of the house downstairs. There were a few old pieces of Mother's furniture in the house, but most of our furniture was the Early American that I had collected.

We had one of those big, old-fashioned kitchens that was such a joy to work in. In later years we modernized it but Everett and I really liked it better the old way. We didn't have a furnace for many years but we did have that lovely old pot-bellied stove in the dining room, the one beside which Everett sometimes fell asleep in our courting days.

Even after we installed an open-air furnace, we still kept that old pot-bellied stove because it brought back so many nice memories.

Everett had completely brainwashed my mother out of her early vague misgivings about "those Dirksen boys." She could not have loved him more if he had been her own son. But she had no background to prepare her for the kind of ambitions my husband had—for that matter neither did I!—so I suppose it was difficult for her sometimes to understand what he was talking about.

She was never able to comprehend why he had to spend so much time in Washington and leave me in Pekin.

The house in Pekin is on a small city lot, only two blocks from the center of town. We always had flowers blooming in a little garden in the backyard. From the very beginning of our married life in Pekin, Everett loved puttering around a garden. He seemed to need flowers the way birds need wings, to help him soar in that big new world of his, a world that more often than not was strange and incomprehensible to my mother and me.

I was becoming active in PTA and other local activities and did not spend too much time in Washington in those early years. I found myself living from one "adjournment" to the next, and those happy times when Everett could be back in Pekin for a while.

But even when he was home he was always working. There seemed to be people always wanting to see him. When we divided our house in Pekin into two parts, we had put some special care and attention to the little section that was to be his waiting room and study. I noticed that when he was home this room was nearly always filled with people wishing to see him, and so to keep them occupied while waiting their turn, I began filling shelves across two walls with our interesting collection of antique bottles.

It started with my interest in pressed glass. On our drives around Illinois, or later our cross-country trips, I always watched for antique shops. At first Everett would just patiently wait while I browsed through the pressed glass collections, but then he became a collector also. He liked to tell people that he became a bottle collector in self-defense—and from boredom in waiting for me to finish browsing in pressed glass.

In any case he accumulated a lovely collection of antique bottles. Some are reflections of history, with portraits of Washington and Lincoln pressed into the glass. One of Everett's favorites was a little brown bitters bottle imprinted with "Tippe-canoe and Tyler Too," referring to the historical presidential campaign in 1840 of William Henry Harrison (hero of the Battle of Tippecanoe) and John Tyler.

Those "bitters" bottles, as they were called, contained the home remedy for whatever ailed you. One swallow and all your aches and pains disappeared. They were about two-thirds alcohol, Everett said, but the bottles were beautiful.

Then there were his barber's bottles, those delightful old-fashioned bottles we used to see in front of the mirror on the counter in the barber's shop. They are made of beautifully glazed enamel, with tiny enameled flowers on them. Some are lettered in graceful Gothic—for such plain names as Bay Rum and Witch Hazel.

When all of these different kinds of bottles were lined up on the shelves in a big open floor-to-ceiling cupboard, they formed quite a lovely grouping and were a constant source of fascination to my husband's constituents, who passed the time looking them over very carefully.

Nearly everyone who came to our house in Pekin admired the lovely lace doilies my mother crocheted for the backs and arms of chairs and sofas, and as table centerpieces . . . And my husband loved coming home to the heady odor that flowed from our kitchen, the smell of homemade bread in the oven and my fried chicken a-frying. He used to say that our kitchen in Pekin had the most fragrant odor on earth, even more beautiful than orange blossoms . . .

That was a pleasant and placid life we had in Pekin, a sweet life, and I wanted it never to end.

During those "adjournments" when Everett was home, we took long drives through the country. It was during these drives that I felt my husband's attachment to the Land of Lincoln most strongly. At first he was the one who always drove the car but eventually I became the family chauffeur, which gave him the opportunity to gaze endlessly out of the window upon the prairies and farmlands he loved so well. He was always interested in crops and cattle and hogs and corn and everything about farming. Farming had been such an important part of his early childhood, and he never lost his attachment to the soil.

He loved Washington. But he could hardly wait to get back to Pekin and his 16th District to look over his beloved prairies and see his cornfields freshly planted or in blossom . . . And his fields of soybeans!

Everyone knew of Everett's dedication to the marigold, but not so many knew that he was also a champion of the lonely little bean, especially the soybean. Long after he became a senator, he wrote the preface to a cookbook, of all things, called *The Complete Bean Cookbook* by Victor Bennett, and the preface was reprinted in the *Soybean Digest*. It was an amusing little essay which illustrates my husband's rather wry sense of humor and his ability to laugh at himself, as well as his knowledge of such basics of life as beans. Although it was not written until many years later, after he became a senator, I think here is the place to preserve it and share it with you, for here is where it really began, on the prairies of Illinois.

Preface to *The Complete Bean Cookbook* by Victor Bennett. Also reprinted in the *Soybean Digest*, February 1967.

HOMAGE TO THE BEAN
(*Everett McKinley Dirksen*)

It was many years ago that a very dignified and slightly belligerent Senator took himself to the Senators' dining room to order bean soup, only to discover that there was no bean soup on the menu. This dereliction on the part of the Senate dining room cooks called for an immediate declaration of war and the Senator promptly introduced a resolution to the effect that henceforth not a day should pass when the Senate was in session and the restaurant open that there would not be bean soup on the calendar. It has, therefore, become an inviolate practice and a glorious tradition that the humble little bean should always be honored.

There is much to be said for the succulent little bean. In fact, there is much to be said for any kind of a bean, be it kidney, navy, green, wax, Kentucky, chili, baked, pinto, Mexican or any other kind. Not only is it high in nutriment, but in that particular kind of nutritious value referred to as protein—the stuff that imparts energy and drive to the bean eater and particularly the Senators who need this sustaining force when they prepare for a long speech on the Senate floor.

I venture the belief that marathon speakers of the Senate going back as far as the day of the celebrated "Kingfish," Senator Huey Pierce Long of Louisiana, and coming down to the modern marathoners in the forensic art such as Senator Strom Thurmond of South Carolina and Senator Wayne Morse of Oregon, both of whom have spoken well in excess of 20 hours and felt no ill effects, would agree the little bean had much to do with this sustained torrent of oratory.

In my enumeration of the bean varieties, I forgot to include one of the most celebrated of all beans, namely, the soybean. Not only has this little Oriental product sustained a civilization in China for perhaps thousands of years, but it has been broken down into so many components that, like Atlas, it fairly carries the weight of the world on its tiny little shoulders. The soybean today produces soya cake for cattle feed which is highly prized by dairymen and beef producers. Its oils are used for preparing table spreads and cooking oils. It is low in unsaturated fats and is prized by dietitians and that vast host who devote so much of a lifetime to keeping a svelte figure. Its oils are further broken down for use in house paints and the soya cake can now be compressed so hard that it makes door handles and gadgetry without number.

Some day some historical bone-picker seeking a subject for a world-shaking thesis that will live as long as Shakespeare will hit upon the lonely bean. What a welter of knowledge he will develop in his research and I am sure he will come to the conclusion that without the bean, the earth would have long since slipped into orbit and disappeared among a galaxy inhabited by bean-eaters. Hail to the bean!

Such was the delightful minutiae of a man whose mind oftentimes was burdened with the gravest problems of those years. Perhaps I am prejudiced because he happened to be my husband, but it does seem remarkable to me that a man like Everett Dirksen could find occasion in his political career even to think about the soybean and the marigold, much less write about them.

I knew those golden days in Pekin must come to an end. I knew at the end of his first term and his re-election for a second that my husband was destined for something bigger than being a one-term congressman. I must confess that in one part of my heart there was a deep-down secret wish that he would come back to Pekin to stay—for good. At the same time it would have been unbearable to see him lose an election, to give up the goals he had set his heart on.

It was only my own timidity and insecurity that made me dread moving to Washington. A wife is very important to her husband's career. I did know that. But I knew nothing about Washington politics or Washington social life. I knew that my husband was going far. Would I be able to keep up with him? Could I learn enough to be helpful to him? I had a business head, yes, I had proved that with the bakery. I had clerked in a store, I could add and subtract, I could operate a comptometer, and I could sing a little. That was the extent of my worldliness. I was a small-town girl with no experience to prepare me for the life of a wife of a congressman in the nation's capital.

But I knew that wherever he went my place should be at his side and that is where I wanted to be.

I was timid and afraid of the world he now moved in and the things he talked about—bills and appropriations.

And sometimes I worried that I lacked the proper clothes, the proper silver and china for the wife of a Washington congressman.

So I put off moving to Washington as long as I could, and I lived from one adjournment to the next.

Everett wrote me a letter or a card every day during the years that we were separated. From his letters I could tell that he was often homesick, and that he looked forward to those adjournments as eagerly as did I.

And though he cared for me a great deal, I think I also fulfilled a need in him when we were separated. I was his link with the Land of Lincoln that he loved so deeply.

Chapter 7

Love Letters and Others

Through the years I have kept all the letters my husband wrote to me. Among the ones I treasure most are those he wrote every day while he was in Washington in the early years when we were separated.

Others might not consider them love letters, but I do.

His letters were always written to Joy and me together, and although he usually signed them simply "Daddy" or "Pops," his imaginative mind found infinitely varied terms of endearment for the two of us.

Should I blush? I thought about it. But no. This is the story of my life with my husband, and his letters give an insight into the man my husband was.

They show his affectionate devotion to his family. But more than that, they provide a unique personal commentary of Everett Dirksen's activities and observations on the social and political scene during a critical period in American history, our involvement in World War II.

It would be an enormous task to sort through all the bushels of his letters I still have, many in his extremely fine and barely legible handwriting, but I have selected a sampling of letters spanning a ten-year period, from 1935 through 1945, to include here.

1935

January 2, 1935

Darling Mumsie and Punkin:

. . . Today we had a number of preliminary meetings. It's like getting back to school after the summer vacation is over and shaking hands with all old friends and meeting new ones . . .

We had our party caucus this morning at eleven. It was a perfunctory affair but anyway I got one thing I wanted—member of the National Republican Congressional Committee . . . All is in readiness for tomorrow. The lights are up and loud speakers will be on hand for the opening of another Congress. However, it's not going to be so hot as I see it. We know in advance that the old gag rule and the steam roller will flatten us out plenty from time to time but anyway, we'll fight them the best we know how.

Suppose the galleries will be filled as usual. Each member gets but one gallery seat and I don't know what to do with mine . . .

January 4, 1935

Darling Mumsie & Joyly:

Just this minute got your very sweet birthday telegram. I sort of felt that it would come and that's why I stuck around the office after the short session today. Just for that, I send you a whole bundle of love and kisses. Well, the great ceremony is all over. Wasn't so hot altho I suppose it is of some import to the many new folks who have come to Washington to see the President. The First Lady, as usual, was in the gallery knitting. I could be awfully catty about that but I won't. There was the usual array of long tailed formal morning attire mixed with the ordinarily attired low brows like myself. I wore my "Bankers Gray" (How I like to say that) with the soft red tie to go with it, spats and a lot of fuzzy hair. Swimming makes my hair wilder than ever and I guess I gotta start having it braided. The message didn't impress me very much (but that's off the record). It was the usual

political speech but I doubt whether it will go down as well with
the folks who are still on relief and waiting for jobs. In a good
hour, the whole thing was over, and like a lot of schoolboys, we
were given a holiday for the rest of the day. (That is to say, a
holiday to go back and work and chase errands.) . . . I feel a
lot older and a lot more dignified now that I've got another
birthday [his thirty-ninth]. Guess I shall have to put on dignity
and act my age, what? Do so hope that you're feeling better and
that this will find you up and around again . . .

I told the First Lady you had the "flu" and she said she sends
her very best wishes. How's that? But I'll do much better. I'll send
you whole oodles of hugs and love and kisses.

January 9
5:30 p.m.

Darling Mumsie and Punkin:

. . . Talk about fog—we're still having it. This is the third
day. Misty and rainy all day and very gloomy. But there's sunshine even in gloom. Just informed that I was certified to the
Banking & Currency Committee.

Sunday.

Darling Mumsie & Joyly-Boyly:

. . . President's message was received just so-so. We've had so
many of these prophecies, while people are still looking for jobs
that it doesn't ring the bell like it did two years ago when the
Adm'n was just starting out.

January 16, 1935

Darling Mumsie and Punkindoodle:

. . . Your daughter is right. 'Maginary hugs ain't nearly so good
as real hugs but I'm hugging you anyway. Feeling pretty good
again. Just hitting the stride. Two committee meetings today.

Talked for an hour and ten minutes on the floor today. Lots of compliments. Feel a bit used up however and now I gotta correct the silly thing. It looks like a book . . . It's ten o'clock. I've been working for 3½ hours correcting the manuscript of that hour and ten minute speech I delivered. Huey Long is on the air tonight and I want to get home and hear him . . .

Sunday Morning.

Darling Mumsie Sweet and Punkin-Pie:

. . . The fun begins Tuesday when we consider the 4 billion dollar works bill. Gag rule and all that sort of thing . . .

First meeting of our Banking & Currency Committee takes place this week. Between three committees, floor work, letters, magazine articles etc. I'm a busy guy, eh what? For every rain drop today, I'm sending you a hug and a kiss and a big juicy kiss for the Snickle-fritz.

Wednesday, Jan. 23, 1935.

Darlingest Mumsie Pal and Punkin Cabbage:

. . . Kinda tired. Been on the floor all afternoon, made a speech, expect to vote against this 4 billion dollar bill because it's bad, and will probably catch cain. However, it's just like the Economy Bill. Maybe he who laughs last laughs best . . .

January 25, 1935.

Darling Mumsie and Joyly-Boyly:

. . . Awfully tired. Another long day on the floor. Made a short speech. Had a long Committee meeting this morning and quizzed Mr. Jesse Jones, Chairman of the RFC.

We adjourned tonight until Monday . . . Believe I shall go to a movie tonight. They're showing "The Life of a Bengal Lancer" and having read the book years ago, it sort of appeals to me as exciting.

. . . Nighty-night, sweetie pie and a big kiss for you and a big kiss for her majesty, the Queen of the Ranch.

Sunday. February 3.

Darling Mumsie and Cabbage:

Today is filing day, clean-up day, reading day, odds-and-ends day. It's just five o'clock . . . Wish I could see the Joyly with her lumberjack and her sled. She must be a card, with red cheeks, coasting in this cold weather. It's good for her. Just the exercise that she needs.

I am looking forward to the big events and to the Joyly's birthday . . . Week from today I expect to be giving you a big hug and kiss and also your coasting daughter. Until then, I'll send a lot of samples . . .

Feb. 19, 1935. 8:30 a.m.

Darling Pal and Little Pal:

Thought I'd write you first thing this morning. Last thing I looked at last night before going to sleep was your picture, hanging on the wall and the last thing I heard was the radio playing "On the Good Ship Lollipop" so I just sort of drifted off to sleep. Slept right well and was I tired . . . Am enclosing some things which might be of interest, especially the booklet on Let's Make a Garden. That makes me homesick . . . Love and hugs.

March 1, 1935

Darling Pal:

. . . Weather is springy this morning and believe it or not but I walked to work. Had an appetite like a horse when I got to the capital and ate mush, bacon, honey, and coffee for breakfast . . . Going to the home of Congressman Hamilton Fish of NY tonight for a 7:30 stag dinner. Leaving Tuesday at three for Philadelphia to make a speech and will be back early Wednesday morning in time for work . . .

March 2, 1935

Darling Mumsie Wumsie and Punkin:

Thought sure I'd get a bit of rest today but no such luck. Stuff piled up as high as ever.

Went to Mr. Fish's dinner last night. There were nine of us there and was it swanky. Must tell you a little about it. First we had cocktails before dinner together with stuffed olives and hors d'oeuvres of some kind or other. Stood around and finally went into the dinner room in order of seniority. The room had lots of large oil portraits of Mrs. Fish's ancestors. Silver candelabras with black candles. At dinner they served sherry, chilled white wine, mint on ice, and whiskey. First course was soup. Then lobster. Then beef with green peas and wild rice. Then came salad. Then came a kind of jelly in which roquefort cheese had been dissolved. Then came ice cream and Blue Bristol deep finger bowls, cigars etc. Those deep finger bowls are funny. You dip your finger in the water and start rubbing it around the edge of the bowl and it sounds like a sweet sounding bell. You must ask me about it. Seemed to use a hundred different plates to serve dinner. The dessert by the way was served on gold plates and were they swanky.

Arose early, and walked most of the way to work. Bought your daughter a globe—that is a geographical globe. You must brush up on your geography and teach her accurately about latitude and longitude. I think there is an information book with it. Also, am today sending a large wall map of the U.S. on linen. It's a pretty big affair but you can probably rearrange the study to put it up on one of the walls.

. . . Believe it or not, I bought a flower this morning for my desk. Was poking along and saw these potted pink hyacinths so I had to buy one and have it standing right in front of me. Makes me feel better and more cheerful. I like the perfume and the gay tone that it lends to the office. Guess maybe it's kind of silly, what?

Hugs and kisses and much love . . .

March 3, 1935

Darling Palsie-Walsie and Punkin:

. . . Had a big affair yesterday. Open house in our office. About a dozen assorted newspapermen, dozen secretaries, virtually all of the Illinois members of Congress, and a few members from Ga., Miss., etc were in. Just informal. They all drank but remained decorous and talked incessantly. It keeps one in the good graces of the Democrats and always yields big dividends . . .

My flower looks so pretty and pert and gay. Must give it some water too sometime today . . .

Hope your sweet perky littly precious daughter likes the globe. You gotta get out the encyclopedia now and brush up ACCU-RATELY on geography. That'll do you a lot of good. Between the map and the globe and you two guys studying, what chance will I have to match wits with you. Not much? . . .

Friday night.

Mumsie Sweet and Punkin-cabbage:

. . . My hyacinth is turning a bit yellow and the blooms are gradually fading. Guess maybe I've forgotten to water it and I'll do so as soon as I've finished this letter . . .

Didn't adjourn until six-thirty tonight and will be in session tomorrow. We have our Home Loan bill on the floor and the fur has been flying all day . . .

Did you hear Huey last night? He's setting them on their ear and is a real menace to Democratic success next year. They'd like to dump him in the ocean if they dared . . .

Sunday morning.

Sweetie Pie and Cabbage:

This is Sunday morning. Got up about eight o'clock. Lolled around for a change, drank some grape fruit juice, made some coffee, made an egg and bacon sandwich, took a bath, read the newspapers, then walked out Rhode Island to New Jersey, down New Jersey to the Plaza, across the Plaza to the office. Got kinda tired but the walk is a great stimulator for the mind. Feeling tip top and expect to spend the entire day in the office getting out letters and looking over books and making some notes . . .

I think you've done a splendid job with the family budget and just for that I'm giving you a great big long hard kiss. And I'm throwing in a couple of hugs for good measure . . .

1938

My birthday. (Jan. 4)

Honey Sweeties:

Well, I'm forty-two years young. Feel younger every day. Feel full of vigor and zest. That's because of you. That's because you never grow any older. It's a grand thing. Keeps me younger too . . .

Guess I fall in love with you all over again, every time I see you . . .

Had a brief session today . . . The President looked pretty good but lacked punch. Too much smirk about him as he delivered his message. The applause was rather scattered. He didn't go over. What applause was there was largely out of respect for his position as Chief Executive. First Appropriation Bill (mine) comes up Thursday. Will be busy on that for a week . . .

Jan. 10, 1938

Sweetie Pies:

. . . Well, today was The Day. There was a great tension. Only 20 minutes of debate under the rule and then we proceeded to vote. The score was 209 to 188. The House has spoken but the issue lives on. If the members are afraid to stand up and be counted when this sort of a proposal comes along, how much can the people of the country expect if the President asked this

Congress to sanction a war. In the same paper tonight which announced the House Kills War Vote Proposal was another headline article to the effect that "The President will ask Congress for $200,000,000 for planes and ships." There you have the answer. Don't be surprised if within three or four months, we may be asked to sanction a course of blockading Japan along with Great Britain. All of which means to me that this situation is bad. Cordell Hull, Secretary of State, told some small group of members a short time ago that we had to lick Japan. So, get ready the wreaths when that time comes. A Democrat from Kansas told me that never in his career was so much pressure put on the Demo members. The Speaker and the Leader spent the morning calling the boys in and even Mr. Farley and other Cabinet officials phoned them all morning that they had to go along with the President or else. All of which will be aired when the time comes.

March 4.

Darling Mumsie and Toe Wiggler:

Did you know that today is the fifth anniversary of my membership in the House of Representatives. It was five years ago that I joined Uncle Sam's official family and what an amazing five years they have been . . . After five years of public service, it is a bit interesting to become introspective and look back over the years. So much has happened. So many amazing things have taken place. The country is so unreal and so different. Not by the greatest stretch of the imagination could one contemplate all the things of great import that have taken place . . . And over it all is the iridescent glow of a beautiful and hallowed family life, built on love and understanding and blessed with beauty. And to you My Sweet I can whisper that our love is undiminished and shines with that same constancy that has made it so wonderful. I don't know what the years hold for us but whatever my attainments might be, they will be because of you and your fidelity and inspiration and love. And for that a precious kiss and another one for that other precious person—The Punkin . . .

Saturday afternoon.
[He did not always date his letters]

Honey Mumsie and Honey Toots:

. . . There is the feel of spring everywhere . . . We must make haste to get ourselves that farm even if it's only 80 acres because we want that feeling of security that comes from having a spot of earth where one can dig and scratch and develop a livelihood. I don't like this war business that is going on and don't like the thought of the regimentation and dictatorship that goes with it. I shall feel infinitely better when we get a bit of land with a snuggly little house on it and be able to say—Come what may, here we shall till the Good Earth and raise food and provender.

March 18

Honey Bunches and Honey Punches:

. . . Your precious daughter will be interested in knowing that Deanna Durbin sat in the gallery yesterday. She wore a blue dress, blue turn-up hat and a red bow at her throat. Last night they had a party for her at the Mayflower and a lot of children appeared for autographs. The assistant manager told me she was a bit snooty and refused to autograph any books because she was tired. Maybe that's what they call temperament but if so, I shall scratch Miss Durbin off the list.

Saturday morning

Dear Sweetie Banker:

. . . Yes, darling, we're making progress. Little by little, the property is being cleared of debt . . . and soon we must start on the farm . . . I get quite a kick out of the precious Toots wanting to carry bus fare. There's diligence and foresight for you. It shows rare independence and the desire to be punctual. I could worship her for that.

April 19

Darling Mums and Toots:

Well, Mother Nature has really been kind to us today and sent a glorious, sunny day with all the proper trimmings such as music of the birds and perfume of the flowers. She's just making up for her derelictions of yesterday. You know they had the opening ball game yesterday so we shut up shop and sallied forth under gray skies to see the game. There was a huge crowd and a lot of ceremony as the President pitched the first ball but it began to drizzle and the game wasn't much . . .

May 13

Darlings:

. . . The other day the barber put some tonic on my hair and combed it back so it was flat and shiny. Did I get a razz on the floor and then the argument began as to whether I looked better with sleek hair or fluffy hair and whether I looked younger one way or another. It never was settled but my hair is wavy again and I guess it will continue that way . . .

May 20

Darlings:

Your activities are fairly breath-taking. I'm not sure but what you can give cards and spades to a lady named Eleanor . . . Finished the Flood Control Bill last night about six fifteen. That's another thing out of the way . . .

May 25

Honey Bunch:

This is the last letter. I start winding up. Tonight I pack . . . Felt like a steam roller ran over me last night. We were in session until nearly eleven o'clock and that's an ordeal in a chamber where the air is so stuffy and bad. More coldish gray weather. Weather man is getting to be terrible. Anyway there will be sunshine when I get home—perpetual sunshine.

June 8

Mums and Mumps:

. . . So you're spending beyond your income. Guess I gotta call you Eleanor or Franklin. Anyway, darling, you must take what you need. So the punk and your ma need some clothes . . . It's late. Just got off the floor after a long and hard day . . . Still hoping that we make it by Saturday. Never can tell.

Monday night

Hi-yuh Sugars:

It's cold. Rained this morning and snowed a bitsy . . . Just my kind of weather . . . Made a short speech on the Farm Bill today. It's been a kind of tussling day on the floor. Tempers are still a bit short. The President comes back tonight I 'spect on account of his toothache. Apparently nothing serious. Only disagreeable . . . Heard a rather interesting sermon yesterday. Church was full. One thing I don't like about that Covenant Presbyterian is the formality. Just a little too much. If the Lord came to earth, He could hardly get in there unless He had on a cutaway and striped pants.

1939

October 6

Darling Tootsies:

. . . Must stop off at PWA and also WPA in the morning on a couple of projects. So I've got my work in fair shape. I want to be on hand in the Senate when the debate begins and have a notebook with me. It should prove instructive and should develop a lot of careful research material.

The opponents to the embargo have been saying that they have more than enough votes to repeal it. I learned today that four have switched to the other side and it's by no means certain that even the Senate will repeal it. In fact, it's even money for the moment at least that they don't . . .

[*In the events leading up to World War II, Germany had invaded Poland on September 1, 1939. President Roosevelt proclaimed a limited national emergency and urged a special session of Congress to repeal the arms embargo which had prohibited the export of arms and munitions to belligerent powers. The Neutrality Act of 1939 repealed the embargo. The bill passed the Senate on October 27 and the House on November 2.*]

Some of the members went home and came right back. Seems that the people insisted that they get back down here and save the country. There is much of that feeling right now . . . I don't hear a word about the candidates who are running for Governor. It would appear that the war has sort of crowded them off the front page . . . I hope you become a swell typist and a swell stenographer because I can think of all sorts of work for you to do . . . Guess maybe I better close up my workshop now . . .

[*Undated*]
[*Early October*]

Honey Pies:

. . . That Laboratory dedication comes on Wednesday the 18th at 11:30 in the morning. Secretary Wallace will be on hand. The dedication service will be short and the Secretary will deliver his principal address at night in the Shrine Temple. It should draw a great crowd.

Depending some on the nature of the schedule here, I may come a few days sooner than the 18th. I have an idea that the Adm'n felt it could put this bill over in a hurry and now it's run into something of a snag. In talking with Senator [*Charles*] Tobey [*of New Hampshire*] today, he intimated that lots of time would be taken in debate. Most anything could happen including the end of the war. Wouldn't that be a business. . . .

The headliners today were Connally of Texas for repeal and Vandenberg* against repeal. Connally made a messy speech, full of sarcastic remarks and illogical statements. It was a two hour sample of school boy oratory. He ended six times before he sat down. Vandenberg followed his manuscript. It was an excellent speech, well tied together, well-reasoned, and to the point. I believe it stamps him as the Republican nominee in 1940. After making due allowances for his love of words and rhetorical embellishments, it was still a great speech. It should stir up the temperature of the country.

The amazing thing about this embargo business is that everybody agrees (including the Pres.) that it's to help the allies. But they don't dare say so in public. If they do, there will be another emotional wave go over the land . . .

Oct. 27, 1939.

Honey Bunch:

I made my speech. It was excellently received. It has disturbed the leadership, I'm afraid. It will read well. Somehow I think it's convincing. One member from Mass. walked out after the first few paragraphs. Later he came to see me and said, "I had to walk out on you. I have been on the side that favors repeal of the embargo and I'm afraid you might make me change my mind." I thought that was a high compliment. At the moment, there is a growing disposition that the embargo will not carry in the House. Wouldn't that be something . . . [*But it did.*]

Gonna have a luncheon tomorrow in the House Restaurant for the Rep. members from Illinois to discuss Illinois politics. Some of them are still away. Saturday is a good day for that kind of fat chewing. It probably won't result in anything much but will serve a bit of a purpose . . .

* Senator Tom Connally and Senator Arthur H. Vandenberg of Michigan.

Dec. 7, 1939.

Sweetie Pie:

. . . Today, we have a variety of things before the Committee which will take all day.

Tomorrow we have Secretary Wallace.

If the pressure keeps up, I shall fool them by going to a movie tonight and forgetting all about this business for a few hours.

Dewey made an interesting speech but the real test comes when he seeks to explain in detail how it shall all be done . . .

The Gridiron is Saturday . . .

Friday.

Honey Kids:

. . . Did a bitsy shopping last night for about an hour. The stores are jammed to the guards. Apparently folks have money to spend for Christmas.

About coming home, there is every likelihood of leaving here Wednesday the 20th and arriving in Chicago via the B&O on Thursday morning. Guess you can sort of count on that arrangement unless I wire you otherwise. Couldn't think of anything quite so interesting, stimulating, delightful, absorbing, felicitous, inspiriting and rehabilitating as to have youse kids there at the train to meet me. Will doctor up my cold so I'll be feeling good when I arrive . . .

. . . It will be such a delight & joy to be home & enjoy Christmas as only we can do—at home, together, filled with the true spirit of the occasion. Then too, there is our wedding anniversary. As the years march on, I find you so absolutely indispensable. But more than that, I find as I search the recesses of heart and soul for a real evaluation of my attachment for you, that I love you more and more with each fading year. It will be ever that way, Tootsie Darling.

1940

(*The following two letters were undated but can be pin-pointed by their contents. German troops entered Paris on June 14, 1940.*)

Monday Morning

Darlings:

The pictures are on my desk where I can always look at them. I think they're grand. I think you and the Toots are grand for so sweetly remembering me on Father's Day with such an appropriate and highly acceptable remembrance. Couldn't think of anything I would rather have. Kisses for both of youse kids . . .

The headlines are black today. France surrendered. There will be even greater insistence that we remain here on duty . . .

My work is now cut out for me and I shall devote myself to the job of building a larger majority in Congress and getting some extra Republicans from Illinois . . .

Monday Evening

Darlings—

How fast the world moves. In a single day, the Germans approach Paris, the Italians join the war and the President makes a name-calling speech which cannot help matters. Truly a big and momentous day in world history.

Already, I observe editorials suggesting that Congress remain in Wash. The Peoria Star for Sunday so proclaimed Democrats who would normally vote to adjourn are in doubt. Anything can happen.

I entertain a sense of dread as I hear members—especially seasoned members—say that soon we shall be in war. It's a bit of irony! To have served in one war and perhaps be called to vote on another, 23 yrs later. Let us hope & pray that it will not be.

Tonight the lobby is filled with high school graduates. They're so young and virile! What a shame that in other lands, youngsters of that age are in uniforms.

Tonight it is cool and comfortable. Ears will be glued to radios for even more war news. And so by easy, self-imposed discipline, the spirit moves to frenzy and reason goes out of the window. And now I feel better after having written you. Much love.

1945

(Early in 1945, toward the close of the Second World War, Everett was sent on a four-month inspection tour of several countries, studying the operation of lend-lease, UNRRA and also agricultural conditions. The tour took him to Europe, Africa, China, Burma, India and the countries of the Middle East. He left the United States on February 21, 1945. By this time I had moved to Washington and had become involved in my own wartime activities. His letters were addressed to me there, at the Mayflower Hotel, where we lived at the time.)

February 23, Montreal.

Honey Kids—

. . . Except for the uniforms one would hardly know in Montreal that a war is on. Plenty of meat (all varieties), canned goods, clothes, shoes, jewelry, etc. Even butter and sugar seem plentiful . . . This is the province (Quebec) which has resisted conscription. It is quite an issue and the Northwest Mounted Police have been around arresting some of the young men of draft age . . . Had a lovely luncheon yesterday with the Consul and his staff. All of them are career men and fine folks . . .

February 27, London

Sweetie Pie—

. . . Churchill came at 12:00 and spoke for an hour. Age and fatigue begin to show. He halts and repeats a good deal. Still sparkles, however, and has a sense of humor . . .

March 1, London

Darling Kids—

. . . Visited Oxford. Beautiful place. Saw the boys in their colored sweaters playing hockey . . . Today I did a hospital and saw about twenty lads from Illinois. None from our area. It's something. You realize there's a war on.

Ran into Sam Goldwyn, the movie magnate . . .

Embassy called. Ambassador Winant wanted to see me before I left. Spent an hour with him. A strange mystical austere man. Like Lincoln. The under secretary for foreign affairs and the Soviet Ambassador came. Winant asked me to remain a while and visit. Enjoyed it . . . (*John G. Winant was Ambassador to Great Britain, 1941–46.*)

March 2, London

Darling Toots-Poots—

. . . Traveling in war time is not too pleasant but then I did not expect it to be.

The British have been very gracious and kind. I met quite a few officials of government and also military men. Civilians. They make every effort to be helpful. Lunched with several members of Parliament. When all is said and done, it is not so unlike Congress . . .

March 3
En Route Paris to Marseille

Sweetie Pie—

. . . Paris is dim, austere, cheerless and seems unhappy . . . Quite a lot of soldiers who are well-behaved, well groomed and orderly . . .

Tues. March 6, 1945
(Cairo to Karachi)

Darling Kids—

I'm sitting in a transport plane looking out of the window. We're at 8000 feet en route from Cairo to Karachi a distance of 1600 miles. We should make it in 5 hrs. 30 min. . . .

Soldiers, generally, are rather resentful about strikes back home. They've read in the "Stars & Stripes" (the service newspaper which comes out once each week) about the strike in Detroit and it nettles them a good deal.

All seem anxious to bring the war to an end that they might go home. They are no different from the men in the last war in that respect . . .

Delhi
Sunday, March 11, 1945

Darling Kids—

So this is Delhi! . . . Moving right along. Had a rough trip from Bombay yesterday afternoon . . .

At Agra we circled over the famous Taj Mahal and had a superb view . . .

Training planes are constantly roaring overhead. Birds are also noisy this morning.

I'm still fascinated by all that I see . . .

March 13, New Delhi

Darling Kids—

. . . Yesterday afternoon I attended the session of the Indian assembly which corresponds to our House. It was interesting. The session closed at 5:00 and thereafter we had tea with Dr. Ambedkar, the leader of the untouchables. He's a graduate of Columbia and an extremely able, well-read person . . . The highlight of the day, of course, was the dinner at the Viceroy's palace. Will not endeavor to give you details now but it was truly regal. The place is one of amazing splendor. Lady Wavell is quite charming . . . (*She was wife of Archibald Percival Wavell, then British field marshal and Viceroy of India, and commander in chief of the Middle East during the Second World War.*)

Teheran, Iran
Saturday, March 24, 1945

Honey Kids:

. . . The trip from Karachi to Abadan was rather tiring. It was about an eight-hour trip at 8500 feet on the so-called bucket seats which are nothing more than deep scallops in a long seat made out of metal. Since we did not have blankets, there was nothing to use as a cushion and those seats got quite hard.

Several Colonels were on hand to meet me and we at once went to the guest house where after a lot of conversation, I went to bed and slept reasonably well . . .

Across the river from Abadan is Khorramshahr which was the big base port for supplies. I inspected the barracks, hospital, mess halls, docks and other installations and in the afternoon, we took a boat ride to Basra . . .

. . . So here I am in Teheran. Made an inspection early this morning—visited the hospital, the cemetery, the University, the mosques, the old quarter of the city, lunched with General Booth, had a long session with Ambassador Morris. Will go back to the Embassy later today for tea.

I went to see the hall in the Soviet Embassy where Churchill, Stalin and Roosevelt met at the conference . . . (*Referring to the Teheran Conference of November 28–December 1, 1943, a meeting of President Roosevelt, Premier Stalin and Prime Minister Churchill, held to strengthen the cooperation of the United States, Great Britain, and the USSR in the Second World War.*)

Teheran, Sunday
March 25, 1945

Sweetie Puddin—

. . . Last night, General Booth bestowed upon me the official insignia of the Persian Gulf Command. It is a shield with a red scimitar representing Iran and a silver sun representing Iraq with a green background. Quite nice and I appreciate it . . .

Guess that's all for the moment. My next letter should be from Baghdad. Tell Toots I'll look for Ali Baba and the Forty Thieves. By-bee precious. Heaps of hugs and love. Be seeing you before long. Pops-wops.

March 27, Baghdad, Iraq

Sweetie Kids—

At last I arrived in Baghdad on the Tigris River (pop. 750,000) but it doesn't look a bit like the movies. Nor could I find Ali Baba. As for the forty thieves, I'll tell you about that later . . .

Beyrouth
Monday, April 9, 1945

Honey Guys—

. . . As I listen to the various discussions about Russia, Britain, France, post-war plans, oil and what not, it all seems a bit vain and bewildering. Even here, there is a very tight censorship and you get to wondering about this thing called Freedom.

You may recall that Mr. Jordan of Boston (the astrology man) indicated that the problems after the war would be more baffling and of greater magnitude than the war itself. I'm inclined to agree . . .

As soon as I finish this, I thought I might brush up a bit on the journeys of the Apostle Paul. All of this is interesting and historic land . . .

Damascus
Tuesday April 10, 1945

Honey Kids:

. . . We came yesterday over the Lebanon mountains by car at
an elevation of 5000 feet and then down into the broad plain at
the edge of the desert where Damascus is located . . .

Had time only to attend the Parliament yesterday. Like the one
for Lebanon it consists only of a Chamber of Deputies. Had a
visit with the Speaker and then attended the session. While the
externals are of course different, it is not essentially unlike all
parliamentary bodies . . .

Today we have a visit with the Prime Minister and then
lunch with the President of Syria. This afternoon we'll be free
to roam about and see the city and the mosque and also look in
the stores. If the prices are not too outlandish I shall pick up
some silk brocade. Best prices at Jerusalem was $32.00 a yard.
That gives a further idea of what inflation is like. Am informed
that prices are a good deal cheaper in Turkey so I shall also be
on the alert when I get there . . .

Strange mixture here of camels, automobiles and burros. Thus
does the ancient blend into the modern . . .

Ankara, Turkey
Friday April 13, 1945

Darling Kids:

It's me again.

First shock of the day of course was the phone call announcing
the President's death. [On April 12] It is in every sense a shock
and most untimely. There is a strange irony about the fact that he
should be called away when the end of the war was in sight
and on the eve of the San Francisco conference. The American
Mission here declared a formal 30-day period of mourning,
provided arm bands and black ties. During that time, there will

be abstinence from all formal affairs such as dinners, luncheons, dancing etc.

Spent the day inspecting OWI, FEA and the Mission. Had a meeting with all of the staffs—about 35 people.

The course of the plane from Beyrouth here was about a straight line from Beyrouth over the Island of Cyprus and then angled a bit to Ankara. It's quite mountainous and there was snow at the higher levels. Country generally is not too prepossessing.

Ankara is divided into old Ankara which is just an old Oriental town and new Ankara where the Government buildings, legations etc. are located. The town was built by Kemal Ataturk, dynamic Turk who died some years ago.* The buildings were all built by German engineers and are quite "boxy"—if you know what I mean.

Saturday, there will be memorial exercises for the President at the residence of the Ministry and we shall all attend. They had to send to Istanbul (Constantinople) for a preacher. There are neither Protestant preachers nor Protestant churches here.

The Germans have a huge Legation here with a staff of 150, all of whom are interned. They are expected to go home by an exchange of prisoners but don't want to go home. That is quite understandable.

Tomorrow we go to Istanbul by train and will then return here and catch the plane for Cairo on Friday. First thing I shall do is to go into hiding and read all your letters. What a day that will be for me!

The weather is quite agreeable—like spring. Had my first bath this morning in about six days. Bath water is really at a premium.

Prices here are terrific. A drink of Scotch costs $2.50. A bar of soap costs $1.00. A very short jaunt in a taxi costs $2.00. Such are the evils of inflation and you can imagine what a hard time the legation clerks have in making both ends meet when they have to shop locally for items.

Met many of the Turkish leaders at cocktails yesterday. The men are not too impressive. The wives were much more so and dress quite well.

* Kemal Ataturk (1881–1938) was the founder of modern Turkey.

Made some inquiries about silk stockings and learned that they are of reasonably good quality and about $2.00 a pair. Bought a few pairs in Damascus but thought I better purchase a few extra pairs. Rather odd that everything is so outrageously high but that silk hose should be reasonably priced.

It's about bedtime. I should take a walk around the block and stretch my legs and then turn in. So here's a good night kiss and a great big hug and all my love.

Sunday April 15, 1945
(Istanbul)

Sweetie Kids:

I'm sitting in the Park Hotel in Istanbul . . .

When we arrived this morning, the Consul General met us in a motor launch and brought us across the Bosporus to the city. Ordinarily, one would come by ferry boat . . .

Had quite a delegation on hand this morning from the Consulate, the OWI, the OSS, the FEA and the Military Attache . . .

Tomorrow there will be another memorial service here for the President at 11:00 o'clock so I presume we shall all attend. Will take a look at the various agencies and then do a bit of sight-seeing . . .

This is one of the key spots of the world and as time goes on, it will loom larger and larger in the international picture.

Wonder just what changes Truman will make if any. After all, he has a mind of his own and his circle of friends are somewhat different from that of the President. Presume Pa. Avenue was jampacked for the ceremony when the body was returned to Washington. Say what they will, it's amazing how highly the ordinary person in this section of the world thought about him . . .

Here as elsewhere prices are outrageous. Yesterday I saw a shop where glassware is sold and went in to price an ordinary water glass. It was $1.65. Such are the ravages of war . . .

Cairo, Egypt
April 23, 1945

Honey Puddin'

This is Cairo. City of more than one million. All races and
nationalities are found here. It's polyglot . . .

On Sunday I stood at the base of Cheops, the largest pyramid
and gazed on the unscrutable sphinx and wondered what happened to 40 centuries of history.

Today, I took time to go to Memphis and see the tomb and
monument to Rameses. Impressive as the remains of an artistic
civilization which did not endure . . .

Had a session with the Prime Minister this morning. He looks
like a very alert American business man in a fez and speaks
excellent English. He served us Turkish coffee. It's a common
custom . . .

Florence May 2, 1945

Honey Gals—

Weather was beastly yesterday, so we didn't fly to the front.
Instead we inspected a camp for German prisoners of war and a
replacement depot. Rained all day . . .

Big news this morning was the announcement of Hitler's death.
It did not make too much of a stir. Most of the men here
are hardened veterans with long service who want to get the
war over and go home . . .

We inspected a disciplinary center where bad soldiers are
rehabilitated. One of the most interesting operations that I've seen
and so different from the old theory that a soldier who had
fallen from grace was just so much dregs and not worth another
chance . . .

Last night the big news was the complete surrender of the
German armies in the Italian theater. Thank God, that much of
it is over and no more lives must be sacrificed. I'm satisfied
that already the set-up is being made for surrender in Europe.

Talked to hundreds of GI's. They want to come home, now that it's over in this theater. Don't blame them . . .

Rome May 5, 1945

Sweetie Guys—

. . . A tour of the Embassy this morning.

And now—hold your breath—a private audience with the Pope at noon. What a saintly, gracious person! It is high adventure and an enriching experience to have met and visited with him. He speaks English quite well. Has lots of questions to ask. It was a 20 minute session and then he gave me 4 rosaries and 3 medals. Also had some photos taken at the Vatican . . .

There have been several demonstrations here in the last day or two over the efforts to Tito and the Jugo Slavs to take over Trieste. That infuriates the Italians. The Communist picture is not too encouraging either . . .

Paris—Tues. May 8, 1945

Honey Kids—

As this is written, I'm sitting in a sitting room on the second floor of the Hotel Ritz. It looks out upon the Place de la Concorde. In the center of this square is the statue of Napoleon, made of captured cannon. People are streaming through the place. Most of them are moving down to the Champs Elysees. It's the wide boulevard where the Arc de Triomphe is located.

Ever since last evening when we arrived from Rome, people, young and old, have been seeking to cast off restraint. They want to slough off the fatigue and weariness of nearly 5 years of conflict. They've wanted to go on an emotional binge. One could discern the fever rise. Today it burst the bounds as the news was officially proclaimed over the radio. [*V-E Day, May 8, 1945, marked the formal end of the war in Europe.*]

Planes zoomed over the Arc de Triomphe. Flags are everywhere. Youngsters are parading. The bells proclaimed the glad fact of an armistice in this theater. Trucks and jeeps filled with youngsters travelled everywhere. The city is filled with soldiers. Traffic is in a snarl. The spirit has been unleashed.

I presume it was much the same at home, and rightly so.

I had an experience of my own. At 2:30 we drove to Versailles where the treaty of 1919 was signed. The celebrated hall was closed. I talked to the guard and told him who I was. He had but one arm. He lost the other in the battle of the Somme in the last war. We shook hands and I pointed to my Legion button. So he escorted us to the Hall of Mirrors where Wilson, Orlando, Clemenceau, Lloyd George, and the German representatives signed the treaty which officially concluded the last war.

The Hall is magnificent. The murals depicting the triumph of French arms over the centuries are superb. Rotten as the Bourbons were, they had imagination and left a legacy to other generations.

At 3:00 o'clock (10:00 A.M. EWT) I stood where Wilson stood. Outside a gun on a Yank tank began a salute to victory. The bells tolled noisily. Joyfully, a crowd of people several blocks distant sang the Marseillaise. The spirit of victory was in the air; it was everywhere—in hearts, and minds and faces of people. It was over, in part, a load had been lifted.

But the sad face of Woodrow Wilson; the determined face of Clemenceau, the tiger of France; the face of the Little Welshman Lloyd George who passed away several weeks ago; the cold countenance of Orlando; the cynical faces of the Germans came wraith-like out of the mirrors. There they were—affixing their signatures to a document designed to end all war.

How ironical it all seems. I saw our troops in the stinking heat of India and the mud of Italy. I've seen them in the bleak stretches of North Africa and in the desert wastes of Iraq. I've visited with 5000 of them if I've talked to one. Magnificent soldiers they are, asking little and giving much. I've seen them in the hospitals—legless, armless, sightless—the grim human wreakage, washed up by the waves of conflict. They conjure up a vision of the millions upon millions of men, women, and children—civilian and military who are the casualties of this struggle, and as I see them marching along in grim, ghostly columns, I think of where I stood this day and what a miserable job this generation has made of a peace that all hoped would endure.

In Italy I saw buildings of grandeur along the ancient Arno River reduced to rubble. In Florence, scene of culture and enlightenment, I saw how the monuments of antiquity crumbled before modern weapons. At Verona, where Shakespeare laid the scene of Romeo and Juliet, I saw humble people with what remained of their furnishings slowly trekking back to a city of debris and destruction. I saw the grass healing the very bosom of earth and trying frantically to cover the scars of shell holes and bomb craters. And as I meditated upon this indescribable destruction and misery, I saw Wilson again at Versailles, in company with Lloyd George, Clemenceau, Orlando and the rest. What a failure it has been; here are the bells and guns of another victory to prove the failure of a generation ago when I was in uniform and served in this very same land against the same enemy.

Will we succeed this time in building a structure of peace that shall have full and fair opportunity to endure? I wonder. I've seen some things, Mumsie, that are disturbing. Already I see Freedom being mocked and leeched away in certain places. I see the vigorous propagation of certain ideologies which imperil the very thing for which young Yanks have died. I see the selfish grasping for power, for economic advantage which can only weaken and then destroy that sense of fairness and that faith which is so requisite to a well-ordered and contented world.

In any event, I believe I see more clearly than ever before what is needed—and needed now—if we are to sterilize the seed of World War III.

Will go to Germany while I'm here and then come home. I'm getting closer and closer. It won't be too long now and then we shall have a celebration of our own—that of sweet reunion. Love

Augsburg, Germany
May 12, 1945

Darling Kids—

It's Sunday—and what a lovely day. Weather is perfect. We spent the night with General Patch* at his billet. He occupies a

* Lieutenant General Alexander M. Patch, Commander of the U. S. Seventh Army.

castle. It's gorgeous. Birds are singing. Flowers bloom. I see fine looking cows. There is a perfect Sunday stillness. Wish you could be here.

From Paris we flew to Augsburg and looked at the desolated city. It's indescribable. The General then drove us to Munich. It's a ghost town. It's impossible to describe a city of 800,000, completely destroyed.

We visited at the Bierhall where Hitler began. Also the Bierhall in Munich where they attempted to assassinate him two years ago. What a lot of water has gone under the bridge since that time.

In the afternoon we went to the notorious prison camp at Dachau. It's quite impossible to describe—the charnal house where these human wrecks were first gassed to death; the crematory where they were burned and the rest of it. While inspecting the crematory, a truck arrived with more dead, broken bodies. It was a revolting thing.

There are still 32,000 persons in the camp. They are the slave laborers from everywhere—Poland, Russia, Austria, the Balkans. They cannot be released until some disposition can be made of them. The hospital wards are still filled with wrecks of people. One marvels how long the spark of life continues to flicker in such wasted bodies. The whole thing recalls Ingersoll's expression of "man's inhumanity to man."

To say the least, it was a full day and I was glad to return to the General's billet for dinner and rest.

As I contemplate the destruction of these great cities—the utter desolation of bridges, railroads, homes, business buildings and what not, I have a feeling that European civilization is done. The whole condition is now ideal for engulfment by Asiatic communism.

Not a happy thing to write on Mother's Day. Wish I could send you a cable today but it's a bit difficult from here. But if I could, I would say "I love you."

Heaps of huglets and kisslets. It's 8:30 A.M. (our time—2:30 A.M. your time) and we leave now for Wiesbaden. By-bee and a heap of hugs.

Chapter 8

Pulling Up Stakes

I mentioned that those letters from 1945 were written to me after I had finally moved to Washington.

When Everett was re-elected for his fourth term in 1938, I knew that my time for decision had arrived. I realized that I must pull up roots from Pekin and make the permanent move to Washington. I belonged there, with my husband. I could not expect to remain a commuter-wife forever.

So, Everett came home to help me pack. Friends had warned me about the "social" life in Washington. They said I would be expected to do a great deal of entertaining at home. When I took inventory of our worldly goods, I realized that we had no silver or crystal, that my china was most inexpensive and my linens limited.

But Everett reminded me, "Spiritual wealth brings more happiness than material wealth. We will have each other and we will make do with the rest."

Our first home in the nation's capital was a small one-bedroom apartment on Rhode Island Avenue. It had another hideaway bed in the living room, a dining alcove and walk-in kitchen. We lived there only a brief time. With the war clouds gathering, we decided to move into a small housekeeping apartment in the Mayflower Hotel. Actually, it was the late summer of 1940 before I could bring myself to face the reality of moving to Washington. We left Joy with her grandmother in Pekin so she could continue school there. I knew that my mother could take care of Joy as well as I could, and I knew that I would be coming back to Pekin often. But knowing this and leaving my child were two quite different things. The move from Pekin was a real wrench for me, although I tried not to let on to my husband.

I made a firm resolution. I would spend every possible moment improving myself in ways that would be helpful to my husband's political career. I had always been a good listener. I would be an even better one so I could learn more about the workings of our government and that world to which my husband had committed himself.

I would work hard at overcoming my small-town timidity. I would learn to entertain. I would learn to help Everett with his speeches. I might even learn to make speeches myself . . . I had no wish to compete with my husband. He was the principal actor on his own political stage. But I would learn how to play the best supporting role any woman ever played.

In time, I did develop enough confidence in myself to play a more active role both politically and socially than I had ever dreamed was possible for me. But it was only by sheer dint of determination. I simply made up my mind not to waste time on irrelevant matters.

Fortunately for me, the timing was right—if I may be forgiven for saying so—because I was immediately plunged into the various and sundry women's activities that arose with our entry into World War II.

There was plenty of women's work to be done and I was grateful for anything that would keep me occupied and help me over my homesickness for Pekin and Joy.

Hazel Vandenberg, wife of Republican Senator Arthur Vandenberg from Michigan, took me under her wing, introduced me to other congressional wives, suggested that I join the Congressional Club (a bi-partisan club for wives of congressmen, and senators), and helped me get busily involved in the Red Cross and in civilian defense.

I shall be eternally grateful for Hazel Vandenberg's friendship in those early years. She made me feel welcome in Washington, and wanted and needed, also. She would call every morning to ask how I was and how everything was going. She was a warm, friendly, outgoing person who did a lot to pull me out of my shell of small-town shyness, and make me feel important. She was devoted to her husband and very knowledgeable about political affairs. I learned a great deal from her, and her friendship gave me genuine pleasure during one of the crucial times in my life. Also, thanks to Hazel, I felt that I, too, was contributing something worthwhile to my country in the war effort.

Hazel was publicity chairman for the Red Cross in Washington, and I became chairman of Camp and Hospital service. I wore a uniform and went to work every day, just as on a regular paying job.

I also enrolled in courses in civilian defense, and almost before I realized it I was even teaching blackout procedures and other aspects of our Civil Defense programs back in Pekin at various intervals when I returned there to visit. Both Hazel and Everett encouraged me in these wartime teaching programs. For a while I seemed to be doing a better job of keeping in touch with my husband's constituents back home than he was, for there were some years during the war when Congress was in continuous session and he did not get home at all.

The social life that I had worried about had been curtailed by the war. About the only "entertaining" we did, if you could call it that, was to invite our "home folks" from Pekin to dinner in the Mayflower dining room when they were in Washington, and then spend the evening visiting with them.

I learned early enough not to be too disturbed at my husband's sometimes sudden change of plans. There was the time, for example, when he said he was tired of eating in the hotel coffee shop and he was hungry for some pork chops and raw fried potatoes, one of his favorite dishes. So, I was preparing dinner in our hotel kitchenette. He had called from his office to tell me he was on his way, and the pork chops and raw fried potatoes were on the stove. He liked them crisp on both sides. We were both looking forward to having dinner in our room instead of the coffee shop.

But Everett arrived at the Mayflower and ran into some friends from Chicago in the lobby.

He called me from the lobby and asked me to come down. I reminded him that our dinner was cooking.

"Well, why don't you just put it aside for a little while and come on down?" he said.

I put the pork chops and raw fried potatoes in the oven, turned it to low, and went downstairs to join my husband and his friends—in the Mayflower coffee shop. When we returned, hours later, the pork chops and potatoes were dried to a crisp. A congressman's wife has to take these things in stride.

The Mayflower's coffee shop was a popular gathering spot because a number of other congressmen and a few senators also lived at the hotel. And after our evening meal, we would repair to the middle reception room for our daily evening get-togethers. Usually the men would sit together talking over the affairs of the day, while the women sat on the sidelines and listened or discussed their own mutual interests. Gradually, I began to feel that I was part of an important political family.

Soon after I had settled into my new role in Washington, with my new resolution to expand my horizons, I went to hear Eleanor Roosevelt speak at the Congressional Club. She made a deep impact on me with a little story she told on herself and I shall never forget it.

She arrived wearing a conservative dark blue suit and black cotton hose and hard shoes, just as everyone else was doing because of the wartime shortages. They did nothing to enhance her appearance. Mrs. Roosevelt, it will be recalled, was not known for her beauty, and I thought as I sat there listening to her that she was more painfully aware of this than anyone else.

The theme of her talk was a wife's responsibility to help her husband in his career, and I of course was all ears.

She told us that she had been very shy as a child because she was an "ugly duckling" and grew up shunning the public limelight. It was not until after she married FDR that she realized she must overcome these feelings of inferiority so she would not be a handicap to her husband. She deliberately set out on a program of self-improvement completely dedicated to helping her husband's political career.

One of her goals was public speaking. She told us how difficult it had been for her when she was first called upon to make speeches for her husband from a platform. At first, a Roosevelt aide always went along with her to provide "fortitude," or to give her moral strength when she spoke.

After one of her speeches, the aide said to her cautiously, "Mrs. Roosevelt, at this particular point in your speech, I noticed that you laughed. I guess I missed the joke. Did you mean it to be funny?"

No, she did not mean it to be funny, she said.

And I remember so well thinking how much courage it must take for Mrs. Roosevelt to make this confession:

"He pointed out several other places in my speech where I had laughed but the audience didn't, and I had not intended it to be funny. It was then I realized for the first time that I had a nervous giggle which was difficult to control. But I knew that I must . . ."

Even as she told us this story, we could see that she was still bothered to some extent by this little nervous giggle. I don't believe she ever lost it entirely. It was not easy for Mrs. Roosevelt to make speeches. But if those speeches were necessary to help her husband in his political career, then speak she must! And she did!

How well I remembered her message many years later when my husband, by then Senator Dirksen, was suddenly called back to Washington by President Kennedy during the Cuban missile crisis of 1962, and I had to carry on his re-election campaign. Mrs. Roosevelt, I'm sure, never knew it but it was her speech that helped me through my own crisis while my husband was off on a more important one. I had remembered it all those years, and I still do.

It was that same speech, in fact, that inspired my own public-speaking career, along with my husband's and Hazel Vandenberg's encouragement. I accepted every opportunity to go back home and talk to women's clubs, church groups, or anyone who would have me. Everett was delighted to have me do so. I never made speeches on politics or national issues. That was Everett's department, not mine. I confined myself to the woman's point of view, trying to answer questions that the average housewife in Illinois would like to know about what it was like living in Washington.

By now I was beginning to see Washington, as well as myself, in a new perspective. Washington, D.C., was an incredibly lovely city back in those years spanning the mid-'30s and the '40s. Somehow it had maintained the quiet dignity of the South, and the pace was that of a slow-moving southern community. I felt a new sense of serenity and happiness there, and I actually found myself wanting to tell the people back in Pekin all about Washington and our activities there.

Everett often helped me with ideas and topics to talk about. And I learned to help him with his speeches.

He once told someone, "I do not write speeches. I find a quiet room, sit at a desk and stare at the wall. If there is a crack in the wall, so much the better; there is no greater stimulus to the imagination. How did that crack get there? Does it go completely through the plaster? The mind seeks the answers and out of this reflection you make a start, you lay out a text, you develop it, and you prepare the final clout."

But there was more to it than that, and that is where I came in. I was, again, his sounding board for helping him expand his ideas and putting them in outline form. Sometimes he would scribble his ideas in a little black book, or sometimes I would. We had dozens of these little black books filled with "ideas for speeches" and through the years we worked out a relatively simple routine of preparing each speech.

We would sit down together, Everett at the typewriter and I with my pad and pencil. He was a two-finger typist but he could put words to paper faster than anyone with the ten-finger touch technique.

He would peck out a few paragraphs to use as his guide. Then using our own system of Roman numerals, small numerals, capital letters and small for headings and subheadings, we would formulate the outline of the speech on my pad. When it was all thought out and organized, I would type the outline for him. He would always memorize the speech from this outline. He never carried the written outline to the platform, never wrote out entire speeches, and rarely used notes. This often limited press coverage, as he did not have advance copies to distribute to reporters. He was a great one for improvising or adding to the original outline in his head.

He had no patience with banquet toastmasters or speakers who ran through the standard stock of jokes merely to take up time. Funny stories, he felt, should only be included if they illustrated a point; otherwise they were worthless.

One of his favorites was about the man who bought a parrot that could speak six languages. He paid the shop owner $35 for the bird, another $15 for the cage, and asked for the bird to be delivered to his home that afternoon. Later the man bounded up the steps to his house, opened the front door, and called out to his wife, "Did the bird arrive?"

"Yes," his wife replied.

"Well, where is he?"

With great composure she said, "I've got him in the oven."

At this point in the story, the audience would always gasp and then Everett would continue, "The man turned beet red and shouted, 'But dear, he was a rare bird! He could speak six languages!'

"'Well, why didn't he speak up?'" was her unruffled reply.

Everett used that story to encourage people to speak up when they had something to say, whether they agreed with him or not. He never liked silent critics. And his audiences never tired of his talking parrot story.

Besides helping him with his speeches and being the family bookkeeper, I also took on a new role as my husband's part-time secretary. That is I often performed secretarial duties for him at home. I never actually went to work for him in the office. Even before I moved to Washington, I had decided that I might be of some help to Everett if I knew how to type and take shorthand. So I enrolled in a course at Brown's Business College in Peoria, and I did fairly well in typing, but not so well at shorthand. I would have stuck it out, though, if my teacher had been more encouraging. But one day she said to me, "Well, I'll try to teach you if you want to go on with it but I don't think at your age you'll ever learn to do shorthand very fluently."

This certainly did nothing to build up my ego. I left the

course. But I did work up my own shorthand system and it came in very handy. There were many times when Everett would dictate to me at home at night and then take my work into his office the next morning. Fortunately, his wonderful secretary, Glee Gomien, and two other girls in the office could read my improvised shorthand and type up the letters for him to sign.

Of course I was not paid for these services. It may be remembered that there was a great deal of criticism of Bess Truman for being on the government payroll while her husband was a senator.

I would never have considered accepting a salary for the work I did for my husband. For me it was reward enough to know that I was helping my husband.

When Joy finished her sophmore year in high school in Pekin, we brought her to Washington to be with us. We were still living at the Mayflower Hotel, and we put Joy in boarding school at Mount Vernon Seminary for her last two years of high school. We were all much happier to have our little family together again.

How the years flew! The war had ended, in 1945, and my husband was still a congressman! By now it looked at though he might be "representing the people" permanently, and he was getting more restless to have that "bit of land with a snuggly little house on it."

We began looking around the countryside and finally found a little cottage on Chesapeake Bay. We only rented it. We did not feel that it was exactly what we wanted to buy and I was not sure that we could afford it. I was never one to jump into things in a hurry. But the cottage was within easy driving distance of Washington and in a beautiful location. We would drive down for long weekends, or sometimes after Congress adjourned, for a little vacation and relief from the confines of hotel living in Washington.

Everett especially needed to get away from his work once in a while, although he never forgot about it completely. He had so much energy and a seemingly limitless capacity for working hard. I saw to it that we got away to our little cottage on the Chesapeake as often as possible.

We spent many happy days there. We enjoyed just sitting on our screened-in front porch and watching the waves roll in, or wading out in the water looking for soft shell crabs, or digging for clams. We were enchanted with the little shrimp beds and oyster beds, something we never saw back in Pekin! And I even learned to prepare seafoods, something I had never done in Pekin.

Was it possible that I actually was beginning to enjoy being a congressman's wife?

You must understand that those words at first had seemed unreal to me and did not hold the same meaning as my being Everett Dirksen's wife.

But living in Washington had expanded my horizon. It was possible that if Everett continued to be re-elected every two years, I might even enjoy spending the rest of my life there with him.

Chapter 9

The Faith That Sustained

It was Memorial Day, 1946.

Everett and I had returned to Pekin for a few days from Washington because he had been asked to deliver a patriotic speech at a Memorial Day picnic in Peoria. He was known as one of the last of the great patriotic-day-picnic orators, capable of holding picnickers quiet and spellbound for hours, and this Memorial Day was no exception.

I noticed nothing different about him during his speech, but on the drive back to Pekin I felt that something was wrong with him. He was not himself. We got home and in the house and still he said nothing. It wasn't like him not to confide in me when he was troubled.

Finally I questioned him, and he told me, rather uneasily, that he thought there was something wrong with his eyes. When he looked out at the crowd from the speaker's platform, he said, everything was one big blur. It was like "cobwebs" in front of his eyes.

This was the beginning of a critically low time in our lives, and a turning point in his career.

He was losing his vision.

We had survived the wartime blackouts. This was a blackout that would require far more personal strength and courage for both of us.

Politically Everett had continued to grow in strength and stature throughout all his terms in office. He had been on many important committees, was in great demand as a public speaker, had been chairman of the District Committee in the House, which made him then the real Mayor of Washington, and he had made many friends among Democrats as well as Republicans.

Many by now were aware of his increasing influence across party lines. Some of his GOP colleagues had even drafted him to try for the presidential nomination in 1944. He was unsuccessful, which bothered him not at all. He was one of those who seconded the nomination of New York's Governor Thomas E. Dewey to run against FDR. And we all know what happened. Roosevelt won his fourth term, and at his death on April 12, 1945, Harry Truman succeeded him.

Everett's grasp of government affairs had increased enormously. He had earned the respect and admiration of many for his handling of various legislative matters. He had served a long apprenticeship in trying times and was at the point in his career when he had much to give to his country. He could become one of its great leaders.

Now, here he was on this Memorial Day, 1946, with the "cobwebs" in his eyes.

We consulted doctors in Chicago, New York, Washington, Detroit, and at Johns Hopkins hospital in Baltimore and the Mayo Clinic in Minnesota. He went through a variety of tests, as well as a variety of opinions. The doctors could not agree on a diagnosis. Neither could they give him any encouragement that his eyesight would improve.

He accepted chairmanship of a congressional committee that was sent to Europe to study some of the problems of the war and its aftermath. While there, he visited eye specialists in Vienna and Paris. They reminded him that the United States was far ahead of them in men and machines. "After all, we have been at war and have not progressed in research, either men or medicine," they said.

As the weeks and months wore on, his eyes became worse, until finally he could no longer read. He still had a small amount of vision in one eye and was able to make out objects such as lamps and tables. He was not yet stumbling about and he still went to his office and tried to do his work.

But for a man who was as voracious a reader as he was, and whose work required long hours of reading legislative records, bills, and many documents that contained fine print and small figures, the loss of his eyesight was a real tragedy.

We went home again to Pekin for the Christmas holidays, and it was here on Christmas Eve of 1946, our nineteenth wedding anniversary, that we received the sad news from our family doctor in Washington.

He telephoned us long distance to tell us that the diagnostic reports were all in from the top eye specialists at both Johns Hopkins and the Mayo Clinic, and they had finally agreed on a diagnosis.

The medical term was chorioretinitis, a degeneration of the retina which was believed to be caused by cancer.

The malignancy had started in the right eye but would in time travel to the other eye.

Everett was advised to go to Johns Hopkins and condition himself for an enucleation. This is the medical term for the removal of an eye.

It would have been tragic news at any time. But coming at Christmas, that special time of year when emotions are so close to the surface, made it seem even more so. My heart ached as I heard Everett ask the doctor, "Is there any alternative?"

The alternative, he was told, would be total blindness.

He gave his permission for our doctor to go ahead with arrangements for the operation. It was to be performed by one of our greatest eye surgeons, who is no longer living.

It was with heavy hearts that we returned to Washington after the holidays.

The decision had been made.

But in the train en route to Baltimore, he decided to have a little talk with God. He had been a man of great faith all his life, and this faith had helped him meet many challenges and overcome many adversities. He needed that faith now as never before. He got down on his knees in his train compartment and prayed as he had never prayed before.

He arrived at the hospital, underwent a final examination, and then was ushered into the eminent surgeon's office.

The surgeon was rather brusque. He shook hands with Everett, and then said, "Well, let's get on with the business at hand . . ."

"And what is the business at hand?" Everett asked, as if he didn't know.

"Removing your eye," said the surgeon. He added that the operation should be performed immediately. Obviously he was ready and waiting, and anxious to get it over with.

Everett looked the surgeon straight in the eye and said, "Well, Doctor, I've changed my mind. I am not going to have my eye removed. On the way here I enlisted the services of another doctor."

"What? . . . Who? . . ." The eminent surgeon seemed a bit miffed.

"The Big Doctor up there," Everett said, pointing a finger upward. "The One upstairs, the Doctor in the Sky, Who watches over all of us . . ."

The great eye surgeon "downstairs" got the message. "Oh? Indeed? And what did He tell you?" he asked with raised eyebrow.

"He told me to keep my eye, that I should not have it removed," Everett replied.

The eye surgeon looked at his watch impatiently and said, "Look, Mr. Dirksen, I have other things to do. Please make up your mind." He made a movement forward.

"I have made up my mind. Keep your cotton-pickin' hands off me, sir, and goodbye!" said Everett, and he walked out of the office.

As he explained later, "I just had this little conversation with God. It was very simple, very practical, and perhaps I should confess a little tearful. I simply told Him I hoped I would not have to yield an eye, but if it was His way, I would accept it. What I really wanted to know was whether to permit them to proceed with the operation. On my knees in that train, I got the answer."

Once Everett had made a decision, that was that, especially one made with God's help.

He caught the next train back to Washington, and found an invitation awaiting him to address a Lincoln Day dinner, one of the most prestigious events of the year, and a new plume in Everett's political cap. To my surprise he turned it down and proceeded to make arrangements for a trip to Florida. A Chicago friend had offered us the use of his house in Palm Beach for three weeks. Everett at first had said he was too busy to take advantage of this nice offer, and when he changed his mind about it of course I was delighted. But I knew also that he was praying for a little miracle, a "rest cure" that would restore his sight.

His good friend, Joe Martin, Republican Minority Whip and later Speaker of the House under President Eisenhower, telephoned Everett and asked, "What's this I hear about you turning down the Lincoln Day dinner invitation?"

Everett told him he was going to Florida for a "vacation."

Joe Martin knew Everett better than that. A few minutes later he was in Everett's office, demanding to know, "What is this all about? Now, tell me, why can't you make that Lincoln Day address?"

Everett had managed so far to put up a good front and not let others know the seriousness of his eye trouble. But he confided in Joe Martin, who listened earnestly and then said, "Where's your calendar? Look here, you have a little more than three weeks before the dinner. Go to Florida and take your rest cure, but come back here and make that Lincoln Day address. We need you."

Everett agreed to do it.

We went to Florida and lazed around on beach chairs, soaking up sand and sunshine and working on his Lincoln Day speech. He collected his thoughts and ideas on Lincoln, and as he spoke them to me, I would write them down for him. This was one occasion that required a typewritten copy of the entire speech for the press, which made it doubly difficult for Everett who was accustomed to using only an outline. This time he would need to memorize his speech word for word and stick to it, for with his eyesight so impaired he could not possibly read his own words.

The brief "rest cure" in Florida did not produce the minor miracle we had hoped for, and we returned to Washington for the Lincoln Day dinner.

Everett's faithful secretary, Mrs. Gomien, had used the largest type available for his script but the glare of the kleig lights turned the copy into one big spot. I sat in the audience that evening, aching with the knowledge of what he was going through, knowing that those bright lights were an anathema to him, praying for God to help him and He did. Everett did not falter over a single word that he had committed to memory. He did not need the script. He remembered it word for word as we had written it.

On that Lincoln Day, February 12, 1947, as he stood there tall and somber and sightless, his words pouring forth with a majestic ring, I knew that my husband, the Congressman from the 16th District of Illinois, extolling the greatness of the sixteenth President of the United States, was also destined for greatness, as Lincoln had been.

There was something exquisitely rare and wonderful in the way he held his audience that day. One could hear a pin drop. And for the first time I think I realized that my husband truly had the ability to be a giant among men. Even without eyes he stood taller than most men with 20-20 vision. He was more than a congressman, more than a "politician." He was a statesman, a leader of men, and born to be one of the great ones. The word "destiny" kept gnawing at me. With some psychic sixth-sense I knew he was "destined" for a place in history, as was his boyhood idol from the Land of Lincoln.

And I sat there choking back tears and praying with all my strength that God would somehow restore his sight and let him carry on his work.

I believe that behind every memorized word of that Lincoln Day address my husband was praying also.

When he stepped down from the platform a number of people, as always, were waiting to greet him. One was an elderly gentleman who stepped up and said, "Mr. Dirksen, I have heard every address since this Lincoln Day dinner was first held. Yours tonight was the greatest of them all." As Everett thanked him, he went on, "But I came especially to tell you that three Novenas a day are being said for you at the Cathedral. Our country has great need of you."

It was only a short time after this Lincoln Day address that Everett made the agonizing decision to retire from the House. He could no longer see well enough to carry on his work. He felt that it was not fair to his colleagues and his country to stay in office with this handicap.

All the spirit and exhilaration of his dreams were suddenly quieted, much to the distress of the many friends he had made in both the House and the Senate.

On the eve of his departure from office, Republicans and Democrats bade him the fondest farewell. Sam Rayburn, then the Democratic floor leader, gave Everett a special accolade that was widely quoted in the press:

"If they are going to send Republicans to Congress, let them send Republicans of the Everett Dirksen kind."

Little did Mr. Rayburn realize how that wish would be fulfilled. For when Everett did recover and decided to run for the Senate, he used all those nice things Mr. Rayburn and other Democrats had said about him.

How was his eyesight restored?

No one could have convinced either of us that his sight was not restored through Divine intervention.

We left Washington and went to live for a while in our little rented cottage on Chesapeake Bay, hoping that complete rest away from work and phones would help. Our cottage had no telephone. Only a narrow rutted road led to the shore from the highway. We discouraged visitors, especially those who might bring work and problems. I must admit that at first we had self-doubts about disagreeing with all the doctors. We both believed in the wonders of medical science. And there were many moments when we remembered with anguish our doctor's answer when Everett asked, "What is the alternative?" and he replied, "Total blindness."

Everett's eyesight seemed to be getting worse, but he was not yet totally blind. He could see to move around. We were both filled with anxiety and it took us several days to settle down and relax, to adjust to the peace and quiet of Chesapeake Bay. For Everett, who was always such an active energetic person, the transition to doing nothing was a difficult adjustment to make. But eventually he did. He rested. He fished. He grew flowers. That was all. Just as the doctors did not know what caused his vision to blur, they did not know what to prescribe for a cure. And neither did we—except faith.

I became Everett's eyes. Even though he still had some vision, I wanted to help him save it whenever possible by not using it any more than he had to. So I tried to make it easy for him to get around, by guiding him, by not leaving things in his way for him to stumble over. I walked him down to the shore and went fishing with him. I helped him plant flowers. I would read to him hour after hour, day after day.

And then gradually the miracle happened. Yes, I believe in miracles for a miracle happened to us there on Chesapeake Bay that told us our faith and prayers had not been in vain. As I was reading to Everett, he reached over and gently took the book from my hand.

"I can see the words," he said quietly.

He could not see the tears trickling from my eyes as I cried silently, "Thank you, God."

He could not see the words well enough to read as yet, but he could distinguish the type, whereas before a page had been only a blur.

Little by little, each day, his eyesight continued to improve. We knew that God was with us and that after a few months, Everett was going to be all right.

When we returned to Washington, Everett went to see the doctor, and he was astonished. He could not believe it, but he had to. The change and improvement were that remarkable.

I would never have quarreled with the doctors' diagnoses that there was a malignancy. There were too many doctors involved and I respected their professionalism. I think that if it had been my eye and all those specialists had told me it had to be removed, I might have had it done. But Everett was so determined not to give up his eye—and how well he remembered that day on the train from Washington to Baltimore when he took his case to the Supreme Doctor and prayed all the way.

And how well I remember that Lincoln Day dinner address when I sat there praying all the way through it for God to give him back his eyes and let him carry on his work.

How could we not believe that his recovery was one of God's miracles?

Both of us believed then, and I will always believe, that my husband was healed by God because he was still needed for work in the service of our government, work that he could not do without his vision.

His eyesight was not perfect. There was still scar tissue on the retina, and his peripheral vision was impaired. He could not see to the left or the right without turning his head. There were certain things he could not do; he could not drive a car or catch a ball. But he could go back to work, get back into action. And we gave thanks to the Lord.

There is an epilogue to this chapter in our lives which I think can best be told by a very fine Negro gentleman and a friend of my husband's, Archibald J. Carey, Jr., who was elected a Judge of the Circuit Court of Cook County (Illinois) in 1966. He was formerly a member of the City Council of Chicago and was a member of the United States Delegation to the United Nations in 1953. He became the first Negro-American to head a White House Committee, when President Eisenhower named his Chairman of the President's Committee on Government Employment Policy in 1957.

He was a pastor for thirty-seven years, and from 1949 until 1967 he was the minister of Quinn Chapel, African Methodist Episcopal Church, the oldest congregation established by Negro-Americans in Chicago.

Arch and Everett had developed a deepening friendship across the years. They had exchanged ideas on the campaign trail and in many intimate conversations in Chicago, Washington or southern Illinois, on the plane or in the car on motor trips, or in the Senate Dining Room. He had been a guest in our home on many occasions, and we had been dinner guests in his home. I know that he and Everett regarded each other with great affection.

But let our good friend, Judge Carey, tell it:

Everett McKinley Dirksen was a man of deep religious faith, and so was I. Out of such an association, he shared with me some private sentiments such as he might not disclose freely to others.

On one occasion he telephoned me and asked me to come and see him because he wanted to ask my advice on something. When I got to his suite in the La Salle Hotel [in Chicago], he was alone. At first I thought it was by accident, but as his story unfolded, I concluded that it may have been by design.

He related and reviewed for me the story of his difficulty with his eyes. He told me of the medical efforts, of the experiments, of the trials and failures, of the places he had gone, and of the baffling and frustrating struggle he had been through.

He also told me of his prayers. I recall vividly his saying, ". . . I had a number of talks with God."

Then he said, "Arch, during those days I promised God that if I could recover my sight and continue my work in gainful employment, I would give a substantial portion of my income to help others."

He told me about praying all the way on the train from Washington to Baltimore, and back. Then he said:

"I made a promise to God. I intend to keep it. I have asked you to come over to help me decide to whom I might give a portion of my income. I want to put some of it in your community. But I have decided now that I will leave it up to you. I am going to put it entirely in your hands."

With that, he handed me a check for $1000.

I was stunned.

Here was a man who had fought his way back through a devastatingly expensive affliction, and who had just come through a rigorous and expensive state-wide campaign for office in which he had won out over the popular and powerful Majority Leader of the Senate, Scott W. Lucas.

In time, Everett Dirksen was to become a colossal figure of influence as one of the most effective Minority Leaders in the history of the United States Senate.

But at this moment he had been a senator less than three months.

I was completely taken by surprise by his most generous offer, and I protested that this was too much responsibility for me to exercise alone. But he insisted. The only qualification he imposed was that I give the matter no publicity whatsoever.

He repeated, "I am just keeping my promise to God."

After considering the matter a day or so, I reported back to him with a number of organizations and projects that could benefit from various sums of money. I asked for his advice and suggestion, but he demurred, saying, "Distribute it as you see fit."

His insistent refusal to permit disclosure of his gift distressed me somewhat. The election was over, and I felt the community should know of his interest and generosity.

One day I again made a determined effort to obtain his permission to publicize the matter. I put forth my arguments vigorously but all to no avail. Finally, I appealed to him on a more personal basis, telling him the story of how one couple, Joseph Bryan and his wife, Mattie, had launched the Colored Big Brothers (to redeem unfortunate boys before the courts) almost alone, with some help from their pastor who was my father, Bishop Carey.

I told him of the case histories I had known of boys who had become good citizens under the guidance of the Colored Big Brothers. I told him that Mr. Bryan had died, but that Mrs. Bryan was carrying on in a big but drafty house at 45th and Indiana, and I said, "Ev, if you would but let me tell what you have done, it could be one of the biggest boosts they ever had."

(I had decided to distribute the $1000 thusly: $300 to the Colored Big Brothers; $200 to Ada McKinley House for unfortunate girls; $300 to the South Side Boys Club, and $200 to Provident Hospital, the principal hospital serving the community of Negro-Americans.)

He finally relented and posed for a picture with me which

appeared on April 14, 1951, in the Chicago Defender, our Negro publication. The picture bore this caption, "Gifts totaling $1000 are donated to various institutions of the South Side by Senator Everett McKinley Dirksen."

So far as I know this is the only word ever to reach the public of this religious manifestation of the character of Everett McKinley Dirksen.

I can only add to Judge Carey's comments my personal gratitude here for telling this in his own words, for I was not present at their meetings.

I can confirm that my husband's frequent and usually well-concealed gestures of generosity to help his fellow men were never done with any thought of public notice.

From his mother he had learned that he owed his church a share of what the Lord made it possible for him to earn. He always tithed. He gave regularly and as substantially as his means would allow.

It came as no surprise to me that he had promised God a substantial portion of his income to help others if he could recover his sight and continue working.

Besides that $1000 to the then Reverend Carey for Negro charities, I know that he gave equal amounts at the same time to Catholic and Jewish church charities, as well as his own Reformed Church.

I also know that once the campaign was over and he had won his first election to the Senate, he gave one-third of his first year's salary as a United States Senator as a first installment of his payment to God for restoring his eyesight.

I do not believe that anyone else knew this except possibly his close friend and administrative aide, Harold Rainville.

My husband certainly would not have wanted it publicized at the time. He won his elections on other merits. But now that he is gone and there are no more elections to win, I can shout it to the world: He did pay his debt to God. And I loved him for it.

Chapter 10

My Husband, the Senator from Illinois
(The Fifties)

It was 1948 when the curtain rang down on Act One of my husband's political career.

He announced that he would not seek re-election. It had been a painful decision to make. But with his eyesight in the balance, he felt that he could not be of any value to his party or his country.

Those two years, between 1948 and 1950, were the only years that Everett did not hold office in a political career that spanned forty years. There were only those few months, eight or ten at the most, of almost total blackout when he had to remain inactive. Then as his eyesight gradually improved, I could see the wheels beginning to spin in his head. I knew he wanted to get back into action.

We were spending a lazy summer at our cottage on Chesapeake Bay, and giving thanks each day that his eyesight was returning. He would wander among his flowers, overjoyed that he was able to see them again, as well as smell them. There had been months when he could not distinguish one of his beloved flowers from another, except by feel and smell.

Once again he was able to see the waves as they rolled into shore, and see the stars shining down on the water. And he was so happy to be able to read again!

It was toward the end of summer that he received word

from Governor Dewey, asking him to come to Albany to meet with his advisers and to help plan his presidential campaign.

The 1948 Republican Convention had been held in Philadelphia in June, and had again nominated Governor Dewey as their presidential candidate, this time against President Truman and his running mate, Alben Barkley.

Everett, of course, jumped at the chance to get back into action, and he felt that his eyes were now sufficiently improved so that he could be of some help in the campaign. I stayed at our Chesapeake cottage while he went to Albany.

When he arrived, he found himself mapping out strategy with several of the more sophisticated eastern politicians, including John Foster Dulles. Every evening this group of men would get together for something they called the "Children's Hour," to rehash the various ideas and programs that had been presented earlier in the day, and to coordinate and combine them.

These Children's Hours were always held during the cocktail hour, over drinks. Everett was a very simple man in his tastes, and did not care much for fancy cocktails. Each evening he watched in fascination as John Foster Dulles paced the room gently cradling his martini shaker. Finally, Everett could contain himself no longer and blurted out, "Foster, why don't you give that thing a good shake?"

Mr. Dulles gave my husband his best patronizing smile and said, "Everett, anyone who knows anything about the requirements of a good martini knows that you do not bruise the gin and the vermouth."

Everett always repeated this story with theatrical flair, and with a very amusing mimicry of Mr. Dulles's patronizing expression and tone.

After some days in Albany, Everett returned to our little home on the Chesapeake, but not for long. Soon came a call from California. The policymakers out there wanted him to come to Sacramento and help Governor Earl Warren get his campaign underway. He was Dewey's vice-presidential running mate.

The Dewey people insisted that Everett write some hard-hitting speeches for Governor Warren. But that did not last long. Governor Warren and my husband were never in agreement in their thinking. Everett's statements were too strong and Mr. Warren reduced them to platitudes, so Everett was not very successful in helping launch Earl Warren's campaign. He came back home, discouraged.

"The feel isn't there," he told me.

The presidential campaign got under way with the Republicans confident that the Democrats were at long last on their way out, and that a GOP victory was in the bag.

The press, radio, national polls and just about everybody, it seemed, except Harry Truman himself—and my husband—thought it was impossible for Truman to be re-elected.

Outwardly, my husband went along with all the victory slogans and fanfare that our party was caught up in, and he did everything he could to help the victory slogans become a reality. But in private he said to me often in those last few days of the campaign, "The feel just isn't there."

Election Day 1948 came. Can anyone ever forget it? The Dewey forces were so confident of victory that the Chicago *Tribune*, "the world's greatest newspaper," committed a memorable journalistic faux pas with an early edition banner headline, DEWEY WINS. When all the votes were counted, Harry Truman, who almost alone thought he could be re-elected, was still our President.

1950 . . .

The beating the GOP took in November 1948 had a decided impact on my husband and marked another turning point in his career. He had formally "retired" from politics, but he had never actually retired. In retrospect I think it would be more accurate to say that he was only out on "sick leave" for a while.

Although his party lost the election, his work in the 1948 campaign at least proved to him that he was still wanted and needed, that his accumulation of experience and knowledge was still of value to his party, and that his eyes need no longer be a handicap.

Soon after the 1948 defeat, we began a reassessment of our situation with some quiet soul-searching. Everett now had the time to use that law degree that he had worked so hard for by going to night school in Washington—at my insistence.

Should he return to politics? Or play it safe and practice law? There was no doubt in our minds that he could do well at it. We debated about it. But not for very long. We both knew what he really wanted.

Quite a few people thought Everett was out of his mind when he had the temerity to start campaigning for the 1950 United States Senate seat against the incumbent Senator from Illinois, Scott W. Lucas.

Scott Lucas was then the Majority Leader of the Democrats in the United States Senate, and Everett's campaign against him was regarded as absolutely hopeless by all political savants of the Washington press corps, as well as everybody else, including his own Republican party. The disintegrated GOP in Illinois were half-heartedly looking and hoping for a candidate for the 1950 senatorial campaign, but the consensus was that no one could beat Scott Lucas. Everett would not stand a ghost of a chance.

But then back in 1932 no one thought "that baker boy from Pekin" had a ghost of a chance against that incumbent Congressman from Peoria, Ed Hull.

In a sense, this was history repeating itself. When Everett lost his first (and only) primary election, he was out next day campaigning for the next term. And won.

Similarly, he lost no time after the GOP defeat of 1948 making up his mind to run in 1950, and he started campaigning early in the spring of 1949.

It was apparent from the start that he would not have much support from his party.

So our daughter Joy and I decided to make up for it.

Joy had just graduated from Bradley University in Peoria and was free to help with the campaign, and we became Everett's two leading helpers. In fact, with so little support from elsewhere except for Harold Rainville carrying on in Chicago, it was virtually a one-man, two-women campaign. Joy and I tried in every way possible to give him the encouragement that he did not have from his own Republican leadership in Illinois.

We traveled with him, drove for him, attended meetings with him. On some trips Joy would stay at home answering the telephone and typing, and we would call her every night to collect messages, discuss projects, and let her know where we would be the next day. When I became too exhausted, Joy and I would exchange jobs. She would drive her father from place to place and I would take over the home office duties. No one could accuse us of "wasting" campaign funds. It was probably one of the most inexpensive senatorial campaigns anyone ever waged.

In eighteen months, we drove 81,000 miles, wore out three cars, and Everett made 1300 speeches.

It was a joy for me to watch him once again looking out at his audiences and actually seeing them, without the "cobwebs" in his eyes. His old confidence had returned completely.

I did not always go in to listen to his speeches, because there was more important work for me to do. Quite often I would remain in the car with a typewriter on my lap, writing out releases to leave for the press.

Then he would jump in the car and away we would go again.

Many times I would drive until eleven or twelve o'clock at night—after a day of driving from meeting to meeting in town after town—in order to make it to a hotel in another area so we would start out early the next morning.

There was one most amusing incident that occurred during this first senatorial campaign. Rather, it is amusing now; it was not so amusing then.

Everett received a call from Colonel Robert R. McCormick, publisher of the Chicago *Tribune*. The Colonel wanted to see him in his office as soon as possible. Strong men have quaked at being summoned by the Colonel and my husband was soon to learn why. He went over to Tribune Tower, took the elevator to the Colonel's own private ivory tower on the twenty-fourth floor, and stepped off the elevator directly into an outer waiting room. When a secretary announced him, a paneled wall slid open and he found himself flanked by two huge police dogs, one on either side of him.

"Come. Sit down," ordered a sepulchral voice from the far end of a cavernous room.

Everett walked across the vast space quaking every step of the way. The police dogs were right beside him. Gingerly he sat down. The dogs stood like sentinels, never taking their eyes off him.

Behind a massive desk sat the giant, heavy-jowled, white-haired Colonel, one of the most legendary men of the publishing world, and then among the most powerful. He came right to the point.

"Young man," he said, "of course we think you can't win, but we could give you a little newspaper help. However, there are certain things you could do for us in Washington if by the wildest chance you should be elected."

He stopped, indicating that it was now Everett's turn.

The dogs had not moved.

"Thank you, sir," said Everett. "*When* I am elected [and he emphasized the *when*, not an *if*], if there is anything I can do for you in Washington, I would be very glad to do so . . . But not for a price."

"Good day," said the Colonel.

"Good day, sir," said Everett.

The two police dogs escorted him to the paneled wall which quietly and mysteriously slid open again, and then closed behind him.

He was still quaking in his shoes when he came home and told me of his experience.

Everett was so much his own man. He wanted to be beholden to no one.

Our pace increased as the time for general election neared. The weeks flew by. As it came closer to Election Day, he became more and more confident, almost jubilant. In the final days of the campaign, he often said to me, "The feel is there."

There were occasions when I felt that my husband's optimism and confidence were shared by no one else but the Dirksens.

I think even his good friend and campaign manager Harold Rainville might have wavered a wee bit, for I remember a discussion they had on the eve of that 1950 election. Harold was trying to reassure Everett. But the way he worded it indicated that he was not really as confident as Everett.

"I'm sure you're going to win," he said. "But I hope that if you don't, you won't be too upset. I'm something of a fatalist, and I believe that whatever happens, happens for the best."

"Rainey," my husband said, "I'm a fatalist myself, and if I don't win, I will be happy to practice law." Then he added emphatically: "But—I *know* I am going to win. The feel is there."

And on that memorable November 7, 1950, Election Day, when the votes were all counted, President Truman's majority leader was out and my husband was in. Everett McKinley Dirksen was the new Senator from Illinois.

I was often asked if our home life changed when my husband returned to Washington as a senator.

Yes. Joy and I now called him Mr. Senator. And after ten years of living at the Mayflower Hotel, we finally moved into an apartment. When we returned to Washington after the 1950 election, Everett realized that he now had six years ahead of him until his next election, so he decided we should have an apartment of our own.

He leased one at the Berkshire Apartments on Massachusetts Avenue. Joy moved in with us, and went to work for her father as a receptionist—without pay. She emphatically repeated that "without pay" every time she had an opportunity. She and Glee Gomien shared two of the adjoining desks in her father's office, and many people remarked about the office containing both Joy and Glee.

Glee often commented on what a delightful person Joy was to have around because of her excellent sense of humor and wit—like her father.

Joy lived with us at the Berkshire until her marriage to Howard Baker, Jr., on December 22, 1951. Her romance with Howard reminded me of our own early courting days when Everett and I were the Prince and Princess in the play at the Pekin Centennial. One of Joy's friends among the "Congressional children" was Mary Baker, daughter of Congressman Howard Baker, from Knoxville, Tennessee.

One year both girls were chosen to be princesses in the annual Washington Cherry Blossom Festival. Joy was the Illinois princess and Mary was the Tennessee princess, and during the long hours of rehearsing for the Festival they became closer friends.

Escorts were generally provided by the Festival committee, but Mary suggested her brother Howard for her own escort. He was just back from service in the Asiatic Theater, and eagerly accepted his sister's invitation to come to Washington for the Cherry Blossom festivities. But by the time the Festival was over, Mary had another escort and Howard was escorting Joy. That is how their romance began.

Their wedding took place in the First Presbyterian Church in Pekin, with a blinding snowstorm outside. But it was still a beautiful wedding. Many of our friends came from Washington and Illinois and Howard's family and friends came up from Tennessee. I remember what a time they had coping with all that snow.

Joy and Howard made a beautiful bride and groom and I'll never forget what a handsome picture the father of the bride made as he stood out there in his formal swallow-tails, courtesy of Chicago's tux-rental tycoon, Ben Gingiss, directing traffic in front of the church in that snowstorm.

Yes, our home life had indeed changed. My husband, the Senator from Illinois, could now afford a Ben Gingiss full-dress coat for his daughter's wedding.

1952 . . .

The year 1950 was a special one for me because that was the year my husband became a senator.

But historians probably will record 1952 as the year Senator Everett Dirksen really made history at the National Republican Convention in Chicago when he dramatically pointed his finger at Tom Dewey and charged him with "taking us down the road to defeat."

Reams and reams of newsprint have gone into reporting this incident. Hundreds of newspaper cartoonists and columnists had a field day with it, and for that matter they still do in every election year.

Yes, I was there when it happened. I don't think that either of us quite realized the impact of his words until we saw all the headlines. It was like the shot that was heard around the world. The new Senator from Illinois had stolen the show at the convention.

Apparently it was my husband at his theatrical best so it seems appropriate to include my version of it here.

First, it is important to review some of the events leading up to the convention. It is not necessary to be a political savant to understand the general outline of history in those years. The Democrats had been in power for twenty years, and the Republicans, including the new Senator Dirksen, sensed certain victory in 1952—*if* only they would pick the right candidate.

"The feel is there," Everett kept saying in 1952.

"The feel isn't there," he had told me privately in both 1944 and 1948 when Governor Dewey had run against FDR first, and then against Truman. But Everett had been one of Dewey's best campaigners both times.

It might also be remembered that in 1944 my husband had first campaigned throughout thirty states seeking delegates for the presidential nomination for himself—at the insistence of other congressmen and party leaders. But when he lost out to Dewey he graciously began campaigning for him.

The senator and Governor Dewey were still friends, but I think Everett felt that being a two-timer loser was enough, and by 1952 he had become one of the principal backers of Ohio's Senator Robert A. Taft.

Meanwhile, on the political scene had arrived a late and reluctant entry fresh from the battlefront, a man wearing the halo of a hero's return from D-Day and the Normandy invasion, a man who was the choice of the GOP's eastern "kingmakers," who felt they had found the one man who could take over the presidency of the U.S. for the Republicans—because, so the tune went, "Taft can't win."

That man, of course, was General Dwight David Eisenhower.

Instead of seeking the nomination for himself again, Governor Dewey was throwing his support to General Eisenhower, while my husband led the pro-Taft forces.

Meanwhile, Everett's encounter with Colonel McCormick apparently had impressed the Colonel, as indicated in a column written by the late Drew Pearson, in which he actually pays the ultimate compliment to my husband.

Col. Robert McCormick, potent publisher of the Chicago *Tribune*, is working on some secret strategy which he hopes will throw the presidency of the United States into his lap in 1952.

On the surface, McCormick gives all signs of backing his good friend, Senator Bob Taft. Actually, however, McCormick favors his able, up-and-coming protégé, Senator Everett Dirksen, recently elected from Pekin, Ill.

McCormick's strategy in this situation is quite simple. At the Chicago convention in '52, he will work for a deadlock between the two leading candidates—probably Taft and Eisenhower. Once he's maneuvered the convention into a stalemate, he will pass out word the only way to break the deadlock is to nominate Senator Dirksen.

If this deadlock does develop. Dirksen might have a chance of securing the nomination. He's a well known and well liked figure in top Republican circles. And since the convention will be in Chicago, there's bound to be a lot of Dirksen support in the ever-vocal galleries.

NOTE—The irony is that Dirksen by himself would make a good President; Dirksen bogged down by Chicago *Tribune* policies would not.

(From the Washington *Post*, June 9, 1951)

Needless to say, that deadlock did not develop, but I think it was interesting of Drew Pearson to say all those nice things about my husband. He didn't do it very often. The Chicago *Tribune* did support Bob Taft in the campaign, as they had supported him in the two previous campaigns, while Everett had supported Dewey.

But my husband had become disenchanted with Dewey's "me, too-ism." He felt that there were too many Republicans of the "me, too" variety . . . I believe it was my husband who invented that "me, too" tag for Tom Dewey. If he didn't, he surely helped pass it along.

He admired Senator Taft, who was a Midwestern conservative

and an outspoken individualist. And Taft had worked long
and hard for the nomination.

I personally remember Senator Taft with very warm feelings
because of his devotion to his invalid wife. We were at the
plane to meet them when they arrived in Chicago at O'Hare
Airport. We saw him carry her off the plane in his arms
and place her in a wheelchair, and we watched him wheel her
up the ramp to the amphitheater. In fact, he was right there
supervising when they put up the ramp. Much as he wanted the
presidential nomination in 1952, once Martha Taft arrived at the
convention, Bob Taft forgot everything else to make certain
she was comfortable.

His concern for her well-being was touching to see. I shall
never forget it.

I was proud that my husband had come to the convention
as a Taft man. I was proud of him when he made the second-
ing speech for Taft's nomination. It was a beautiful speech,
and I still feel one of his best.

But it was largely forgotten in the uproar over Everett's
outburst at Dewey.

I suppose millions of television viewers saw my husband
at that 1952 National Convention, when he pointed his finger
directly at Tom Dewey and said, "We supported you in 1944
and 1948 . . . We followed you before and you took us down
the road to defeat!"

This really brought the GOP convention to its feet, both
booing and cheering.

The convention became so noisy that the acting chairman
had to rap for order. Everett drew a big laugh when he said,
"I assure you that I didn't mean to create a controversy."

Governor Dewey sat there frozen-faced, sipping from a soft
drink bottle. And he delivered his big New York delegation to
Eisenhower.

No one could ever call Everett Dirksen a poor loser. He
accepted his defeats and disappointments philosophically.

When General Eisenhower won the nomination over Taft,
Everett became one of Ike's best campaigners. In fact everyone
not actively involved in an election campaign of his own
was put into action to tour the country for Ike. The National

Republican Committee mapped out a program for Everett to campaign in the Far Western states. Our first stop was Billings, Montana, for a nighttime rally. We stayed overnight and took off early the next morning in a small plane for Hobbs, New Mexico. This plane was not pressurized and our ears began to stop up. By the time we landed at Hobbs, we were barely able to speak to the welcoming committee. Once we got past our "Hellos," we had to ask for a doctor.

From there on, the planes we flew in were always pressurized, but the damage was already done. Our ears pained us terribly. Every stop we made after that, our first request would be to see a doctor hoping for relief, and the doctor would always say, "Don't fly for two or three days." This of course was impossible. There were times when we were almost completely deaf. This campaign tour lasted about three weeks, and we both were never without pain in our ears.

But came November 4, 1952, and we felt that we had contributed our bit toward putting a Republican in office, after twenty years of the Democratic regime.

Although General Eisenhower was not our choice for a presidential candidate, in time we developed a deep admiration and affection for both Ike and Mamie. Of all the Presidents my husband served under, and the First Ladies I knew, I suppose we really saw more of them. And among all the Presidents' wives, my relationship with Mamie Eisenhower has remained the closest through the years—perhaps partly because we became so well acquainted through our husbands' several illnesses.

We finally went to our first Inaugural Ball. We had attended other inaugurations, but not the balls. It was not until Eisenhower was elected that we had any great part in any kind of festivities. A Republican in the White House, for a change, was cause for celebration.

I think I had one of the loveliest dresses I ever owned for my first Inaugural Ball. I bought it at Marshall Field's. I even had them design it especially for me. It was a white lace gown with a big yellow bow in the back and streamers that hung down from the bow. It gave me a sylph-like figure.

In spite of a certain sense of sadness for Bob and Martha

Taft, I was thankful for a Republican victory and for the first time I felt that we were really "in" in Washington.

1954 . . . The McCarthy Hearings

Anyone who missed seeing Everett on television at that memorable 1952 Republican National Convention in Chicago certainly had a chance to make up for it during the summer of 1954 when the much publicized and televised McCarthy Hearings created such an uproar. The whole country was caught up in the controversy over whether Wisconsin's Senator Joe McCarthy should be impeached for his disclosures of Communist infiltration in our government. My husband shared McCarthy's hatred of communism and voted against impeachment. And my goodness, what an avalanche of mail that brought! It wasn't all assault-and-battery, though. This time thousands of women wrote to Everett just to tell him how much they were enjoying watching the McCarthy Hearings—and especially *him* (my husband, not McCarthy)—on TV.

From the sound of their letters I don't think too many women got too much of their housework done during those hearings. Some said they moved their ironing boards into their living room, where their TV sets were, in order not to miss anything. Some admitted that their husbands were a bit irritated to come home from work tired, to find nothing for dinner but cold sandwiches.

Of course there was the usual amount of abusive hate-mail from the anti-McCarthy forces.

It took several months to answer all those letters, but the whole staff pitched in, and I helped also, and between us we answered every piece of mail that came across the senator's desk.

No matter how crudely written, misspelled, or grammatically incorrect, no matter whether written on brown wrapping paper with stubby pencil (as was often the case), each message always received the personal attention of Senator Everett Dirksen, the complaints no less than the compliments. Throughout all his terms in public office he stuck to this policy that all letters addressed to him must be read and answered. This was his contact with "the people."

1. "The Dirksen Boys"—Benjamin Harrison, three years old, standing, and the year-and-a-half-old twins, Thomas Reed on the left and Everett McKinley on the right.

2. The Dirksen home place.

3. The home of Mrs. Lillie Carver. Mrs. Dirksen still lives here part of the year.

4. Everett Dirksen at sixteen.

5. Second Lieutenant Dirksen during World War I. He was twenty-two years old.

6. First campaign picture taken on February 11, 1929,
the day after his daughter Joy was born.

7. Congressman Dirksen taken in 1939 in front of the Carlton Hotel in Washington.

8. The senator greets Generalissimo Chiang Kai-shek.

9. The Senator from Illinois beside the Lincoln Monument, in the Lincoln Memorial, Washington, D.C.

10. Senator Dirksen with granddaughter Cynthia in his arms, and grandson Darek Dirksen Baker standing in front of his mother, Joy. Photo was taken in 1962 after speech at Republican Club in Pekin.

11. The Dirksen twins, Everett and Tom (far right) celebrate their sixty-sixth birthday in 1962 with their wives Louella (beside Everett) and Mildred. Louella's mother, Mrs. Lillie Carver, helps cut the cake.

12. Senator Dirksen in his familiar lotus position on top of a desk in the Senate Press Gallery. (UPI Photo)

13. The Dirksen family at home in Pekin. (Sitting, left to right) Senator Dirksen, granddaughter Cynthia, Mrs. Lillie Carver (the senator's mother-in-law); (Standing, left to right) grandson Darek Dirksen Baker, Dirksen's son-in-law, Howard Baker, Jr., Mrs. Dirksen and daughter Joy (Mrs. Howard Baker).

14. Senator and Mrs. Dirksen beside the wrought-iron fence in front of their country home in Virginia.

15. Senator and Mrs. Dirksen in one of their marigold gardens in Virginia.

16. Former Vice-President Hubert Humphrey admires Senator Dirksen's tie while President Richard Nixon looks on.

17. The Nixons greet Senator Dirksen at his last birthday party. Beside the senator is Mrs. Dirksen; to his left are close friends Mr. and Mrs. Ben Regan.

18. Louella Dirksen with a glass globe containing the Dirksen marigold. (Photo by Frances Kuhl)

If they chose to attack him on certain issues, at least he was pleased that they even cared enough to take the time to write to him, and they deserved an answer.

By now, these letters from "the people" did not bother me as much as they once did. I was pleased that so many felt free to express themselves to him, good or bad. He always received more mail than any other senator, which was an indication of his popularity with the public. And if they did not approve of everything he did, that was to be expected.

What still bothered me to a certain extent were the attacks made on him by his colleagues and the press. That was one of the things about politics that I never liked; there are always so many personal attacks on those in the public eye. But I had to learn to cope with it. Otherwise I would have been a very unhappy lady for a good many years, wouldn't I?

1956 . . . Second Term

The year 1956 was a memorable one for us for reasons both political and personal.

Not only was it the beginning of my husband's second term as a senator, but it was also the beginning of a period of deep contentment in our lives. We had weathered the transition years. We now had a sense of *belonging*. We were even thinking of putting down roots. After long and serious soul-searching we had decided to do some land-searching in earnest, to try and find that piece of land Everett had wanted for so long. We loved our little Chesapeake Bay rented cottage, but we had decided to give it up as soon as we could find a place we could afford to *own*. This was a very special chapter in our lives, and I am coming to it later.

I mention it here because it seems now in retrospect so intertwined with Everett's election to his second term in the Senate which brought us—or at least me!—that certain sense of permanency, security, which I believe most women want. And certainly politics is the last place in the world where you would expect to find it.

But Everett won his second term in the Senate! My thrill for him was as great the second time around as the first.

My all-time favorite bumper sticker was the one in 1956, in red, white, and blue, which read D I R K S E N, with

I K E emphasized in the name. For it was Ike's second term, also.

1959 . . . *Another Milestone*

Everett was elected Republican Senate Leader, thus attaining the official recognition he so well deserved as his party's leader in the Senate. His most important work was yet to be done. He was on the threshold of the stage where his star shone the brightest. And how proud I was of him.

AN EARLY MORNING

A few days ago—on an early morning—I walked out to get the morning newspaper. As I started down the driveway I felt a stillness. Yes, there are no cars and no sirens in the country, but this was a stillness which only Mother Nature creates, and as I looked about I realized I was in fairyland. The grass was white and covered with sparkles. Tiny icicles, like chandeliers, hung from the trees. Others pointed upward and looked like candles with flaming tips. The moon was high and cold, but beckoning. The air was still.

Suddenly I heard a whir of wings and a bright red cardinal settled on a branch close by. As he did so, little diamonds fluttered to the ground. He began his morning song. Within another instant there was another whir of wings and a blue jay perched on another branch and more diamonds fell. He had a raucous cry.

As I looked at these two harbingers I said to myself: These are the colors which Betsy Ross fashioned into our flag. She used the red of the cardinal, the white of a frosty morning, and the blue of the jay—and it is a symbol to our people everywhere, of the beauty of their homeland. While I stood there with my hand on the mailbox, I knew that when I carried the paper inside it would tell of crime and war and accidents and death. I paraphrased from Browning's *Pippa Passes:* "God's in His Heaven, and all *would* be right with the world if we could only make it so."

I stayed a little longer, wanting to hold onto this moment. But as I looked to the east I saw the first rays of the sun followed by a ball of fire. As it rose higher, the trees began to drip and the diamonds slipped from the blades of grass. Then

I knew truly that Mother Nature was at work. The water would trickle down into the earth, where there were tiny seeds and bulbs—and the sun would warm them and soon there would be a garden of colorful flowers. And as I walked toward the house I knew that on an early morning I had seen a miracle. Mother Nature had taken her fairy brush and touched everything about me once over lightly.

(No, the above was not written by Everett Dirksen. But it might well have been. It was inspired by him and written by his wife, Mrs. D. I delivered it as part of an address to the Capitol Speakers Club of Washington, D.C., and I include it here because he loved it so and often said it expressed precisely his own early morning feelings about our "Heart's Desire." He even told me he could not have said it any better himself, which was the ultimate compliment, coming from the Senate Minority Leader from Illinois. But then how can you live with a man like that for all those years without subconsciously absorbing a part of him through osmosis?)

Chapter 11

Heart's Desire

By 1959 we had finally achieved Everett's dream of having a "bit of land with a snuggly house on it."

We had found the property while driving around the countryside on weekends, an idyllic spot on a branch of the Potomac near Leesburg and Sterling, Virginia, an hour out of Washington.

It was only three-and-a-half acres, not the eighty Everett once had in mind, but it would suffice.

We cleared most of the grounds ourselves. It was a jungle of overgrowth and dead trees when we bought it. We spent a good many hours cutting out those dead trees, with me on one end of a cross-cut saw and Everett on the other. And I spent a good many hours in pain from a long siege of poison ivy!

But it was worth it.

I designed our "snuggly little house" with some help from Everett. He insisted on a big Tennessee stone fireplace that would hold five-foot logs, and picture windows that would let him look out over the grounds and feel close to the earth. He had never liked our eighth-floor Berkshire apartment. He always said his feet were too far off the ground.

So I purposely designed our one-story house in a two-story (southern style) neighborhood, so Everett could have easy access to the outdoors he loved so, and in cold weather could see and feel his outdoors from inside.

We named it "Heart's Desire" because that's what it was. He had wanted it for so long.

And he could grow his flowers and putter around his gardens to his heart's content.

Everett could make anything grow . . . Not only flowers. He planted fruit trees and a vegetable garden. And he kept me busy canning all the fruits and vegetables from his gardens. Later we bought a freezer so we could have fresh-frozen peaches, cherries, pears, strawberries . . .

Everett saved a large section of his garden space for vegetables, for to him nothing tasted quite so good as home-grown tomatoes, corn, radishes, lettuce, beets, and of course his beans. He never forgot his boyhood in "Beantown," back in Pekin . . . And I must add that his vegetable garden grew the longest cucumbers I have ever seen.

But his flowers, of course, were his real joy, his morning glories and snapdragons and verbena, the tulips and daffodils and rose gardens and marigolds.

Everett was not one to go out picking his flowers and keep them in vases around the house. He preferred to leave them on their stems in the garden, except for that single bud he always brought in to me for our breakfast table. Sometimes he would gather a bouquet of flowers or a basket of garden crops for his office staff, but he always made sure there were enough flowers in his garden for his eyes to feast upon. He seemed to drink in their color and fragrance, which were like nature's gold, frankincense and myrrh to him.

My husband had an early morning ritual which never varied. He would get up and turn off the yard lights. We were both "night prowlers" and always left lights on, both inside and out, which saved us from bumping into objects (and each other) in the dark. Some of Everett's best ideas came to him in the middle of the night, and I would frequently find him working away at his desk at three o'clock in the morning.

We always left the coffeepot on the stove, so he could have a cup or two while he was working. Occasionally he would go into the kitchen and pour himself a glass of milk.

But every morning, after he turned off all the night lights, he would start the coffee (in the drip style glass coffee maker with the filter paper), then go out to get the morning paper and pick a fresh rose or marigold along the way. He liked hearty breakfasts—bacon and eggs and toast and jelly, with crispy fried potatoes, or bacon and French toast with maple syrup. He liked to start the day with a good breakfast, but I think more than anything else he liked to have companionship in the morning. I always sat down with my husband and had breakfast with him.

One of his greatest joys was the after-breakfast morning walk he took over his grounds.

He especially enjoyed watching for that first blade of grass in the spring, or the first little flower buds peeping through the ground. I remember so many of those early mornings when he would come rushing in to tell me the exciting news, "Hey, Mrs. D., the first crocus is up! Come look!"

And then there were his birds and his birdhouses! He was forever filling trays with dried bread crumbs and birdseed, which we bought by the 25-pound sack. And the birds seemed to spread the word that the place to go for a good feed was "Heart's Desire." We had cardinals, swallows, jenny wrens, martins, and quail . . . Everett never tired of listening to their birdsongs or watching them building their nests and hatching newborns . . .

He had many of them named. The crow was Johnny-One-Note. Another he called Teacher, and his favorite was Mr. Red Bird, who was always the last one to say good night.

He began making birdhouses for them. My husband's birdhouses were a source of amazement to all who knew him, including me, because it was a rather well-known fact that he could hardly use a hammer without smashing a finger. My husband was a man of many talents, but he was no handyman around the house. Yet he could make beautiful birdhouses. He used anything he could get his hands on—coffee cans, wooden boxes of all shapes and sizes, and gourds.

Each year when Everett ordered his flower seeds, he would also order a few packets of gourds because it was easy for him to make birdhouses of them. All he had to do was cut a hole in one side, take out the seeds, then gouge another hole beneath it and poke a stick in for the perch, and hang it from a tree. He had birdhouses everywhere, mounted on poles, swinging from tree limbs, single-family, dormitory, or condominium-type dwellings for our "little boys," as he called the cacophony of birds that swirled about "Heart's Desire."

An important part of Everett's daily morning ritual was his fifteen-minute meditation period. My husband had learned about meditation long before "transcendental meditation" came into vogue. He always set aside fifteen minutes for meditation each morning, which he felt was very important to help him start his day off right. After his daily morning walk around the grounds, he would sit quietly on the patio and meditate. It was a time for peace and silence. And there was only one person who ever interrupted. That was President Eisenhower.

The President had the habit of calling eight o'clock breakfast meetings in Washington every two weeks or so for the leaders of the Republican party. When those calls came from the White House, Everett would not have time for his meditation period, and he regretted that very much. But other than those times, or when he was ill, he never missed his morning meditation.

He had an affinity for the electrical storms we frequently have in Virginia. It may sound strange to some but I remember that we used to sit out on our patio and watch the streaks of lightning spreading over the night sky and listen to the loud claps of thunder. If the rain was light, our big patio awning was protection enough but when the rain was heavy, we huddled back against the picture window, and sometimes we were driven indoors.

Our dear friend, Lee Naegel, from Florida, who was like one of the family, was always a little nervous during these electrical storms. I recall one time when Everett lured her out on the patio in the midst of one of our fiercest electrical storms and proceeded to give her a little philosophical speech about the beauty of the storm.

"You should enjoy this part of Nature, when it's so noisy," he told her, "Because it's at this time that Nature is dominating

and man is only a little part of the general scene. There is a
reason for the thunder and lightning. It is God's way of express-
ing Himself."

Among the happiest times we had together at "Heart's Desire"
were our little fishing trips. We had our own dock and we always
kept a small motorboat there so Everett could go fishing, which
seemed to relax him. But as often as not he would just sit there
fishing off the dock and meditating—almost as though defying
the fish to get on his hook. He didn't really want to be interrupted
by having to pull in the line and take the fish off the hook . . .

Everett suffered his first heart attack in 1957, only a mild one,
but he was convinced that having our place in the country had
saved his life, or at least prolonged it and hastened his recovery.
The doctor had ordered him to get away from the office for a
while and rest quietly. Our "Heart's Desire" was the ideal place
for that. After a short period of recuperation, he was strong
enough to go back to work, but he still had to spend his weekends resting until he was fully recovered.

One of our greatest joys was in having our new little family
visit us in Virginia, for by now we were grandparents. Joy
and Howard had given us a grandson, Darek Dirksen Baker,
born April 5, 1953, and a granddaughter, Cynthia, born March
26, 1956. Everett called her Cissy. He derived great pleasure
from his grandchildren, and they worshiped him. I think they
were enthralled by his voice. He would talk to them as though
he were the Chief Justice of the Supreme Court, and they
would not know a word he was talking about but they would
listen to him by the hour.

I remember one of the things that he began telling them
long before they were old enough to understand—that he was
going to see to it that they had the same opportunities and
the same freedom their "Grandpappy" had when he was growing up.

On one occasion when Cissy was sitting on his lap and he was
solemnly orating to her, she looked up at him and said, "Gramps,

you sound just like Mr. Ed." (Mr. Ed was the talking horse of a television show.)

I can still hear him ask, "What's for supper tonight, Mrs. D.?" He never called it dinner.

My fried chicken was his favorite dish. He always said no one else in the world could make fried chicken to taste like mine, and the truth is he was so spoiled that even when he was in the hospital he insisted on having my fried chicken.

Everett was ill a great deal and he was always put in Ward 8, the VIP ward at Walter Reed Hospital. There were only ten beds in Ward 8. It had its own little parlor and dining room off one end, and it had its own chef.

The chef was waiting to see me on one occasion when I went to visit my husband. He told me Everett had not been eating well, and that he had refused to eat the fried chicken he had prepared.

"He said it was nothing personal against me," the chef explained, "but my chicken just didn't taste like Mrs. D.'s. That's what he said." Hesitantly he asked, "Would you mind showing us how you do it the next time he's supposed to have chicken on his menu?

So there I was, in the kitchen of the VIP ward at Walter Reed, frying chicken! I did it often throughout the years of my husband's illnesses.

I have never regretted one penny of the money we spent on the house and grounds of our "Heart's Desire," for it was exactly that to Everett, the fulfillment of a dream. I know that it not only prolonged his life but enriched it magnificently and brought him great contentment while he was living.

And later on, when we were able to afford it, we built a little winter home in DeBary, Florida, and we called this one "Contentment."

POLITICAL REFLECTIONS . . . THE SIXTIES

When Daniel Webster died more than a century ago, a man who differed strongly with him on many public issues rose in Congress to say this in eulogy:

Our great men are the common property of the country.

Everett Dirksen of Illinois was and is the common property of all the fifty states.

Senator Dirksen belonged to all of us because he always put his country first. He was an outspoken partisan. He was an individualist of the first rank. But he put his Nation before himself and before his party. . . . His impact and influence on the Nation was greater than that of most Presidents in our history . . .

President Richard M. Nixon
at Memorial Services in the Rotunda of the
Capitol, September 10, 1969

Chapter 12

The Kennedy Years

I remember the day Everett came home and told me that a very handsome new young congressman had stopped in his office to pay his respects. A bright boy, my husband called him.

His name was John Fitzgerald Kennedy.

Everett still was a congressman then also. Through the years their paths crossed frequently and they developed a genuine affection for each other.

On a personal level it was more like a father-son relationship because Everett was old enough to be his father and in fact sometimes treated him like a son—or perhaps more like a younger brother. He often voiced concern over young John Kennedy's health. It may be remembered that John Kennedy frequently suffered from spinal or back ailments which were the result of his war injuries. And Everett's illnesses always made him more aware and sympathetic to the physical problems of others. I especially remember one fatherly, get-well note that Everett dictated to him while the young Senator Kennedy was recuperating from one of his spinal flare-ups in Florida.

First as a congressman and then as a senator, Jack Kennedy often called on Everett for advice. I think perhaps it was my husband's wit and humor, his old-fashioned style as a senator or "elder statesman" as he came to be known, combined with his ever-youthful zest and spirit that explained the delight and admiration he aroused in young John Kennedy.

And certainly he had great admiration as well as affection for "that Kennedy boy," as he so often called him.

This was the relationship that had grown up between them since John Fitzgerald Kennedy was first elected to Congress in 1946, and then to the Senate in 1952, and again in 1958.

The election year of 1960 marked another turning point in our lives.

Political writers are generally agreed and I believe historians will record that my husband, a Republican, reached his pinnacle of power and influence in the early sixties while the opposition party was in office, under the Kennedy and Johnson administrations.

From a strictly personal point of view I must admit that the year 1960 still holds a special meaning for me also, because it was the beginning of my husband's best years and greatest contributions to his country, and I took pride in all his triumphs in spite of the fact that I felt I was sharing him with the whole world.

Also from a strictly personal point of view, I remember it because of an accident that kept me from attending the 1960 national convention in Chicago with my husband. It is the only one I ever missed, and under circumstances that might have been tragic.

I was especially looking forward to this convention not only because of my husband's newly elevated rank within the Republican party as Senate leader (he would be reigning host at the convention), but also because I had been selected to play the role of Mary Todd Lincoln in a fashion pageant that was part of the women's program for the convention. Evyan Perfumes of New York loaned us copies of dresses worn by Presidents' wives. These dresses were replicas of gowns displayed in the Smithsonian Institution.

I was a member of the program committee making all the arrangements, and naturally, I was very pleased to be the one chosen to wear Mrs. Lincoln's dress. The dresses were sent to us in Washington so that we could have our pictures taken and rehearse our program before going to Chicago.

The day before we were to leave for the convention, Everett

and I had been working around the grounds of our new home. We started to burn a small unsightly mound of twigs and brush. Everett fetched the kerosene and sprinkled it, and I struck a match. Boom!

Someone had mistakenly put gasoline in the kerosene can.

Neighbors heard the explosion and came running and called an ambulance. I was rushed to the hospital in Leesburg, eight miles away, with first degree burns. I was in the hospital for six weeks.

It was a terribly painful experience, and I was depressed and disappointed to miss the convention. But I was delighted to learn that the committee had asked our daughter to be my substitute in modeling the Mary Todd Lincoln dress.

And no matter how busy Everett was at the convention, he always found time to call me and tell me how much I was missed, and "Hurry up and get well."

We both had very mixed feelings about the 1960 presidential election when our party's candidate, Richard Nixon, who had served as Vice-President with Eisenhower, lost out to "that Kennedy boy," as Everett still thought of him.

He had known Mr. Nixon also for many years. Naturally he saw much of him during the years that Nixon had served as a senator, and then as Vice-President.

And in spite of my husband's personal affection for young John Kennedy, he never for a moment forgot his role as his party's leader in the Senate. Of course he was disappointed that the Republicans lost and the White House again was in the hands of the Democrats.

In one sense our disappointment was perhaps greater than in some Republican quarters because it was our own state, Illinois, that defeated Nixon.

I suppose enough has been written already about the stranglehold that Chicago's famous Mayor Richard J. Daley and his Democratic political machine have on the voters. It seems unnecessary for me to recap it here, and that isn't exactly my forte. Besides, Chicago's vote frauds have been exposed time and again *

---

* My collaborator on this book, Norma Lee Browning, in fact wrote her own hair-raising exposé of the Chicago vote fraud in this 1960 election, during which she and her husband, along with thousands of others, were disenfran-

and nothing is ever done about it. I know there was a mutual respect between the senator and Mayor Daley. I know my husband enjoyed the city of Chicago and while he was certainly not in constant contact with Mayor Daley they sometimes exchanged ideas or communicated on matters of interest to either or both.

I am certain that everyone who read the news or watched television following the 1960 election knows that it was the manipulation of votes in some of the Chicago precincts that flipped Illinois into Kennedy's electoral column and gave him the victory over Nixon, with the low margin of only 8858 votes.

But for that, we both knew Nixon would have been President in 1960, instead of John Fitzgerald Kennedy.

And we felt especially sad that it was our own beloved state which threw the election to the Democrats, and by such a close margin.

But Everett was not one to lose much time in regrets. As Senate Minority Leader he began immediately to reorder his thinking. He had been chosen Minority Leader only the year before, under President Eisenhower. Now, with a Democrat in the White House, he was to assume new responsibilities as Minority Leader representing the "loyal opposition."

One of his first duties, and possibly one of his most difficult, was to accustom himself to a little matter of protocol. "That Kennedy boy" was now his new Commander-in-Chief. And I was aghast when I heard him say "Yes, Jack," to the President on the telephone one evening from our home in Virginia.

I do not remember anything else from Everett's end of the conversation, but as soon as he hung up the phone, I said, in a tone of feigned horror, "You called him Jack!"

He looked surprised. After all, he had been calling him Jack for a good many years.

---

chised. For weeks she had served as a volunteer precinct worker, was up at dawn on Election Day to work as a poll watcher, only to find when she took time off to cast her own vote that her name had mysteriously disappeared from the books. She was suddenly non-existent, though she had lived and voted in the same precinct for twelve years. Her experience and subsequent investigation of her status as a disenfranchised "ghost" appeared as a fascinating front-page series in the Chicago *Tribune* (November 23–29, 1960).

I suppose it is difficult for people to realize that a friendship established over the years such as Everett had with both President Kennedy and President Johnson from their earliest years in Washington goes beyond party boundaries.

It is indeed possible for a Republican and a Democrat to become intimately acquainted and on a friendly, first-name basis merely from sitting next to each other in committee hearings over a period of time. Everett and Jack Kennedy had been on a first-name basis for fourteen years. I am sure he was somewhat jarred to be reminded that it should now be "Mr. President" instead of Jack. But it was the first time he had served under a President so much younger than he.

"When he said, 'Hello, Everett,' I just forgot and responded instinctively. I promise never to let it happen again," my husband said apologetically. And he didn't. From then on it was always "Mr. President." The protocol makers probably would have forgiven him for that one slip. I seriously doubt that it bothered the President a bit. But it did bother Everett, for throughout his career he was always cognizant of the fact that the President was the head of his country, and regardless of who was serving in the office at the time, his position was always recognized with respect from my husband.

I am quite well aware of the criticism heaped on the Senator from Illinois by the conservative wing of his party because he supported some of President Kennedy's political policies. In spite of this I must say that my own personal recollection of President Kennedy cannot help but be colored by his genuine fondness for my husband, which he expressed in many ways and on many occasions. What senator's wife would not be prejudiced by this?

And I was quite impressed with the President's thoughtfulness and consideration for others. He was never too busy to telephone at the end of the working day and say how grateful he was for something Everett had done or said, or to express his approval of what had been going on in the Senate, or in a committee hearing. Many times the phone would ring before Everett was home, and it would be the White House calling. When Everett returned the call, the President would come on either to ask his advice or thank him for something. He seemed to be most

appreciative of the help others gave him, and he never hesitated
to express his appreciation, which I happen to regard as an
uncommonly fine (and all too rare) trait in anyone, especially a
man burdened with the responsibilities of the presidential office.

Bay of Pigs . . .

So many people have asked me how my husband really felt
about the Bay of Pigs fiasco and President Kennedy's role in it.
First, let me say that this is not intended to be a history book. It
is a book of memories.

I think history will record quite accurately all the events
that led up to the aborted Bay of Pigs invasion by a small band of
Cuban exiles trying to overthrow the government of Premier
Fidel Castro. The incident took place early in 1961 (April 17),
while John F. Kennedy was in the honeymoon period of his
presidency, and it is a historical fact that he accepted full
responsibility for the defeat.

It would be presumptuous of me to embellish on an incident
of such historical significance. As to how my husband felt about
it, I think he probably thought the President had been ill
advised and things didn't eventuate the way he had planned.

"I'm glad he owned up to it manfully," Everett said, still like
a father speaking of his son.

Jackie . . .

We did not know Mrs. Kennedy well. I don't think anyone did.
I always had the impression that she was in a job she did not
very much like and was trying to make the best of it. She was
quite reserved and I don't believe anyone could ever get close
to her. But she was always a lady and always a gracious hostess.
She entertained beautifully and always in good taste.

Everett did not have the same affection toward her that he
had for the President. For one thing, of course, he hadn't
known her as long. For another, he was a bit piqued when she
made off with one of his favorite chandeliers that hung outside his
office.

The chandeliers in the area of the Senate Minority Leader's
office were rather famous. One was a massive old cut-glass,
beautifully prismed chandelier that hung directly over a huge

conference table inside the chambers. It had once belonged to Thomas Jefferson and was known as the "tinkling chandelier." It tinkled so loudly that it sometimes interrupted important conferences and the conferees, led by the Minority Leader of course, would sit quietly listening to the lovely music of the tinkling chandelier.

It was one of a pair. The other hung directly outside the senator's office door.

As we heard the story later, Mrs. Kennedy came to a luncheon at the Capitol one day, spotted the beautiful outside chandelier, and fell in love with it. She proceeded to go back to the White House and put in motion the details of "borrowing" the chandelier for the Treaty Room of the Executive Mansion.

She invited a few guests in for the formal "hanging" and thoughtfully remembered to invite the occupant of the Senate Minority Leader's chambers, from whence the chandelier had been usurped.

My husband missed that chandelier that had hung outside his office and he never quite got over a slight feeling of vexation that Mrs. Kennedy had exceeded her authority and "tried to dismantle the U. S. Capitol," as he put it.

Although the chandelier supposedly was only "borrowed" for the Treaty Room of the White House, so far as I know it is still there.

Bobby . . .

I have a strong recollection of one very unhappy encounter my husband had with Bobby Kennedy. He had nothing in common with Bobby. I think he felt that he was the most immature and least qualified of the Kennedy brothers, as well as the most temperamental.

I was almost as indignant as Everett was the day he came home and told me about a little temper tantrum Bobby had in his office.

The incident took place in October 1965, two years after President Kennedy's death. Robert F. Kennedy had been Attorney General of the United States and was now the freshman Senator from New York. His other brother, Senator Edward M. Kennedy of Massachusetts, was trying to push the nomination of a Boston politician, Judge Francis X. Morrissey, to the Federal bench.

Everett was a member of the Senate Judiciary Committee and opposed to the nomination. He had checked into the man's record, as was his practice in all such nominations, and found substantial evidence that he was not qualified for the Federal bench.

Although it was Ted pushing the nomination, it was brother Bobby who tackled the Senate Minority Leader in a fit of real fury that embarrassed their mother, Mrs. Rose Kennedy.

As Everett described the scene to me, Bobby was a very angry young man as he paced up and down the floor raging against what he deemed a malign conspiracy to defame him and his family, and berating foes who seemed intent upon frustrating him and his brother.

Suddenly he wheeled around and leveled an accusing finger at Everett.

"You!" he shouted. "You have always hated the Kennedy family!"

What a preposterous thing to say to Everett Dirksen who was never in his life motivated by personal hostility to any member of the Kennedy clan. If he had wished to do so, he could have reminded Bobby that his brother, the late President John F. Kennedy, had had numerous occasions to thank the providence which put a Dirksen in the Senate as leader of the opposition party.

Instead, my husband said, "Young man, don't be a fool." He turned and pointed to a bust of the late President displayed behind him on the top of his cupboard, and quietly asked, "Would I have that up there if I hated the man? I will always have an affection for him." He paused, then added pointedly, "And his mother."

As for the Morrissey nomination, which was coming up on the Senate floor the next day, he warned Bobby, "If you push this thing tomorrow, I will throw the book at you. And there's more in the book than you may realize."

The Kennedy brothers' fight for the nomination was dropped.

A few days later he came home and told me that he had received a very interesting long distance telephone call from

Mrs. Kennedy, Mrs. Joe Kennedy, the remarkable mother of the Kennedy boys.

"I know how much you thought of my son, Jack, and how much he thought of you," she said. "I'm sure you can understand why, as a mother, I appreciate it so much that you did not say anything unkind about my son Teddy or vilify his name in any way during the Senate arguments on this Morrissey nomination. I want to thank you for it."

Everett was quite pleased. He said that Mrs. Kennedy was most gracious over the telephone to him. It isn't often that the mother of two senators calls a senator in the opposition party to thank him for not saying unkind words about her offspring.

Personally, I think Rose Kennedy is one of the most remarkable women I have ever met, and has been underestimated in the overall picture of the Kennedy family. It was always her husband who got most of the credit for imbuing his sons with political ambition. I'm not so sure that it wasn't the driving ambition of Rose Kennedy that shaped their futures. She is a woman of great will power, great determination and strength. Her endurance through all those family tragedies, in fact, would indicate that she is the strongest of the Kennedy clan. No other mother in U.S. history has sent three sons to the Senate, one of whom also became President. We felt sure she wanted Bobby in the White House . . .

Mrs. D. Takes Over . . .

My most vivid recollection of the Kennedy years is the one in which I was most personally involved, and it happened because of the Cuban missile crisis of October 1962.

This was the year of more than one Dirksen crisis, also. First, it was the year of another senatorial re-election campaign (his third) for my husband, and for the first time in our married life I strongly opposed his running again. In fact, I had fully made up my mind that I was going to put my foot down, I would not permit him to run for re-election. I now know how wrong I was. But wives who love their husbands do get selfish sometimes.

I thought we should have more time to spend together. He was working much too hard and his health wasn't good. It was nothing serious at the time—only that he expended so much of himself that he became fatigued easily. And I knew that this one was going to be a hard campaign.

I wanted him to save his health, and himself.

"I would just like to have you around longer," I told him. It was as simple as that.

I lost my campaign—and he started his.

That was the year a militant Chicago Democrat, Representative Sidney R. Yates, a devoted Kennedy follower, had decided to run against Everett, and there were rumors circulating that President Kennedy had promised to campaign in Illinois for Mr. Yates. But his heart could hardly be in it, as everyone knew.

One top administration Democrat was quoted as saying, "I like Sid Yates. But my party would be in a hell of a mess— Kennedy would be in a hell of a mess—if Dirksen got defeated."

There were other printed rumors that President Kennedy favored my husband over his Democratic opponent, all of which added up to a rather sticky campaign.

As it turned out, Congress had been in session so late that year, Everett hardly had any time to campaign. He had about three weeks to cover Illinois.

I remember the day the telephone call came in our hotel room. I knew it was important from the intense way Everett was listening. He hung up, then carefully, deliberately picked up his campaign schedule and his notes, and turned them over to me, saying, "Well, Mrs. D., you're taking over this campaign. That was the President. He wants me back in Washington. He's sending his plane for me. It's urgent."

I had a panicky feeling inside me which must have shown on my face.

"You can do it. You have to! You can do it just as well as anyone else . . . Better!"

He gave me a reassuring kiss and with that, the senator's wife who was not going to permit him to run for re-election found herself in charge of his campaign.

Now, how vividly I recalled Eleanor Roosevelt's admonishment of some twenty years earlier when she spoke to our Congressional Wives Club and told us of our responsibility to help our husbands, no matter how difficult it might be. I remembered the story about her nervous little giggle. At least I didn't have that as a handicap!

If she could face large audiences to speak for her husband, so could I.

That memory of Eleanor Roosevelt, and the fact that I had some three decades of experience traveling with Everett during his campaign trips provided me with the extra confidence I needed to do the job.

During the following days the newspapers were filled with reports on "the Cuban missile crisis," as it was called—referring to the discovery of Soviet missile bases being built in Cuba. President Kennedy had called on his defense and military leaders, as well as key members of the Congress, for a series of bi-partisan advisory conferences during this "crisis." He ordered a naval and air quarantine of Cuba and notified Khrushchev that the U.S. was prepared to sink their ships in the ocean unless the missile bases were dismantled. What this amounted to was that he dared nuclear war over the missile bases, and it was regarded as the boldest stroke in Kennedy's presidency. The "crisis" was resolved when Khrushchev backed down and ordered the missile bases dismantled.

In checking back over these few bare facts in another historically significant turn of events, I find that the actual dates given for the Soviet missile crisis were from October 22 to October 28, 1962, so it was during those few days that I took over my husband's re-election campaign while he was in Washington.

Now I would have to tell my audiences why they should re-elect my husband, without getting into party politics or legislative matters as he could.

However, this turned out to be not as difficult as I had thought it might be. I played my role honestly even though there were times when I had to play it by ear.

There was, for example, in the schedule Everett had given me, a night meeting on the far south side of Chicago in what is known as the "black belt." A friend had given me the use of his car and driver for the evening, so that I would not have to be driving by myself in an unfamiliar section of the city. We arrived at the meeting hall to find that the driver and I were the only white persons present. This in itself did not bother me. I had no fear of my audience because of their color, but I was quite aware that Everett had never had much support from Chicago's Negro population in spite of the fact that he was one of the leaders in the Civil Rights fight.

I was not quite sure what approach to use with them, but fortunately I think I instinctively chose the right one. I was introduced by the Republican candidate for Congress from that district, who told the crowd that the senator had been called back to Washington because of the Cuban crisis, that I had come in his place and would be happy to speak to them if they wanted to hear from the candidate's wife.

They clapped politely, then listened attentively as I talked. I started right off by telling them that when we were married, we repeated the vows to love, honor, and obey. In this particular instance, my husband had requested me to take over his speaking schedule and I was obeying his orders. That is why I was there with them.

Strangely, the men and women were seated separately on opposite sides of the hall, but immediately the cheers went up from both sides, "Amen, sister!" "That's what you should do, sister!" And from there on I had no problem. I came away satisfied that I had done well at the meeting and had won a few votes for my husband.

In the opposite direction, some miles north of Chicago, Everett was scheduled to speak to a group of political science students at Mundelein College, a Catholic girls' school. I had planned what I felt was a very informative and helpful speech about actual working campaign procedures for this particular audience, since they were students majoring in political science and I thought they would be interested in a more serious talk than some of my audiences.

I was completely taken aback when their teacher and faculty adviser greeted me with, "Hello, Mrs. Dirksen. I'm so glad you are here to represent your husband. I admire him so much. I'm a good friend of Senator Paul Douglas and I think the two of them think so much alike that I can't wait to hear what you have to say."

I wanted to shout, Good Heavens! Anyone teaching political

science in college certainly should have known that the only thing Everett Dirksen and Paul Douglas had in common was that both were Senators from Illinois.

Paul Douglas was a Democrat and a liberal at that. He was a professor at the University of Chicago, known as one of the strongholds of liberalism, and he had written some books with a decidedly liberal viewpoint.

Everett and Paul Douglas were friends. In fact one of the last telephone calls Everett made before his last illness was made to Paul Douglas because he had heard that Paul was ill. Everett spoke to both Emily Douglas and Paul. (He is retired now and well, as I write this.)

But their friendship did not change the well-known fact that Everett and Paul Douglas never agreed in their basic thinking.

I was thoroughly appalled that anyone, and especially a teacher of political science, could say that those two thought alike. And if that was what she was teaching her students, I was in serious trouble. As we walked from the car to the auditorium, I mentally debated whether to abandon my original speech outline and try to explain to the students the differences in the Dirksen-Douglas political thinking. I decided against it. Everett was not running against Paul Douglas, who was already a senator. He was running against Sidney Yates, who aspired to be. And besides, I did not wish to embarrass the Sister, nor to cast doubts upon her competency as a teacher.

I decided that I would stick with my original outline and then answer questions. It seemed to work out well. But I have often wondered how far that faculty adviser led her students astray in their political thinking.

It can get cold in Chicago in late autumn. (Or any time, for that matter.) I remember the bitter cold October night that I shared a platform at a shopping center with Dick Gregory, the Negro performer. The platform had been hastily set up on top of a truck in the middle of the parking lot. It was in an unsheltered area and the wind was whipping around us and I was shivering.

It seemed even colder to me than it actually was, because I realized the crowds had come to see Dick Gregory, not me.

My teeth were chattering from the cold as well as from my nervousness, as I stood up there to present my husband's campaign program. As I made my shaking, shivering opening remarks, a kindly gentleman who was with Dick Gregory removed his overcoat and placed it around my shoulders. It was a wonderful gesture of compassion and I shall never forget it. I finished my speech with a feeling of warmth in spite of the chilling winds from Lake Michigan.

But I was relieved when Everett returned from Washington to resume his own campaign. We both were amused at the little irony of the situation—that the one time I had objected to his running again, I was his substitute campaigner!

On the way back from the airport I asked him if the President had said anything special to him. He lowered his voice and told me that after one of the Cuban-crisis meetings, the President had stopped him and asked him to stay a little longer. Everett said he had to get back to Illinois to finish his campaign.

And the President said, "You don't need to campaign. You know you're already in. I don't think we [the Democrats] are going to hurt you very much in Illinois."

There was a sharp-eared newspaper reporter riding in our airport limousine, for this juicy tidbit leaked out and was played up in the press. What an uproar that one caused. President Kennedy even had to issue a formal statement declaring that the Democratic President did not favor re-election of the Republican senator.

How relieved was I when that 1962 election was all over. And of course Everett was back in the Senate.

We were preparing for our Thanksgiving holidays at our "Heart's Desire" in Virginia when we heard the news that stunned the world, that President Kennedy had been shot. We spent the next few days shocked numb and immobilized at the horror and the sad, gray pageantry surrounding the death of our young President. Along with the real personal loss, Everett was disturbed to realize that our country had fostered a climate which could nourish such a violent act as assassination.

Chapter 13

The LBJ Years

Certain years and events stand out in my memory better than others because they mark turning points and highlights in my husband's political career.

It is easy, for example, to remember 1932 as the year he was first elected to Congress, 1950 as the year he became a senator, 1952 as the year he accused Tom Dewey of taking us "down the road to defeat" during his nominating speech for Bob Taft at the Chicago convention.

It is easy to remember that he was chosen Senate Minority Leader in 1959. I thought it was about time! And I remember 1962 as the year of the Cuban crisis only because that historic incident tossed me into the political arena, substituting for my husband in his re-election campaign.

As Everett's wife and number one supporter (except for those first tentative reservations in 1962), I naturally felt a close sense of identification with all of those events.

Now comes 1964, the year my husband was heralded as the saviour of the historic Civil Rights Act, under a Democratic President, Lyndon B. Johnson. History has already recorded this as Everett Dirksen's "finest hour," an accolade reaffirmed by none other than Senator Mike Mansfield of Montana, Democratic leader in the Senate.

My political memories of that historic year, 1964, are admittedly colored by some highly personal emotions that have no place in the history books. For this was also another presidential election year, and in retrospect I must say it was the most turbulent one of Everett's political career.

It was the year in which my husband more than any other senator labored long and hard putting through a civil rights bill which might as well have had his name on it—and then turned right around and pledged his support to the man who cast the most noted vote against it, Senator Barry Goldwater.

It was my husband who made the nominating speech for Barry Goldwater at that famous Cow Palace convention in San Francisco in the summer of '64. I still regard it as one of his best. He was fond of Barry Goldwater. Everett had almost singlehandedly persuaded Goldwater to run for the Senate.

We had had our ups and downs in more than thirty years of life in the political jungle, and we had developed thick skins. Criticism was part of the game.

But I can remember no other time when more vilification was heaped on him, and no time when it affected me more.

In politics, as in baseball, yesterday's hero is today's bum. That transition was never quicker than for my husband who was an idol of the Washington press corps one week and a target of derision, ridicule, and scorn the next.

Actually, it was a little longer than a week.

The date of Everett's final Senate floor speech immediately prior to the historic Senate vote on the Civil Rights Act was June 19, 1964.

He made his announcement for Goldwater on June 30 at Chicago's O'Hare Inn, where the fifty-eight members of the Illinois delegation to the Republican convention met in caucus.

It was this Illinois vote, led by Everett's endorsement, which all but crushed Pennsylvania Governor William Scranton's chances for the GOP nomination.

Governor Scranton, it may be recalled, had been the last-ditch hope of the eastern "liberals."

And it was largely the "liberal" press corps that began crucifying Everett. At his first press conference after the Illinois caucus, he was assailed with angry and sarcastic questions.

Did he regard Barry Goldwater as God's gift to the party and the country?

Was his memory so short that he had forgotten his civil rights speeches aimed at Goldwater?

What was he getting in return for this—the vice-presidency?

Nearly everyone seemed surprised that my husband had no interest in the vice-presidency.

"I would have to dedicate roads and courthouses and bow to visiting princes and kings," he said. "I am not a candidate."

He tried not to show irritation at the unfriendly questioning, but when one reporter referred to his age, which was then sixty-eight, and his "condition of health," Everett informed him that newspapermen assigned to cover his campaigning for Goldwater in the fall had better be in good physical shape to keep up.

Throughout it all, Everett remained cheerful and optimistic when he discussed the events of the day with me at home. But to me they were depressing days, hearing and reading some of the cruel and senseless things the press was saying about him.

The New York *Times*, for example, which only days before had elevated him to a lofty pedestal for his contribution in rallying support for the civil rights bill, was now saying he had deserted his "high principles."

I believe the majority of Washington correspondents had a personal liking for Barry Goldwater but they made no secret of their opposition to his conservative policies. And they were simply transferring this hostility to Everett.

To make matters worse, at least from my personal point of view, he had just gone through a long siege of attack from members of his own party for the help he was giving Democratic Presidents, present and past, on important issues of the time. Although he had opposed much of the late President Kennedy's New Frontier programs, it was only with Republican votes, marshaled by Everett, that JFK achieved any wins at all. And although he opposed the new President Johnson's Great Society, he was given the credit for taking LBJ off a hot spot in the civil rights battle.

In both the John F. Kennedy and Lyndon B. Johnson administrations, the rule of success was "Clear it with Dirksen."

As news commentator Howard K. Smith once said of him, "He is not a senator. He is *the* senator—the man who gets legislation passed or stopped."

My husband, let me repeat, was the staunchest of Republicans. He did not believe in obstructionism for the mere sake of obstructionism—of opposing Democratic proposals because they originated with the Democrats instead of the Republicans. And while we're on the subject of origin, if I remember correctly the first civil rights acts were introduced in 1957 under the Eisenhower administration, then again in 1960 and 1963 under President Kennedy, and only came to fruition under LBJ, with Everett's help.

Some of his Republican colleagues seemed to forget how much of the Kennedy-Johnson regime of the New Frontier and the Great Society he opposed. They were not concerned that he was a Republican leader in the cause of "bi-partisanship." And some of their attacks, I felt, were as unjustified as those of the "liberal" press.

None of them should have labored under any illusion, for despite his help to Democratic Presidents, my husband had said, "When the time comes, when the chips are down, I'll show what kind of a Republican I am."

This he did, in an act of high conscience and courage, when he announced his endorsement of Arizona's Senator Barry Goldwater.

A few pertinent facts should be recalled. President Johnson had been in office only a few months when the historic Civil Rights Act was passed, having taken the oath of office only hours after the tragic death of President Kennedy.

He was thrust into the presidential office by fate, and not by popular vote of the people. Because 1964 was a presidential election year and Lyndon Johnson was only in his first year as a "substitute" President, there was a very strong feeling even among Republicans that no one would have the remotest chance of winning against him in the November presidential election. After all, you can hardly depose a man without giving him a fair run at his job. So the sentiment went.

My husband did not go along with this sentiment. He wanted a Republican in office, and one who could help get more Republicans into the Senate.

Only those who did not know the senator well were surprised

when he announced his support of Barry Goldwater. He had been saying for months that he would back the candidate who would most help the election of Republican Senate nominees. He realized that Goldwater's nomination might hurt the chances of some of the Northeast Republican incumbents, but at the same time he felt that the Republicans' best chances for picking up Senate seats lay in the Midwest and Far West states, where Barry Goldwater carried a lot of weight.

There were other reasons also. Everett and Barry Goldwater had been good friends in the Senate. Everett was instrumental in making Goldwater chairman of the Republican Senatorial Campaign Committee in 1955, a job that put Goldwater in constant contact with Republicans all over the country and gave him hundreds of far-flung pulpits from which to preach his views.

As for the civil rights issue, Senator Goldwater had voted against the bill only because he felt that certain parts of it were unconstitutional, and it was no secret that he had gone to see Everett a number of times to discuss his stand on the matter and to promise that he would enforce the bill if he were elected President.

Everett felt that Goldwater had earned the right to the nomination because he had worked hard for it and that he had a good chance of beating Lyndon Johnson. He also knew Barry Goldwater as a man of strong conservative convictions, like his own.

When a reporter asked him why he chose to back Goldwater, my husband proudly and defiantly replied, "Well, because I wanted to."

Need he say anything more?

But there was one incident which I am sure influenced his decision. That was Governor Scranton's little trip to Washington to see Everett and to urge him to become the "favorite-son" presidential candidate from Illinois, an obvious ploy to withhold the Illinois delegates' votes from Goldwater at the national convention, and to let Everett know that he would be welcome as a vice-presidential running mate on the GOP ticket.

Everett couldn't care less about being Vice-President because he loved his role in the Senate and wanted to stay there. But Scranton's other suggestion really annoyed him.

"What does he think I am? A rookie? I certainly am not impressed," he said, and I certainly did not blame him.

Actually there was nothing inconsistent in my husband's choice of Goldwater as the candidate. Everett always had been and still was a Midwestern Republican, which is an entirely different brand from the eastern "liberals." He was not known for his admiration of the GOP's Northeastern "kingmakers," as they were sometimes called, and Scranton's overtures to him did nothing to enhance his feelings in that direction.

It was soon after Scranton's visit that he let the world know he would endorse Barry Goldwater, thus incurring the wrath of both the GOP "kingmakers" and the press.

Henry Cabot Lodge, who was a Scranton supporter, took it upon himself to remind the public, through the press, that Everett had nominated Senator Robert Taft for President at the 1952 convention—and that General Eisenhower "ran away with the show." He implied that this would happen again, with Scranton coming up the winner.

Everett's reply was simple. "Sometimes the history book rises up and smites you," he said.

Indeed there were striking similarities between the 1952 and 1964 Republican presidential campaigns, and the starring role Everett played in each of these dramas. These two, in fact, were the most dramatic in my memory, and not only because my husband made a nominating speech at each convention. Both conventions were torn with bitter intraparty animosities—between Taft and Eisenhower backers in '52 and the Goldwater and Scranton forces twelve years later. Emotions always run high at political conventions but I cannot recall any more divided than those two.

I believe anyone who was there, either in Chicago or San Francisco—or perhaps both—would agree with me that the most memorable sight and sound at each of these conventions was my husband dramatically pleading the cause of Bob Taft at one and Barry Goldwater at the other.

There were even a few similarities between Taft and Goldwater. Both were outspoken individualists and identified with the conservative wing of their party. Perhaps because of their Midwestern (Ohio) and Southwestern (Arizona) backgrounds, both shared my husband's lack of enthusiasm for the eastern "liberal" or "progressive" Republicanism of the Scranton backers.

In 1952 the eastern Kingmakers were saying "Taft can't win."

In 1964 they were pulling out all the stops for a "Stop Goldwater" campaign.

Everett and I were both very much aware that his nominating speech for Goldwater would have to be a good one. A nominating speech rarely sways many delegates because most of them are already pledged to a candidate. But it can influence the millions of television viewers, who are also voters.

We realized that he should have a very strong and effective speech to counteract the anti-Goldwater feeling that was gaining momentum, engendered by the eastern "liberal" Republicans and press.

We began working on the speech together at home long before the convention. I worked more closely with Everett on this speech than on any other, because my good nature was being sorely tried by the barrage of criticism hurled at my husband. He was taking it cheerfully, but not I. I think any wife is hurt when someone criticizes her husband. In politics we learn to expect a great deal of name-calling and mud-slinging and to bear up under it. But this was a bit much. The same people who glorified him for his civil rights stand had turned on him, cruelly, and were treating him like a traitor because of his support of Goldwater.

It is a wife's instinctive nature to come to her husband's defense. I wanted my husband vindicated. I feel that I contributed something toward achieving this by helping him write the speech nominating Goldwater. We discussed our ideas together and worked them out carefully, almost paragraph by paragraph.

A great to-do was made of the fact that Everett broke political protocol in that nominating speech by not waiting until the end to mention Goldwater's name. Instead, he almost opened with his name and kept repeating it at every mention of Goldwater's qualifications for the office.

We had discussed this at home before the convention. It seemed ridiculous to wait until the end of the nominating speech to name his candidate when everyone already knew, and when there was such a bitter intraparty battle raging over it. He believed that by frequent mentions throughout the speech, he could better make his listeners remember the qualities and qualifications he meant to dwell on. I think he was right because by knowing who the candidate was from the beginning, the audience could hold its attention on the points Everett was trying to make.

He made them well. It was a very effective speech and, in my opinion, one of Everett's most impressive ones.

And this time history did not repeat itself. In 1952 his candidate lost. In 1964 his candidate won.

But that was only the GOP presidential nomination. There was still the national election in November. History has recorded the disastrous consequences of that one—disastrous for the GOP.

Everett believed Senator Goldwater was a man of courage, conscience, and convictions. When the race was over and Goldwater had lost, he took it philosophically. He did not aim any words of direct criticism at Goldwater, but rather blamed the party for staying on the defensive and not selling "our merchandise." Everyone knew that "our merchandise" referred to the Republicans' congressional record.

LBJ—MR. PRESIDENT . . .

When Everett first went to Washington in 1933, Lyndon Johnson was then a doorkeeper in the House of Representatives. He later was a secretary to one of the congressmen and soon after that was elected to the House of Representatives himself.

Their friendship in later years caused much comment and consternation, but it must be remembered that their intimate association stemmed from way back. Everett had worked with Lyndon Johnson for years, both in the House and in the Senate, where Senator Johnson was Majority Leader until he chose to run on the Democratic ticket as Vice-President under John Kennedy in 1960. And he had worked under Johnson when he took over as President after Kennedy's assassination in November 1963.

They were for the most part political adversaries but they were also close friends.

I alway appreciated his concern for Everett's health. How well I remember the inaugural luncheon, shortly after he was sworn in. I looked up to see the President coming toward my table and when he got right in front of me, he peered down into my face and said, "You've got to take care of that man. We need him."

After the luncheon he cornered Everett and told him he should slow down and only work two days a week, a proposal which we both greeted with some merriment.

Everett certainly did not approve of Lyndon Johnson's "Great Society." He called his State of the Union message "a blueprint for paradise."

But by and large they maintained the good working relationship they previously had even after Lyndon Johnson became President. It was common knowledge that they sometimes made six or seven phone calls to each other in a single day. And there were many times when Everett went to the White House at the end of his working day to meet with the President, including that memorable time I have already mentioned when the President caused him to miss our dinner party.

I know that my husband was very forthright and outspoken with the President in a way that others close to him wouldn't dare to be, either because they were too protective of him or in awe of him. As a friend Everett felt obliged to tell him—and often did so in no uncertain terms—when he thought the President was doing something wrong, and why he disagreed with him. The President seemed grateful to have Everett's viewpoints on certain issues. If, however, they did not always see eye to eye, Everett would accept the President's decision and make the best of it because, after all, his friend Lyndon Johnson was now also his Commander-in-Chief. No one had greater respect for the office of the President—no matter who was occupying it—than Everett.

In explaining how they had worked together as Senate Minority and Majority Leaders, Everett once put it very well when he said:

"We both knew that it was necessary for us to cooperate, in the interest of the country, so that the Senate could turn in a useful and productive piece of work. We always went on the theory that the leaders had to cooperate unless we wanted to convert the Senate into a shambles. All, of course, of no benefit to the country. We could always fight, hard and clean, but always make the Senate operate."

They still maintained this same working relationship after Johnson became President.

The Johnson Ladies . . .

We had known the Johnsons for so long and had watched Lynda and Luci grow up practically from the time they were babies. Everett was especially fond of the two girls and they were especially fond of him. Luci would always drop in to see him when she came up to Capitol Hill. She regarded him with great affection, and he always took the time to have a little chat with her. We were invited to both girls' weddings. Luci's wedding was held soon after Everett had broken his hip in 1966, and he was still on crutches. He wouldn't have missed her wedding for anything. And what a picture he made struggling up that steep bank of steps of the church. Everyone wanted to assist him but he brushed them all aside and made it up the steps by himself. It was a lovely wedding . . . and so, too, was Lynda's wedding which was held in the White House on December 9, 1967.

Of course I had met Lady Bird when our husbands were still in the House but we became much better acquainted while both our husbands were in the Senate, and we were members of a group called the Senate Ladies Red Cross, composed of wives of senators. Lady Bird automatically became president of the group when her husband was elected Vice-President. She faithfully attended all our Tuesday morning sessions when she was in town. We made bandages, and sewed for hospitals, and it was a very pleasant, friendly group.

It might be said that Everett and I perhaps had a closer rapport with the Johnsons than with some families because we had known them longer. Yet, one of the truly sad and lonely things about being in politics is that it is impossible to develop really close friendships even within your own party, much less the opposition party. Everett and the President were friends, but they *were* of opposite parties. And wives especially, though perhaps mutually drawn to each other, simply abstain from forming close personal friendships when their husbands are of opposite political parties.

Skin of an Elephant . . .

Please do not ask me why I should have been more piqued at the slurs on Everett's name during the Goldwater campaign than at other times. By now I should have been conditioned to the constant nastiness and viciousness and back-biting that are so much a part of the political way of life. Hadn't I known from the very beginning what to expect? Those rumors about Everett being a wife-beater and neglecting his child in that first campaign back in Peoria and Pekin should have steeled me for anything that followed.

Failing that, I certainly should have been immunized against anything after all those mailbags of venomous insults he received when he dared to "defy" the newly beloved FDR by voting against his NRA (National Recovery Act) back in 1933. The people who loved Franklin Roosevelt, loved him passionately, and got quite carried away in their attacks on Everett. But for a "one-term congressman" he had lasted quite a while, hadn't he?

Then, of course, there was that avalanche of hate mail during the 1954 McCarthy Hearings but nothing bothered me quite so much as the abuse he took for his nomination of Goldwater.

Sometimes I found myself wondering whether certain politicians had ice water instead of blood in their veins, for all the mean, stinging personal insults they could find to fling at one another. Everett regarded politics as the most fascinating business in the world. Perhaps so. But you soon learn it is also a ruthless and brutal business, and in order to survive, you need the "skin of an elephant," as Everett used to say.

Fortunately, I did manage to develop "the skin of an elephant" which over the years helped me through "the slings and arrows of outrageous fortune." I learned to ignore most of the criticism directed at my husband and to concentrate on the more challenging aspects of his job.

I always had the utmost faith that whatever he did was right. So I was not often unduly disturbed by his detractors. I could not afford to let myself be emotionally torn by the words of his critics.

In politics it is very important to develop a high degree of insensitivity, but I must confess that along with my "skin of an elephant" I also developed the memory of one. I have tucked away in my memory treasure chest the names of those who said unkind things about my husband. When I meet them at parties I am polite. Why not? Everett's philosophy was: never let the sun go down without a kind word for those who didn't have one for you!

He was far less bothered by criticism than I. While he did not welcome it any more than any other man, he accepted it as part of the job.

His attitude is best summed up in a brief note he wrote to our friend, Marjorie Kunstadter:

Dear Marjorie: Think nothing of those slanted cynical editorials. On one pair of the crutches [which someone sent him] *on which I hobbled around after I got out of the hospital and wheel chair* [when he broke his hip] *is a little card which says,* "I COUNT THAT DAY LOST WHEN I DON'T CATCH HELL FROM SOMEBODY." *It is a great sentiment by which to live.*

Political Chameleon? . . .

I am well aware that my husband was sometimes criticized for changing his mind, so to speak, or shifting his position on certain political matters. Political writers and columnists had a field day with his well-known "flexibility." They called him the GOP's "political chameleon," to which Everett usually replied, "Change is an inherent way of life. The only people who do not change their minds are in cemeteries."

This remark in many ways epitomized the man, Everett Dirksen, who was the essence of practical politics but managed never to lose sight of the greater goals for the people of this nation.

I do not feel that my husband ever reversed himself in his principles, or changed his basic way of thinking. Rather, he advanced with the times. He was criticized first as an "isolationist," then as an "internationalist." From time to time he was called a liberal Democrat, a conservative Democrat, a neutral independent, an isolationist Republican, a moderate Republican, a conservative Republican, and I cannot remember what else.

One political writer said of him that his positions on issues "have been so varied as to give pleasure at one time or another to practically everyone." And another wrote, "They say he is so nimble in changing position that it is no feat at all for him to enter a revolving door backward and emerge face forward."

Such pleasantries amused us.

I think my husband had the best answer for his "shifting" political position when he said:

"I'm an old-fashioned, garden variety of Republican who believes in the Declaration of Independence, the Constitution, and Abraham Lincoln, who accepts the challenges as they arise from time to time, and who is not unappreciative of the fact that this is a dynamic economy in which we live and sometimes you have to change your position."

I often heard him remind people that "politics is the art of the possible." He always used this as his guideline as he approached the many complex issues on which decisions were needed.

It must be remembered that his position as Senate Minority Leader under Democratic administrations made it necessary for him often to practice the "art of compromise." In fact, during his nearly thirty-seven years in Washington, the Republicans were the majority party only during the last two years of the Eisenhower administration. So, as leader of the loyal opposition he often found himself trying to work out the best possible solutions without completely sacrificing the principles of the Republican party, and it was necessary to fight constantly for the largest fraction of whatever a minority could achieve and to have that fraction composed of the most constructive portions of the desirable whole solution.

As I have mentioned, he did not believe in opposing Democratic proposals merely because they might implement the majority party's program. He did not believe, as some of his GOP colleagues did, in abstaining from participation in the great problems of the day by taking a stubborn partisan stand. He believed that by offering the administration judicious support on certain issues, the minority party not only could develop a positive record but might very well exchange votes for amendments, revisions, or other fine points of legislation which would express something of the Republican view.

It was this philosophy, I believe, that gave my husband such a powerful voice in the government. His thinking was far ahead of the times. Though he certainly knew all the technical machinations of politics, he was always a statesman first and a politician thereafter. I am sure this was a factor in his constant growth and strength, and his increased national stature.

I am sure he often thought of himself as a bi-partisan rather than a partisan leader, always keeping uppermost in his mind the good of the country.

It is my opinion that the charges of his being "indecisive" or "wishy-washy" or an "opportunist" for changing his mind, shifting positions, or remaining flexible on certain major issues are completely unjustified.

One of my husband's great abilities as a statesman was that he did remain flexible on great public issues. He refused to be locked in on a position until he had an opportunity to hear and weigh all the evidence.

He did indeed master the art of political compromise, but always for the good of his country.

He did indeed change his mind with the changing times, but there was always a continuity in his thinking: What was best for his country?

He devoted himself to every task and every subject with such intensity and diligence and thoroughness, so that naturally with the changing circumstances in the world there would develop some change in his ideas.

He gave each of his Presidents support at crucial times that elevated him above partisanship. And he opposed them when he felt he had to in the interests of his country.

I believe anyone who knew Everett Dirksen well would agree that his deep sense of commitment to the country he loved so much, the United States of America, transcended all personal and political considerations.

As he explained it, "You start from the broad premise that all of us have a common duty to the country to perform. Legislation is always the art of the possible. You could, of course, follow a course of solid opposition, of stalemate, but that is not in the interest of the country."

So when it came time for him to vote on a particular bill or piece of legislation, that was the principle behind his every vote, whether it was in the interest of his country. His decision might offend members of his own party. He might be labeled a liberal, a Democrat, or a revolving-door Republican. Labels bothered him not.

His friendliness to some Democratic proposals might cause his Republican associates to grumble, but he refused to bend to partisan pressures. He took a practical view of the lawmaking process and was less concerned with partisan politics than with the deep moral issues of our times.

If I had to choose one key word to describe my husband's greatest asset in the service of the government, I would have to say courage. He often said there was only one debt greater than the Federal debt, and that was the debt that he owed his country. Because of this, he had the courage to change his views, the courage to battle for what he believed to be right for his country, the courage to stand up and cheer his country when it was not the most popular thing to do.

And if I had to choose only one out of all of Everett's speeches to sum up the kind of man my husband was—his character, his ideals, his love of country and God—I would have to choose the one he titled, "What's Right With America."

I have found a copy of the typed outline he used for this speech which he gave at a Chamber of Commerce luncheon in Jacksonville, Florida, on November 21, 1967.

I am including the complete outline here because it gives an insight not only to Everett Dirksen, the man, but to the way he organized his thoughts, underscoring certain words for emphasis. Most of all I wish to include it here because these are his words, his beliefs, and I feel they are worth preserving for future generations who hopefully will profit by them.

FLORIDA CHAMBER OF COMMERCE
Jacksonville Luncheon
Nov. 21, 1967

"What's Right With America"

I. *INTRO.* Greetings – Thanks – *N. D. COW* – To see you – To be seen – *LANTERN*

II. *THIS TURBULENT WORLD. No Bad News*
    LINCOLN and little girl.
    50 YEARS AGO – Lenin
    22 YEARS AGO – Atom
    MARX AND MISSILES – Europe – Middle East – Cuba
    Asia – Africa

III. *THEY HAVE BURDENED A WORLD.*
     DECIMATE – THEN REBUILD – The Walk Back
     SAME FOR A RIOT-TORN CITY – Rebuild.
     WORLD'S GRANARY – India, Spain, Asia.
     WORLD'S ARSENAL – Latin America, India, Pakistan
     WORLD'S BANKER – DEV. BANKS – Devaluation –
     Mid East
     WORLD'S TEACHER – Know-How – Point IV Techni-
     cians
     THE WORLD HAS BURDENED US, OUR PEOPLE
     RESOURCES, SOMETIMES OUR PATIENCE.

IV. *DESPITE ALL THIS, AND DESPITE THE TUMULT*
    AND FEVER WHICH BESETS THE WORLD – What's
    right with America? How quick we are to ask, *What's Wrong*
    with America? Rather ask, What's Right

    A. *HER HEART IS RIGHT* – When Need and Disas-
       ter Strike – At Home or Abroad – Quakes or Floods –
       Tidal Waves or Volcanoes – Fire or Hurricane –
       THERE SHE IS – Food, Medicines, Loans, Experts
       NO QUESTIONS ASKED AS TO WHO

    B. FIDELITY TO FREEDOM – Only so long will she
       tolerate Tyranny, Restrictions, Impairment, Erosion
       and then THE ROLL BACK – The spirit of SAM-
       UEL ADAMS, THOMAS PAINE, PATRICK
       HENRY, PETER ZENGER, ANDREW JACK-
       SON, ABRAHAM LINCOLN still lives, still kindles.

    C. *OPPORTUNITY STILL LIVES HERE.* The *Cen-*
       sus Clock – 200 million – *Centrifugal* and *Centripetal*
       Forces – a Balanced Land – Never Famine – Never
       Starvation – The Migrants – My Mother – *Roman or*
       Greek, Turk or Slav, Asian or African can succeed.

D. *WILLING TO ACCEPT LEADERSHIP – Legacy*
of a decimated world – We *could disdain* or accept –
Only we could handle and fulfill – *VIETNAM.*
COSTLY.

E. *STILL LAND OF LAW AND ORDER* – The exceptions receive the emphasis – *Detroit* is not America; *NEWARK* is not America; *PLAINFIELD* is not America – *THINK OF THE THOUSANDS* of Communities untouched or untainted by disorder and lawlessness and violence – Sporadic, Emotional Binges Happen but the *PENDULUM SWINGS BACK – THE DEED TO YOUR PROPERTY IS STILL GOOD –*

F. THE SOUL OF AMERICA IS RIGHT. What is this soul of America? Not as we think of the soul of the individual endowed with immortality but the activating principle, the energizing force which makes us tick. That soul is still right.
> Still dedicated to the *dignity* and worth of the *individual*.
> Still finds *virtue* in *thrift, frugality, work*.
> Still believes in *prayer* as the greatest of all forces.
> Still believes there is a *Providential force* which helps shape the destiny of men and nations.
> Still believes in *morality* and *character*.
> Still believes in the *Golden Rule*.

V. WHILE WE MAY NOT BE ABLE TO SAY IT OF THIS TURBULENT WORLD, We can *slightly paraphrase* that refreshing sentiment from *Browning's* "PIPPA PASSES":

> The year's at the spring,
>   The Day's at the morn,
> Morning's at seven,
>   The Hillside's dew-pearled,
> The Lark's on the wing,
>   The Snail's on the thorn,
> God's in His Heaven,
>   All's right with America.

Chapter 14

His Finest Hours

Achievements and Unfinished Business

No man is an island, entire of itself;
Every man is a piece out of the continent, a part of the main;
If a clod be washed away by the sea, Europe is the less;
As well as if a promontory were;
As well as if a manor of thy friends or of thine own were;
Any man's death diminishes me, because I am involved in man-
kind;
And therefore never send to know for whom the bell tolls, it tolls
for thee.

John Donne

So many have asked me, what do I feel or what did Everett feel was his greatest achievement as a political figure?

This has to be answered on two levels, from both an objective (if possible) and subjective point of view.

As to the first, it has already been written that when future historians assign credit for passage of the epochal Civil Rights Act of 1964, the name of Senator Everett Dirksen will lead all the rest.

I know that Everett gained his greatest stature, ironically, under the Kennedy and Johnson administrations, and probably history will say that his two major contributions were the Civil Rights Act and the Test Ban Treaty of the previous year, under Kennedy.

Although I have touched on the Civil Rights Act in the previous chapter in relation to Senator Goldwater's vote against it, I should like to add a few personal footnotes here just to keep the record straight.

Not only was Everett the pivotal figure in the passage of the bill, but he practically wrote it. He spent months in doing so, and he was so absorbed in his task that there were times when I felt I was more wedded to that bill than to a husband. I learned quite a bit in the process, though, because as usual Everett discussed his ideas with me and I contributed what I could as his sounding board.

One point I would like to clarify here, this historical Civil Rights Act of 1964 with which my husband's name is so closely identified, was certainly not his first excursion in the field, nor can the Democrats claim all the credit for civil rights legislation. In my opinion, the picture presented to the American public regarding civil rights has been somewhat distorted.

For one thing, everyone seemed so surprised to see Everett Dirksen emerge as a strong civil rights crusader under Johnson's administration.

Anyone who had followed his record must have been aware that he was no Johnny-come-lately in the field. While he was still in the House of Representatives, he voted for anti-poll tax and anti-lynching measures. He also sponsored or co-sponsored a number of bills dealing with civil rights issues.

It may be recalled that John F. Kennedy had campaigned rather strongly—and effectively—on the civil rights issue, but then after he was elected President he did nothing about it—for the simple reason that he knew the Capitol Hill Democrats were far more deeply divided than Republicans on the issue.

After chiding the President for his failure to keep his campaign promise on the civil rights program, a group of House Republicans introduced their own measure in early 1963. Everett read the bill, of course, and said it was much too weak and would obviously have to be rewritten. It was. First by President Kennedy himself, then by a House subcommittee and finally by the President and the committee. GOP Floor Leader Charles A. Halleck pledged support of the compromise bill in return for one thing—that the President publicly acknowledge the GOP contribution. Kennedy agreed. That was in the fall of 1963, just weeks before President Kennedy was assassinated.

Lyndon Johnson took up where President Kennedy had left off. He wasted no time in submitting the bill to the House, urging them to pass it as a memorial to the late President, and he gave the Republicans full credit for their stand.

The measure was approved in February with the majority of Republicans voting yes, standing staunchly behind their GOP Floor Leader.

But the critical test was yet to come—in the Senate. Even among senators who favored civil rights, there were grave reservations over certain parts of the bill. Without going into all the legislative fine points, I recall very well how concerned Everett was with those aspects of the bill that might usurp the states' jurisdiction in these matters and give too much control to the Federal government.

Everett followed the course of the House bill day by day, making copious notes and compiling a list of prospective amendments. Just a few days before the measure was passed by the House, he went to the hospital for treatment of a bleeding ulcer. He took along his worn and dog-eared copy of the bill and began rewriting it in his hospital bed. He continued making revisions during his week of recuperation at our home in Virginia.

As soon as he was up and about, he met daily with his legal aides who helped him go over the bill word for word.

After weeks of work, he came up with seventy-odd amendments, which had been slowly, patiently, and meticulously designed to bring more Republicans into the fold—and to shut off the longest filibuster in Senate history, led of course by southern Democrats who did not want any civil rights legislation.

At Everett's suggestion, Vice-President Hubert Humphrey, acting as President Johnson's "floor manager" for the bill, arranged for a series of bi-partisan meetings between a group of Senate and administration leaders. The meetings were held in Everett's leadership office—under the tinkling chandelier. (The one that was left after Jackie "borrowed" the other.) After five conferences, the House bill was rewritten to everyone's satisfaction, and on May 26, 1964, Everett introduced it to the Senate with the comment,

"I doubt very much whether in my whole legislative lifetime any measure has received so much meticulous attention."

Basically what he had done was change the bill to allow the states more leeway in controlling their own civil rights conflicts, and to safeguard against abuse of power by possibly overzealous Federal officials, such as an Attorney General.

I believe everyone, Republicans and Democrats alike (with the possible exception of Bobby Kennedy who was then Attorney General), agreed that my husband's proposed amendments vastly improved the House bill. Political writers and analysts generally agreed that although others had been involved, it was "Dirksen's bill," as they called it, more than anyone else's.

Then came the day of the historic Senate vote, June 19, 1964.

Everett and I had stayed up late the night before working on the twelve-page speech that he was to deliver on the Senate floor immediately prior to the vote.

I almost knew his speech by heart then and I can still remember a great deal of it.

He used as his theme one of his favorite poems by the English poet, John Donne, which I have quoted at the beginning of this chapter.

"I am involved in mankind, and whatever the skin, we are all involved in mankind. Equality of opportunity must prevail if we are to complete the covenant that we have made with the people, and when we held up our hands to take an oath to defend the laws and to carry out the Constitution of the United States . . .

"Any man's death diminishes me, because I am involved in mankind," he quoted. And then, relating the poet's thoughts to his own, he continued, "So every denial of freedom, every denial of equal opportunity for a livelihood, for an education, for a right to participate in representative government diminishes me . . ."

He went on to say that the poet had "left what I believe was a precious legacy on the parchments of history."

And when it was all over and the votes counted, there were many who obviously felt that on this historic day the Senator from the Land of Lincoln had "left a precious legacy on the parchments of American history."

Overnight my husband was a hero in the great American press.

You would have thought they had "discovered" him, or even invented him.

Suddenly the U. S. Senator from Illinois, Everett McKinley Dirksen, was a "statesman," "one of the great Senatorial Leaders of the century." Suddenly he "has emerged as the most influential man in the Senate."

And suddenly he found himself the fair-haired boy on Capitol Hill, a favorite with the press galleries, the darling of liberals who up to then apparently thought *they* were the ones who "discovered" civil rights as well as Dirksen. News magazines did cover stories on him and editorials blossomed out like marigolds reminding us over and over that it was Everett Dirksen who so "expertly revised and tailored the bill more to the Senate's liking," that it was Everett Dirksen who delivered the Republican votes and ended the filibuster and put the bill across, that it was Everett Dirksen's "finest hour."

These were the events that immediately preceded my husband's involvement with Goldwater in the 1964 presidential campaign, as recounted in my last chapter.

So, as I have said, the hero's "finest hour" ended when he toppled from the pedestal of the liberal press, but this can scarcely alter the pages of history that have already been written on the Civil Rights Act of 1964, which many regard as my husband's greatest achievement.

Test Ban Treaty . . .

History also will probably record that among my husband's major contributions were his labors on behalf of President Kennedy's proposal for the Test Ban Treaty of 1963. Again, he felt it was in the best interest of our country to vote in favor of the treaty. And as with the Civil Rights Act later, he also met with bitter opposition. In Chicago his hotel was picketed by hordes of females from the National Federation of Republican Women.

"I thought those women were going to eat me up. I told them that, come hell or high water, we were going to have that treaty and that I didn't care what happened to me. I plowed in."

He more than plowed in. It was Everett who spent weeks talking to all the high-placed people who objected to the President's proposal, carefully collecting all their views and reasons for their objections. And it was Everett who then painstakingly drafted the letter of assurances to them which President Kennedy sent to Congress.

In simple words, the President's proposed treaty would ban nuclear tests in outer space and under water, but would permit continuation of underground tests.

His critics, however, felt that JFK could not be trusted to take the necessary safeguards to keep this nation strong.

This is where Everett, again casting politics aside, stepped in to support his young Commander-in-Chief on an issue which he believed vital to the safety of our country.

The letter which he outlined for the President promised continued maintenance of weapons laboratories, improved atmospheric detection, and a quick resumption of testing if Russia should violate the treaty.

It was this letter and my husband's own moving speech from the Senate floor which swayed many senators to vote in favor of the test ban.

That speech has been generally regarded as one of his best. He recalled "the bright morning when the whole bosom of God's earth was ruptured [at Hiroshima]. A man-made contrivance we call a nuclear weapon . . . caused a mass incineration such as never before had been witnessed in the history of the whole, wide world. Little did man realize . . . the anguish that would be brought into the hearts of men, women and children. But in the accelerated march of history, how quickly we forget . . .

"Mr. President, that happened eighteen years ago last month. Since then what have we done? What steps have we taken? How far have we moved? I want to take a first step, Mr. President. I should not like to have written on my tombstone, 'He knew what happened at Hiroshima but he did not take a first step.' . . . If there be risks, I am willing to assume them for my country . . ."

At the beginning and again in summary he reiterated. "We advocate an early agreement by all nations to forego nuclear tests in the atmosphere."

He had stated his purpose explicitly: "At the outset, let me say that I shall support the treaty." And then he proceeded to develop his reasons.

There was a record attendance in the Senate for his address. Long-time critical and astute newspaper observers applauded Everett. Senators and newsmen alike agreed that it was "one of the most moving events of recent times."

In fact it was this event, nine months before the Civil Rights Act, which first earned Everett nationwide acclaim for his "statesmanship."

Newspaper editorials commended him with headlines such as, "A statesman emerges . . ." He was hailed as a "man of courage . . . who gave the nation and politicians of both parties a lesson in nonpartisan statesmanship . . ."

Many wrote then, "It was Everett McKinley Dirksen's finest hour . . ."

So, he had two of them. For the history books, that is.

The Test Ban Treaty was generally considered one of President Kennedy's greatest achievements. The date of my husband's speech and the Senate vote was September 11, 1963. A few days over two months later President Kennedy was dead.

14-B—The Right to Work Law . . .

Once when someone asked Everett what he considered his greatest legislative achievement, he replied, "Although it is perhaps a negative distinction, I am most proud of the bills which I prevented from being enacted. The American people can thank God that only six to eight percent of all legislation introduced becomes law."

He realized that the most basic ingredient of democratic freedom lay in the absence of excessive regulation. He knew that it was perfectly possible for a free society to legislate itself to death. He believed that the accomplishments of a government cannot be measured in inches of statutes, and that the freedom of man could not be measured as a ratio of Federal regulation.

Standing high on that stack of bills which he prevented from being enacted was one that made him most proud, one that I am sure he regarded as among his more important achievements. I mean the achievement was in getting the bill disposed of, buried.

He did it by literally talking the bill to death in what Capitol Hill calls a filibuster, but Everett called his "an attenuated discussion."

The bill was known simply as the 14-B bill. Actually it was a bill to repeal Section 14-B of the Taft-Hartley Act, the section which outlaws compulsory "union shop" contracts.

It was a bill which would have legalized compulsory union membership in all fifty states.

The battle on this one took place in the fall of 1965 and the early months of 1966, and it was regarded as one of President Johnson's most severe legislative setbacks.

The labor unions were demanding repeal of 14-B, and it had become one of the President's major goals. He was stunned to learn that Everett was going to lead a filibuster against repeal of 14-B.

"You wouldn't do that to me, Ev?" he asked.

"I'm going to do it and the debate will be long and formidable. It could last until Christmas," Everett told him.

The House had already voted for repeal and LBJ expected the Senate to do the same before giving the green light for adjournment. He had obviously anticipated no problem in the Senate, since Everett had supported him on other controversial issues.

Besides, Congress had been in session eight months, and everyone was tired and wanted to go home.

But Everett announced that he had twenty-seven senators lined up for his "talkathon" and they were all ready to talk indefinitely to prevent the bill from coming to a Senate vote.

President Johnson wailed to Everett, "I thought you were my friend."

"I am," Everett replied. "But remember why Brutus rose against Caesar—'not that I loved Caesar less, but that I loved Rome more.' Well, I love my country more." (*Julius Caesar*, Act III, Scene 2)

The President, as well as all of Capitol Hill, should have known by then that except for the late Senator Taft, no Republican leader of Congress had so consistently stood for what he believed to be the national interest as distinct from partisan advantage.

Everett summed up his attitude toward the 14-B repeal bill in these words:

"It is not a labor issue so far as I am concerned but a pre-emptive issue. If the Federal government pre-empts the power of the states to act in this field, the states will never regain their right to deal with union matters.

"Is there a more fundamental right than the right to make a living for one's self and for one's family without being compelled to join a labor organization?"

So he opened the filibuster and the bill was finally shelved in late October. But under union pressure it was brought up again when Congress convened in January. Again Everett began another "attenuated discussion," a thirteen-day filibuster that was called "the second battle of 14-B."

It was finally buried with the letters RIP (Rest in Peace) on February 10 for the remainder of the session, and for good as far as Everett was concerned. "They'll bring it up again over my dead body," he declared. And so he saved the Taft-Hartley's Section 14-B.

It was one of the President's few defeats.

Unfinished Business . . .

There are many frustrations in politics. One of mine was in watching my husband work so long and hard and not accomplish as much as he wanted to, or not be given the recognition I thought he should. There were technical reasons for most of this, although it took me a while to get accustomed to them.

For example, there would have been many more bills and amendments in Everett's name except for the fact that his was the minority party. The chairman of a committee is always a member of the party in power, and the legislation proposed bears the name of the chairman or one of his party's colleagues. When Everett proposed a piece of legislation, it would go to the Majority Leader and then lie on his desk until it got the required number of sponsors, or he might have to compromise with a Democratic committee chairman to get support from the majority side.

He had great patience, and eventually he taught me to have patience also. Often he would come home and say, "Well, I won a point today," and if I became upset that his entire bill or idea had not been accepted, he always patiently explained how important it was that he "won a point," and we must expect to win only one at a time, step by step.

There are many bills he introduced which perhaps were not of spectacular significance but which we both felt were for the good of the country. Perhaps I'm prejudiced but I still think the bill he introduced dealing with smut and obscenity would accomplish more, the way he wrote it, than any of the other bills in this area which are now pending in Congress.

He also introduced a bill to make it a Federal offense to desecrate the American flag.

And then there was his beloved marigold bill and his Prayer Amendment. But these were more than merely "legislative" matters. They were his unfulfilled dreams, which deserve their own chapter.

To Be or Not to Be?

Did Everett want to be President? It is the inevitable question. I doubt whether any man in public life hasn't at times harbored a fleeting secret desire to be President. Everett sometimes joked about it. Like the time a reporter asked him whether he thought President Johnson should withdraw the nomination of Abe Fortas as Chief Justice and he answered, "I don't know what the President should or should not do. I'm not the President. I should be but I'm not."

Now, if you ask me whether I wanted him to be President, I can tell you that those words of his are precisely the way I felt about it. He should have been. I think he would have made a better President than any of those he served under, and he certainly did the President's work for some of them.

Sometimes I "bugged" him about it a bit. I knew he had the ability and the foresight, and I saw how hard he worked for everyone else. He was ahead of his time in so many ways, and I felt that he might accomplish more if he were in a higher office. When you are already in the Senate, the presidency is about the only place up you can go. I felt that he could have averted some of the problems and contributed much more to shaping the policy of this country if he had been head of our government.

But Everett himself never really had any strong presidential ambitions. Not that he would ever have turned down the nomination! And not that he didn't have strong, driving personal ambition for his role in the Senate. But that was all part of it. He loved the Senate.

How many times have people remarked that Everett really *looked* like a senator and acted like a senator. He looked the way people expected a senator to look. He was everything they thought a senator ought to be, a real statesman-political-orator senator of the old mold.

But that wasn't all. Everett regarded the Senate as an end, an entity in itself.

He felt the Senate was a high calling, and that there was no need to try to go on to be President or Vice-President.

He worked hard at being a senator, a senator from the old days of the body, but he kept the common touch. Even those who had never met him felt friendly and warm toward him. They felt he was someone they knew and liked.

One of his greatest achievements, in my opinion, was that he always found something to praise in the other man's point of view.

It is my opinion also that it was this very quality which frequently made him invaluable to the Presidents he served under, and to his colleagues on both sides of the aisle in the Senate.

Yes, I suppose the Divine Guidance in which he so strongly believed fully intended Everett Dirksen to be a senator, and not a President.

And he had such a truly humble attitude about reaching his pinnacle from such lowly beginnings.

I heard him say it so many times, to me and to others, how amazing and wonderful it was that the son of immigrant parents could achieve one of the highest places in the land.

When he was first elected to the Senate, he used to say to me, "Mrs. D., do you realize that I am now one of only ninety-

six men [before Alaska and Hawaii] who have the most important roles in shaping our government?" It wasn't a boast. He
simply never ceased to marvel at the fact that this could happen in
America. When he was elected Minority Leader of the Senate,
he became one of only four men—two in the House and two
in the Senate—in positions of enormous influence.

To him it was rather incredible that he could have attained
such a position in one of the four chosen spots in the entire
House and Senate. He was most humble and grateful for this
achievement, and content to remain where he was.

I know he savored his role as Senate Minority Leader, and
there are those who say he accomplished more than he might
have if he had been President. Perhaps so.

But when I think of how hard he worked to accomplish
for others, I always remember his words, "I'm not the President.
I should be but I'm not."

My husband was a great believer in the freedom guaranteed
to the people of this country by the Constitution of the United
States, a document embodying the basic law of the land, and
the world's oldest written constitution. It was adopted on September 17, 1787, by the Federal Constitutional Convention, and
immediately sent by the Continental Congress to the states
for ratification.

Of all the hundreds of speeches Everett Dirksen gave during
his political career, I would be hard put to select the most
memorable ones, but certainly high on the list would be one
that he gave on the floor of the House of Representatives
on September 17, 1941, on the anniversary of the signing of
the Constitution.

And as I write this page, exactly thirty years later, on September 17, 1971, I cannot help but think how timely and applicable
his thoughts are today, as they were in 1941. Because we are
nearing the year 1976 and the 200th anniversary celebration of
our Declaration of Independence, I feel it appropriate to preserve here my husband's words of reverence for the Constitution
which he called our keystone of freedom. Not only did he
give this speech on the floor of the House on the anniversary
day, September 17, 1941 but he used it on many platforms

through the years. I think it deserves a place among his finest hours and achievements.

Mr. Speaker, how distressing it is that on this anniversary of the signing of the Constitution so little has been carried in the public press to mark this natal day of a great document. As we wrestle each day with swiftly moving events, one wonders at times whether we, as a free people, are fully mindful of the value, the freshness, and the durability of that great organic law under which we exercise such complete human freedom.

Everywhere in this land, from every platform, there should resound today encomiums on the Constitution of the United States of America as the longest-lived, most virile, and all-embracing organic act in the history of the world.

On many occasions I have tried in my humble way to translate its freshness and application in terms which I understand and which the people understand.

One journeys back to a period in 1917 when the legislature of the State of Nebraska undertook by legislative enactment to interdict and restrict the teaching of a certain language in the public schools of that State. In that State, however, were intrepid souls mindful of the guaranties which are embodied in the Constitution who brought that question to the Supreme Court of the land. They leveled an accusing finger at those who would so restrict liberty of speech and thought and solemnly warned that such an act was in contravention of the very act whose anniversary we observe today.

But a few years ago the legislature of Oregon enacted a statute which required that every child of school age be educated in the public schools of that Commonwealth. At first glance, such a statute seems harmless enough. But what of the law-abiding, devoted fathers and mothers who send their children to parochial schools which are supported entirely from their own contributions? What of their right to educate their children in schools of their own choice where they might absorb the ancient truths of the faith of their fathers? In consequence of this statute, the Society of Sisters launched an appeal, and once more the issue of liberty was reposed before the Supreme Court. Once again that tribunal examined the never-aging law which we revere as the Constitu-

tion and invalidated this legislative effort to infringe upon and restrict the guaranties of liberty of conscience.

But a few years ago in the State of Alabama a group of Negroes were apprehended for the commission of a heinous crime. One of them did not receive that kind of impartial trial by jury which is guaranteed to every citizen by the Constitution. When the sovereign State of Alabama sought to take away his life, he appealed to the Supreme Court, and again the fundamental question of constitutional guaranties was in issue. Did the high tribunal frown upon the appeal of this poor Negro? Did that tribunal, taking note of the mass of unemployment in the land, merely gloss over the case and indicate that one poor jobless Negro more or less was of little consequence and thus lightly dispose of a momentous issue? Frankly, it did not. It examined the document which is as a cloak to human liberty and sternly admonished that State that it must not take the life of this humble person unless he had first enjoyed a fair trial and been given the benefit of every constitutional guaranty which had been written into that living document.

But a few years ago a young man with pockets bulging with communistic literature was seized on the streets of Atlanta. Under an ancient statute he was sentenced to a long period of servitude in the chain gang. Of all places where communism cannot and does not exist, that place would be the highest court in the land. Yet, when one who was disseminating literature and preaching doctrine which had for their purpose the destruction of this Government, he appealed to that same Government whose destruction he was abetting for succor and relief. Once again constitutional guaranties were on trial, and once again the Supreme Court after an examination of the assurances and guaranties which the Founding Fathers bequeathed to us as a great legacy, said to the State of Georgia, "You must not send even this person to penal servitude until he has had a fair trial."

I think of what happened in Germany a number of years ago, when the names of Jewish war veterans who had fought and died for that nation in the World War were, under the impulses of hate and prejudice, expunged from the commemorative bronze tablets which had been erected to the memory of those who perished in that struggle. That could not happen here. The Constitution, whose creation we mark today, is the great shield which protects the basic liberty and conscience of all. Men may raise the ugly banner of hate and prejudice, but what a comfort that the Bill of Rights, which has come to us in all its fresh and unimpaired glory, is still intact and stands today after the elapse of more than 150 years as the citadel of human freedom.

There are some who believe that the Constitution of our land is but a musty museum piece which has outlived its usefulness. There are some who would streamline it and give it the modern touch. The history of more than a century and one-half rises up to proclaim on this anniversary day that the Constitution is as virile, as durable, as fresh, as applicable, and as vital in this year of our Lord 1941 as it was when devised and adopted by those rugged and courageous pioneers who laid the foundations of this land.

Let it never be said that the American people and the Congress of this Nation, every Member of which took oath to support and defend that Constitution before he or she could exercise the responsibilities of membership, shall be wanting in reverence for this keystone of freedom or wanting in appreciation of its value to the continued entrenchment of freedom in our own great land.

Chapter 15

Unfulfilled Dreams

Prayers and Marigolds

I have tried to give an objective account of Everett's most important achievements and contributions, as measured by the yardsticks of political observers and historians, which I am not.

As Everett's wife, I happened to have been very much involved in them, and so my account might not be as "objective" as it should be. But I did try. I am sure both of us would have to agree with all the others on his "finest hours," from the standpoint of the greatest good for the greatest number of people.

But now, if you ask me what was *really* his finest hour—and his saddest frustration—I would have to say it was his Prayer Amendment.

How happy he was the day he came home to tell me that he had finally been able to get his Prayer Amendment on the books as Senate Joint Resolution Number One. That was in the first session of the 90th Congress, January 1967. I'll never forget it. It was one of the happiest days of his life . . . And it was also one of his greatest disappointments that he was unable to get his measure for the right to pray in schools again passed.

With each new session of Congress, his school prayer bill was always one of the first he submitted. It, of course, was not a bill to make prayer compulsory. All he wanted was the freedom to have prayer in schools for those who desired it.

He felt that there had been a gradual breakdown of the

moral fiber of our country, too much permissiveness and lack of discipline in family life. He felt that children should learn early in life the necessity and values of religious worship, and that there should be a place for religious worship in their school life.

This was one measure which we both hoped would be passed without too much delay, but unfortunately Everett died before any action was taken and now it is necessary for someone else to start all over again and present the bill to Congress. As I write this our beloved son-in-law Senator Baker has submitted it to the Senate. I still think the Supreme Court could find some legal precedent to reverse its decision on school prayer —a decision based on a case involving a woman atheist! I am hopeful that the Court will someday reverse itself because it depresses me to know that in a legal battle, atheism won over God.

I wish to include here the story of the Prayer Amendment as my husband wrote it. I do so for many reasons. First, I could not think of writing a book about our life together without including it, for it is the bedrock of everything we believed in. His Prayer Amendment, as you will see, is more than the sheer poetry of his words. It is his impassioned plea for the right of prayer in public schools, the right of a child to ask God's blessing on our Nation, the right of voluntary worship of the Divine Creator who endowed us with certain inalienable rights. Are we going to deny Him even a few minutes of public reverence?

But Everett said it all so much better than I or anyone else ever could. And in pleading the case for prayer he gave one of the most logical and brilliant expositions on the story of Creation, and proof of the Creator, and why Government should have no right to ban public reverence, that I have ever read anywhere.

These words and these thoughts must be preserved, not only because they were his but more importantly because they will be an inspiration to all who read them. And hopefully perhaps one day they will provide the motivation for others to continue the crusade to bring the right of voluntary religious worship back into the lives of our school children.

PRAYER AMENDMENT PLEA

Mr. President, on Independence Day I looked out of the window to see the flag flying in a mild breeze and the lawn drenched in sunshine. Against the rail fence were dogwood, japonica, spirea, hydrangea, and crepe myrtle. Filbert bushes furnished the backdrop, golden marigolds were dancing in the mild breeze. In a center garden incredibly beautiful, canna heads were finding glory under a cloudless sky. In still another garden, double white petunias were the edging for the deep colored zinnias that stood like sentinels in the sun. In a tree row made up of black locust, white cherry, redbud, and dogwood was a mass of wild fern and peeking out from under the cover was blooming mountain laurel.

Along the deep green privet hedge, cannas, red, white and salmon geraniums were shielded by still other white petunias. Along the west lotline, those stately snapdragons—deep red, white and pink were ready to share their color and beauty with every visitor and passerby until frost. There were the fantastic dahlias in all colors, flaunting their beauty to the wide world.

Near the carport were hardy asters, ready and willing to share the last splash of beauty before Jack Frost came to paint the leaves. In the gardens closest to the river, pansies were keeping a last minute vigil before the blooms would fail, asters were ready to take over the job of beauty, hybrid geraniums were making their second or third salute to color, impatiens were asking, twinkling like stars, dwarf marigolds were quietly carrying on, domestic ferns were performing like peacocks.

Close by were the tea roses—deep red, pink, white, yellow, silver and gold—with their lingering fragrance.

Making ready to dazzle the eye and the senses were the shasta daisies, gladiolas, day lilies, lemon lilies, white lilies apsending themselves, with tall zinnias standing like alert guards to shield them.

At the top of the ridge was the vegetable garden—yielding beets and carrots, radish and lettuce, spinach and wax beans, green and pole beans, strawberries building new life and vigor for next spring fruiting. Tomatoes on stately vines were soon ready to provide pink delicacies and pepper plants were pushing for the day when dark green peppers could be picked. Handle gourds were sending their tendrils along the wire fence to provide birdhouses for the purple martins in the next season.

Crows, grackles, sparrows, jays and others were enjoying the feeders. Wrens, sparrows, barn swallows were feeding their broods of youngsters. The purple martins were scolding and warning the intrusive sparrows. The mournful catbird, the lilting meadow larks, bob white, red breast robins were supplying the music for the leafy cathedral on the lower level. Those patient fishermen, the white herons, were back earlier than usual. Above it all was the throaty music of the warblers and the twittering of the wrens.

Presiding over this cavalcade of beauty were the gentle birch trees, the pin oaks, the pines and hemlock, the aged cottonwoods and sycamores, the beech and elm, walnut and maple, hickory and willow, Japanese yew and Greek juniper, Virginia spruce and pyracantha, Chinese tulip and flowering crab, flowering peach and flowering cherry, domestic holly and Norway maple.

Mr. President, who can live with this beauty, this diversity, this color, this salute to the mind, the heart, the soul of man and not believe in God—in a Creator behind it all?

If this needs implementation, then contemplate this almost incredible balanced, ordered world.

The story of Creation, recorded in Genesis, when carefully and leisurely appraised, brings amazement and wonder. It is the story of form out of formlessness, of night and day, of land and water, of grass and every green herb with seed, of fruit trees with their own seed, of days and seasons and years, of sun, moon and stars, of beasts and fowls and creeping things, and of man—incomprehensible man—the only living thing with mind and will and soul and intelligence, to whom was committed dominion over all living things.

One need but be alert to the phenomena of a single day to appreciate this story. There is daybreak and the rising sun, the incredible diversity of all plant life, the endless variety and sheer beauty of the flowers, the matins and vespers of the birds, and the feeling of a complete, balanced, ordered universe that life might be sustained.

If the sun were very much closer to earth, we would be charred into cinders or dust and if it were much further away, we would freeze and plant life could not grow. If the moon were much closer, its attractive power would engulf all of the land areas of the earth by gigantic tides.

If earth's speed on its axis was much greater than it is or if its speed around the sun were much greater, life could not exist.

These are but a few of the amazing phenomena which sustains us and inspires us to but one conclusion and that is that it all fits into complete, carefully ordered design and behind that design must be the hand and the presence of the Designer.

Call him Creator or God, Providence or Presence, Supreme Intelligence or Master, Architect or Engineer—the omnipotent, omniscient hand is evident at every turn. And in the forefront of it all is man himself, whose chemical composition might be had for a few dollars, but whose soul and spirit, mind and intelligence is beyond all finite evaluation. For it is man with dominion over all living things whose brain is the only creative engine under the canopy of Heaven. To believe—fervently believe—that behind this complete, ordered, balanced marvelous universe there is a Supreme Intelligence, a Creator, a God, is the only conclusion to which one can come.

But there is still another and a very important conclusion and that is that the Creator could not, and would not, forsake his creation or abandon that which He created. How could He abandon man—his prize creation—especially in an hour of confusion, despair and bewilderment. How could the Creator set man adrift and let him stand alone without some instrument for coming into harmony and attunement with the Creator.

It must have been the awesome majesty of the universe which inspired Alfred Tennyson to write:

"Flower in the crannied wall,
    I pluck you out of the crannies,
 I hold you here, root and all, in my hand,
    Little flower—but *if* I could understand
 What you are, root and all, and all in all,
    I should know what God is and man."

And here, Mr. President, we come to grips with the matter before us.

PRAYER is the natural expression of the spirit. From its inspiration can come perfection and spiritual development of those divine attributes which carry man closer and closer to God. Prayer in public schools may not have a profound spiritual effect upon children as some cynics contend but it charts the access road to the Creator, lays a foundation for the habit of prayer, keeps before them the simple fact that behind this universal design is a Designer and provides rehearsal for the soul.

So, Mr. President, I submit again a resolution for a Constitutional Amendment to make freely permissible prayer in public buildings and especially public schools.

On two previous occasions I brought before the Senate measures proposing an Amendment to permit voluntary school prayer. While a majority of the Senate voted in favor of these measures both failed to receive the two-third vote necessary for approval of a Constitutional Amendment.

I told the Senate that it was not my intention that the matter would die quietly and that it would not be either subverted or diverted and that the Resolutions would be brought up again. I regard this is of overwhelming importance to the moral fibre of America.

Our spiritual heritage has contributed to the noble endeavors which have made this Nation one of the great hopes of mankind and has been taken for granted for so long that we are in danger of seeing that heritage supplanted in the public schools, where the minds of our children are molded, by what we are told is regarded as a neutrality toward religion but which is in reality an official indifference to religion, sometimes approaching hostility.

We have recently spent a great deal of time and intensive effort in the Congress fashioning an Omnibus Crime Control and Safe Streets Law. The President has appointed a Commission to study the effects of violence which has grown to such staggering proportions as to stun and horrify the Nation.

People everywhere are asking what can we do? They have a right to look to this body for leadership and it is our duty to provide that leadership. It has been said of old that the longest journey starts with a single step. I ask the Senate to take that one step now and to permit the children of America to pray for this country in the schools we provide for them. I humbly suggest that now, perhaps more than ever before, this Nation should not be too proud to admit that we are in grave need of Divine assistance.

Despite much wringing of hands and the lamentations of the opponents, I assure you the pillars of the Republic will not crumble if we should approve this Amendment. It still has a long journey ahead of it in the ratification proceedings required to be undertaken by three-fourths of the States. I urge the Congress to give the States the chance to get to work on this measure.

I respect the honest differences of opinion which exist concerning prayer. I know that many of my distinguished Colleagues in this Body share honest and sincere differences of opinion on this subject. I acknowledge the sincerity of those differing viewpoints. Differences can never be resolved by ignoring them. We must address ourselves as reasonable men of goodwill to attempt a resolution.

What we now have in this country is a religion of secularism, an official Government position favoring the non-believer over the believer. Freedom of religion was intended and it ought rightly to be, a shield protecting the right of conscience of a citizen. It is being used now with the endorsement of the Government as a weapon to strike down the free exercise of religion protected by the First Amendment to the Constitution.

I suggest, Mr. President, that the placing of these words in the First Amendment is significant. They are just before freedom of speech and of the press.

We have heard and seen a great deal very recently about the rights of the people to assemble and to petition for redress of grievance. Certainly these are important, but must we wait for crowds and multitudes to assemble before listening to the voice of the people? Polls taken when this matter was last before the Senate showed that more than 80 percent of the American people favored voluntary school prayer. Must we place ourselves on record in the history books as standing in the way of this vast outpouring of public sentiment?

What is proposed here is a simple restatement of a right slowly and increasingly eroded. Let me read it to you in full. It is only one sentence.

"Section 1. Nothing contained in this Constitution shall abridge the right of persons lawfully assembled, in any public building which is supported in whole or in part through the expenditure of public funds, to participate in non-denominational prayer."

Is that too much to ask?

Section Two is the necessary operating language and is as follows:

"Section 2. This article shall be inoperative unless it shall have been ratified as an amendment to the Constitution by the legislatures of three-fourths of the several States within seven years from the date of its submission to the States by the Congress."

It is a reinforcement of a right we thought we had all the time. It is a right that no one can be compelled to exercise. It is as permissive as anything can be. It favors no religious denomination over another—the prayer, if any be offered, would be non-denominational.

The Constitution has been interpreted by the Supreme Court in such a way as to close the door on voluntary school prayer. There have been a number of such decisions. They have been studied by the Constitutional Amendments Subcommittee in the last Congress when the Subcommittee held hearings on a previously proposed Amendment, S.J.Res.148. Some of these decisions follow:

Engle v. Vitale—370 U.S. 421 (1962).
In a 6–1 decision the Court held that the required recital of an official prescribed, non-denominational prayer in New York public schools was unconstitutional.

Abington School District v. Schempp and Murray v. Curlett
June 17, 1963.
The Court held unconstitutional the reading of the Bible and recitations of the Lord's Prayer in public schools.

In holding these opening exercises unconstitutional, the Court's decision also affected the compulsory Bible reading practices of 13 States; in 24 other States daily Bible reading has been permissive.

Following the above decisions by the Supreme Court, other lower Courts and Commissions have tried to implement the decisions.

In *Stein v. Oshinsky* (New York) an action was brought by the parents to enjoin school officials from preventing the recitation of prayers on the children's initiative. The District Court granted summary judgment to the parents. The U. S. Court of Appeals of the Second Circuit reversed the District Court with directions to dismiss the complaint. The Supreme Court refused to review the Circuit Court decision. The two prayers were:

> "God is great, God is good,
> And we thank Him for this food."

On January 22, 1968, the Supreme Court denied certiorari in the case of *DeSpain v. DeKalb County Community District 428*, the effect of which was to hold that these words—

> "We thank you for the flowers so sweet;
> We thank you for the food we eat;
> We thank you for the birds that sing;
> We thank you God for everything."

were a prayer and forbidden. The decision of the United States Court of Appeals for the Seventh Circuit was in part as follows:

> "We are of the view that the verse is a prayer and that its compulsory recitation by kindergarten students in a public school comes within the proscription of the first amendment, as interpreted by the Supreme Court in the 'school prayer' cases. School Dist. of Abington Tp., Pa. v. Schempp, 374 U.S. 203, 83 S.Ct. 1560, 10 L.Ed.2d 844 (1963); Engel v. Vitale, 370 U.S.421, 82 S.Ct. 1261, 8 L.Ed.2d 601 (1962)."

In the 89th Congress that Subcommittee took testimony concerning school prayer and the hearing record is 884 pages long. In it is contained the decisions of the courts dealing with school prayer. They are long and complex. They are not unanimous decisions. The dissents are brilliant and in scholarly legal language and fairly blister the decisions. The American people may not follow all the complexities of these legal semantics but they do know that through the consistent application of these prohibitions against free non-denominational prayer, it has been barred to their children. There now exists no acceptable substitute for a moment of prayer. I have no doubt whatsoever that if this Congress will only give them a chance the American people will decide overwhelmingly for public reverence.

Americans have been saddened in the past few years as our beloved country has been rent by violence from within, our cities have seen destruction and bloodshed unparalleled in peacetime in any modern nation. Our National prestige in the world may be at a record low. If we are to provide moral leadership for the world, we should not shrink from addressing ourselves to the moral leadership of our own country.

We spend billions of dollars every year to assist those underprivileged and disadvantaged of our citizens. We have taken from the hard-earned wages of other Americans over $120 billion since World War II to spend in Foreign Aid in almost every other country in the world. We have done so because we are told it is our moral duty to help those people.

Is it asking too much to allow our children a few minutes of prayer in our schools? Mr. President, this is not going to cost the taxpayers one cent. We pass measures here every day with price tags in the millions and billions of dollars with scarcely a murmur.

As one Nation under God we have prospered mightily in material things. Are we going to deny Him even a few minutes of public reverence? We have taken pride in our spiritual heritage and have proclaimed to the world that men are endowed by their Creator with certain inalienable rights. Here is one of the most significant differences in our form of government from every other government in the world.

Elsewhere men have only such rights as their rulers see fit to grant—for today—tomorrow they can be taken away. Not so here. We claim our rights to be inalienable, from the Creator. Even our Government cannot take them away. Have we become so proud that we will refuse to permit our children to ask God's blessing for our Nation? I hope not.

The United States has done more to ease the burdens of mankind than has any other country since the dawn of history. We have accomplished great tasks and we have many more before us. We also have powerful enemies dedicated to our destruction and they strive mightily for the minds of men.

Let them not say against us that this great Nation has concern only for material things and that when the time came for the United States Senate to permit a little child in his schoolroom to ask God's blessing on our Nation we refused to act.

Mr. President, the vast majority of the American people are in favor of voluntary school prayer. This amendment would favor no denomination over another. It makes nothing compulsory. It is as permissive as anything can be. I urge its adoption.

And may I add to my husband's plea even now as this book is going to press that the mothers and fathers of this country are still petitioning Congress to pass this Prayer Amendment. If one woman, an atheist, could persuade the Supreme Court to deny the privilege of prayer in the schools, millions of men and women can persuade Congress to approve this amendment before them. And what a great tribute that would be to Everett Dirksen.

I think if Everett were alive to read this, he would like it if I mentioned again here his beloved marigolds and his unsuccessful attempts year after year to have a bill passed that would make the marigold officially our national flower. I realize this would not have been regarded as a major achievement but it was something that was very close to his heart, and I am sure he would like to have seen it accomplished.

Following is an excerpt from one of his pleas for the marigold bill:

A Senator Champions the Marigold . . .

When spring comes, there will be flowers. We shall be delighted with the earlier flowers—the tulips, the daffodils, the redbud, and the dogwood blossoms. A little later will come all the delightful annual flowers, which nature compels us to cultivate every year, but leaves a residue of seed which makes them almost perpetual. They will include the humble but beautiful petunia, the zinnia, and the calendula, and also the marigold.

Two or three years ago, I introduced a joint resolution to make the marigold the national flower. That stirred quite a controversy; and, as a result, the corn tassel and the rose and other flowers were advanced as candidates of our national floral emblem.

But I still find myself wedded to the marigold—robust, rugged, bright, stately, single-colored and multicolored, somehow able to resist the onslaught of insects; it takes in its stride extreme changes in temperature, and fights back the scorching sun in summer and the chill of early spring evenings.

What a flower the marigold is! I am looking forward to the time when these gay flowers will salute and intrigue our sense of beauty.

So once more I find myself impelled to introduce a joint resolution to make the American marigold—its botanical name is *Tagetes erecta*—the national flower of the country.

And following is an article he wrote for *National Wildlife* magazine which explains his own reasons for nominating the marigold as our national flower. This is my favorite of everything he wrote on the marigold. I am sure it will delight marigold lovers everywhere.

I NOMINATE THE MARIGOLD
by Everett M. Dirksen, U. S. Senator from Illinois

In the last seven years and in four successive Congresses, I have introduced legislation to make the glorious American marigold our national flower.

In support of my latest bill, introduced in the 90th Congress on April 17, 1967, I now present the full weight of evidence for this remarkable flower. For the marigold holds a proud place in our cultural—as well as horticultural and floricultural—heritage.

Drive with me down the George Washington Memorial Parkway from Washington, D.C., to Mount Vernon, Virginia, home of the Father of Our Country. Let us walk among the neatly planted flower beds and manicured hedges of George Washington's old gardens. Here, where the first President once walked, we see the American marigold in all its golden beauty.

A different marigold. I hasten to explain that the American marigold, a tall and slender lass 2 to 4 feet high, is not to be confused with several other marigolds. The American marigold blossom is 2 to 4 inches in diameter. Its colors, while predominantly on the sunny side, may range through the yellow-oranges from off-white to deep mahogany. The plant has a shaggy foliage and is known botanically as *Tagetes erecta*. For the benefit of my nonbotanical readers, this means that no other marigold, no other flower, carries this identification.

Among the other marigolds are:

the lovely marsh marigold, a member of the buttercup family, which grows wild in many of our national parks among other places

the pot marigold, or calendula, extolled by Shakespeare and Sir Walter Raleigh

the bur-marigold of the sunflower family

the cape marigold, a South African perennial

the corn marigold, of Europe and Asia

the French marigold, a dainty floweret which regularly takes its appointed place in the succession of floral arrangements at Lafayette, Farragut and other small parks of Washington, D.C.

But none of these species, despite their charms, can match the American marigold. Native to the New World and nowhere else, *Tagetes erecta* is truly the all-American flower. It impressed the Spanish conquistadors so highly that Hernando Cortez carried the flower back to Spain where it eventually spread to North Africa and to other parts of Europe. Brought back to America by European colonists, the flower was a garden favorite of Virginians, soil-minded New Englanders, and especially of the Dutch of New Amsterdam and the Hudson valley.

By Henry Ward Beecher's time, more than a century ago, that worthy New England spokesman could say:

"As for marigolds . . . we shall never have a garden without them, both for their own sakes and for the sake of folks who used to love them."

Now let us proceed from Mount Vernon to the nearby Woodlawn Plantation, once the home of Nellie Custis, Martha Washington's granddaughter. Here we see blossoming marigolds nodding gently in the Virginia breeze. The flowers bedeck the herbacious borders leading through the rose garden parterres in front of the Georgian mansion.

Popular in Washington. Returning to Washington, we find that a senator's humble preference for the marigold is shared by many a Washington home owner—and many a gardener, both amateur and professional. For there are abundant lawns and gardens on the quiet streets and avenues of the Nation's Capital that are enhanced by the American marigold.

And if we drive out to the National Arboretum in nearby Maryland, we will find that the flower has been granted a further distinction. The Arboretum, which specialized primarily in woody ornamentals, has departed from its specialty to reserve a distinguished place for the marigold. Here, in its mixed flower beds of annuals, the Arboretum maintains spun yellow and golden jubilee marigolds.

And the George Washington Memorial Parkway is not the only National Park Service area leading to the American marigold. I have been deeply gratified to learn that three venerated historic sites of the National Park System are rich in marigolds.

How natural that these memorials so enshrined in our history should make the American marigold a choice planting in memory of those who cherished the flower in an earlier day.

At Adams National Historic Site, Quincy, Massachusetts, hardy marigolds bloom from mid-July till frost. The flowers are a feature of the showcase garden maintained at the Georgian home of Presidents John Adams and John Quincy Adams. Mrs. Lyndon B. Johnson visited this historic site in 1967. The marigolds, intermixed with other old-fashioned standbys, fascinate visitors with a riotous display of golds, yellows, and oranges. In the marigold trade, these flashy members of the *Tagetes erecta* family are called the carnation-flowered crackerjack, the chrysanthemum-flowered glitters, and chrysanthemum-flowered orange.

American marigolds also border the rose garden near the

graves of President Franklin D. Roosevelt and Eleanor Roosevelt at the Home of Franklin D. Roosevelt National Historic Site, Hyde Park, New York. A variety known as the yellow diamond jubilee is the choice planting here.

At Saint-Gaudens National Historic Site in New Hampshire some 50 to 100 American marigold plants enliven and beautify the extensive formal gardens of Aspet, home of the late sculptor, Augustus Saint-Gaudens. Described as "large, thrifty" plants, marigolds display deep yellow and orange blossoms.

Saint-Gaudens had a deep appreciation of the marigold. He took particular interest in his gardens, often rearranging the flowers personally.

Today the National Park Service maintains this marigold tradition here by displaying the cut flowers in season in the Saint-Gaudens home.

The imaginative touch of Lois Stone, a prize-winning state and local flower arranger, presents the blossoms in a manner appropriate to the New Hampshire setting of mountains and white birches where Saint-Gaudens created some of his greatest sculpture.

Already the nation's choice. This radiant bloomer, this majestic American marigold, is to my mind already the Nation's choice. No matter where you go in all the 50 states, you are sure to find the tended gardens of America saying it with marigolds.

That the marigold grows so ubiquitously is no accident. American nursery men and seedmen have worked tirelessly for generations to improve the marigold. They have developed a greater range of color, larger flowers, greater hardiness and vigor, and a foliage with a more agreeable aroma so that it might with the least effort and expense be produced in every part of the United States. Thus, it might rightly be considered our national floral emblem.

That is the purpose of my bill of April 17, Senate Joint Resolution 73.

Now that the beautification effort has captured the hearts of the Nation, I can think of no better gesture than to designate the American marigold—*Tagetes erecta*—our national flower.

National Wildlife Editor's Note: The flower which Senator

Dirksen so commendably calls the American marigold has long been called the African marigold. Taken from the New World to Spain by Cortez, Tagetes erecta spread to North Africa where it presumably acquired its name as the African marigold.

In view of the flower's origin in the New World, however, Senator Dirksen's renaming of the plant is well-justified. May his effort to call it the American marigold succeed, whether or not it ever becomes the national flower.

Chapter 16

Mr. Showbiz

I would be remiss not to mention one of my husband's fondest achievements, his re-entry into show business as a recording star, and a Grammy winner at that!

I say re-entry because, after all, he starred in a local theatrical in Pekin, Illinois, some forty years earlier and married the leading lady, remember?

Winning a Grammy, so we learned, is the equivalent of winning an Oscar in Hollywood. The Oscar is Hollywood's Academy Award presented annually for outstanding performances in the motion picture industry.

The Grammy is given by the recording industry's National Academy of Arts and Sciences to outstanding record artists, and Everett won it in 1967 for the "best documentary recording" of his album, *Gallant Men.*

So there he was—and I'll never forget it—the seventy-one-year-old Gentleman from Illinois and second most powerful man in Washington as he was now recognized—standing up there holding his Grammy statuette, along with Lou Rawls, Cannonball Adderly, Bobbie Gentry, Glen Campbell and other teen-age heroes and heroines, on the NBC nationally televised Grammy Awards show.

Everett was the first United States Senator to reverse the performer-to-politician trend and become a show-business personality. He was the first senator ever to cut a commercial record, and to everyone's surprise it became a big hit.

It sold enough copies—over 500,000—to give him a gold record and place him fifth among Best Selling Male Vocalists, above such pop idols as Elvis Presley, Dean Martin and Bob Dylan for that particular period of time.

Of course the press had a field day with this new side of the Senator, and so did Everett, for that matter.

He held a press party to celebrate his debut as a recording star—for Capitol Records—and he told everyone, "I've been speaking for the record [Congressional] for over thirty years. I have merely moved from one Capitol to another."

Actually, this "new" side of the senator wasn't really so new. It had been in the developmental process for a few years.

It all started with that distinctive voice of his, which Bob Hope once described as a duet between Tallulah Bankhead and Wallace Beery. He had been approached by record companies but never seriously considered recording anything until in his mailbag one day he received a postcard from a fan whom he had never met, Arnold C. Pedersen of Minneapolis, who urged:

"With that rich, resonant voice of yours I wish you would make a record of the Lord's Prayer, Gettysburg Speech, Declaration of Independence, the Beatitudes, Allegiance to the Flag, Preamble to the Constitution and some of the other important documents."

This struck a responsive chord in Everett.

Mr. Pedersen added, "You have a unique voice which should be recorded while you are still here to do it."

Everett kept that card in his wallet, carried it around with him for years, and must have pulled it out of his pocket a hundred times.

At the time I was trying to persuade him not to run for re-election in 1962, I built a little home in DeBary, Florida. Years before, I had gone to visit our dear friends Colonel and Mrs. Kessenich who had retired there. I fell in love with a little spot that had pine trees reaching for the sky and a little lake to the back. I purchased three lots and forgot about it.

We had been spending our winter vacations in Miami but as

Everett became better known it was hard to get the quiet and rest which he needed so badly.

He was horrified that we should have a home in Florida as well as one in Virginia. He said, "You'll get me defeated." But he wasn't defeated and he came to love our little home in DeBary which he named "Contentment."

In December of 1965, while he was sitting on the porch in the sunshine, he finally found time to record his reading of the 23rd Psalm, the *Battle Hymn of the Republic*, and something he said he "concocted" himself called *Vietnam in Flanders*.

The quality of these first recordings in Florida was not too good, so when we got back to Washington he did them over again on tape in the Senate recording studios.

Meanwhile, apparently someone else unbeknownst to us had recorded Everett's singing at his seventieth birthday party on January 4, 1966, only weeks after he had made the recordings in Florida. One of our big events of the year always was the Everett Dirksen birthday party, hosted by Everett's close friend, Ben Regan. Everett's birthday parties became quite famous in Washington. He always sang his favorite song, *Danny Boy*, and our favorite, *Song of Songs*—as well as some of the Irish songs he loved so much. Nothing pleased him more than to wear a sprig of shamrock in his lapel on St. Patrick's Day or to sing Irish songs at his birthday parties.

In any case, both the recordings he had made in Florida and those someone else surreptitiously made at his seventieth birthday party triggered more interest from the recording companies.

One company actually wanted him to sing! Everett couldn't quite see himself as a septuagenarian singing senator!

Another company offered him a contract which he would have been quite willing to sign, for he could have recorded all the patriotic and religious messages he wished—but there was a provision for him also to narrate *Winnie the Pooh* and *Peter Rabbit* in the future.

Everett said flatly "No!"

"I didn't think it was consonant with my work in public service for me to be known as a reader of nursery rhymes," he explained to a reporter.

I'm sure I helped him make this decision, for I objected

strenuously at the time to the idea. I reminded him that's all the political cartoonists would need—news that he was narrating *Winnie the Pooh* and *Peter Rabbit*. And then watch for all the cartoons of Everett with rabbit ears or holding a jar of honey. I did not approve of this idea a bit.

He did have that kind of voice that appealed to children. I distinctly remember one occasion when we went to a big Washington party and a woman came up to him and asked in all seriousness if she could possibly hire him to read bedtime stories to her children! This is true, believe me. And he might have made a million dollars by recording children's bedtime stories, who knows?

But we talked it over together and decided he had more important work to do.

When Capitol Records offered him the opportunity to do *Gallant Men*, we were delighted.

This was a saga of the triumphs of American history.

It begins:

"Down through the years there have been men, brave, gallant men, who have died that others might be free. And even now they do it still."

The album includes Everett's readings from the Mayflower Compact, the Star-Spangled Banner, the Gettysburg Address, and the Pledge of Allegiance. It also includes some of the experiences of our early patriots and perhaps part of the album's success was that Everett's heart was really in it. Never mind that some flippant reviewer described it as "a sort of husky Bach fugue." It turned out to be an auspicious start for a senator embarking on a show-business career.

Up to then it had been the other way around, with song-and-dance man George Murphy becoming a senator, and actor Ronald Reagan in the California Governor's chair, and even Shirley Temple Black (Little Miss Marker) running as a congressional candidate.

I remember so well some remarks that Governor Reagan made in introducing Everett at a Republican rally at his (Reagan's) alma mater, Eureka College in Eureka, Illinois, in October 1967, the year Shirley Temple ran for Congress (and lost).

"Politics is already overcrowded with actors, some of them better than movie and television stars," the governor said.

"Shirley Temple, for example, will find just as George Murphy did, that she can't hold a candle to that old trouper, Senator Everett McKinley Dirksen . . ."

One aspect of his recording career that both surprised and pleased us was its appeal to the young people of this country. Everett received thousands of letters from these "kids" who wanted an autographed picture of him. Everywhere he went, they crowded around him, wearing buttons which said, "We luv you, Ev," and "Ev, you melt me." We never did really figure out whether the kids thought the senator was "campy," as the current expression went, or whether they really understood his patriotic messages and liked them. But for a time there, he was a very important part of their lives.

Someone even suggested him as the logical successor to the Beatles, who had announced they were retiring from show business. I am not even sure that Everett knew who the Beatles were, and I also doubt that those boys from Liverpool ever heard of Senator Dirksen.

Some called him the "Grandpa Moses of the recording industry," and a "happening," which was the "in" word of the time.

Through it all we had our many chuckles and fun-times together, and Everett went on to record two other albums after *Gallant Men*. The first was called *Man Is Not Alone*, and it was released around Easter of 1967. On it, Everett used many Bible quotations, linked together with commentary that he wrote himself, and he also read a prayer by St. Francis of Assisi, as well as William Ernest Henley's poem, *Invictus*, The Lord's Prayer, and a one-line prayer which President Kennedy always kept on his desk: "Oh Lord, Thy sea is great, and my boat is so small."

This album, an inspirational rebuttal to the "God Is Dead" trend, did not do very well but I consider it the best one he did. His third album was called *At Christmas Time*. It was recorded on a steaming hot July day in New York, and released at holiday time of 1967, our fortieth anniversary.

This was an especially joyous occasion for us, because we were also taping a Christmas television special starring Everett in an hour-long program—and with the rest of the family acting as his supporting cast. Our daughter Joy, and her husband Howard, and the grandchildren, Cynthia and Darek, were there with us, celebrating our fortieth anniversary at Christmastime in our redwood-and-fieldstone ranch house. And our hearthside at "Heart's Desire" was never happier than on this very special occasion, when my husband, surrounded by his adoring family circle, recited his Christmas Carols from his new album for the television cameras.

I must digress here to mention that Joy's husband, Howard Baker, had been elected a Senator from Tennessee only the year before, in 1966—the first Republican senator ever elected from that state. And, oh how well I remember a little remark Joy made all those many years ago when the two of us, mother and daughter, carried the load of that first senatorial campaign in 1950.

She was then only fresh out of college, but so exhausted and frustrated by all the problems of her father's political campaign that at one point she said to me, "Mother, when I get married I'm going to marry a ditch-digger!"

So here she was married to the Republican Senator from Tennessee.

And how wonderful it was for us to all be together on that memorable Christmas-Eve Anniversary, and how much Joy and Howard and the children enjoyed being a part of that TV special. How proud we all were of our Daddy and Granddaddy!

Only a month after the Christmas program, Everett did another hour-long special with news commentator Howard K. Smith. His reviews on this one from TV columnists around the country were quite good. One especially I still treasure and I am including it here not only because I like it but because it also has more value than a prejudiced wife's review of her husband's performance. It was written by Rick Du Brow, syndicated columnist for United Press International, and it appeared in many papers throughout the country after the show aired in January of 1968.

WHAT A JOY TO SPEND ONE HOUR WITH "EV"

by Rick Du Brow

Everett McKinley Dirksen, the second most powerful man in Washington, D.C., and the fifth most popular male recording artist in the nation, was the subject of an hour ABC-TV program Monday night. It was, simply, a gem.

The broadcast was a finely polished blend of two elements: A personal look at the 72-year-old senator from Illinois, and a tour with him of the Capitol Building in Washington. He was excellent company in both areas. When it comes to talk of political style, let no one underestimate Everett McKinley Dirksen.

Much of the pleasure of the hour was the easygoing, natural rapport and humor between Dirksen and the reporter-host, Howard K. Smith, who went on the tour with the senator. The way they picked up on each other's remarks and anecdotes provided a fluency that averted the stiffness often accompanying programs about politicians.

Furthermore, the unending flow of knowledge about events and people and history in the Capitol, as only Dirksen can express it, gave the hour more real flavor of the atmosphere of the place than any comparable video program in memory.

As the broadcast noted, Dirksen is the last of a breed—or maybe the first. His individualism is a joy to behold, and makes him seem younger than the gray Establishment types half his age. And, as the hour pointed up, an added reason for this is the simple, innate sense of humanity that constantly pops out from behind the spectacular flow of words.

He is an incomparable offhand conversationalist, and his recollections of dealings with five presidents therefore took on an appealingly intimate tone. Adding to this rare flavor of Americana was a visit to his home town of Pekin, Ill., where his two brothers—including his twin—recalled boyhood days.

One of them remembered how young Everett used to practice his oration in the barn, and how you could hear him from the barn to the kitchen. His mother would say, "Now just listen to him talk," and you could say the same today.

Dirksen described himself as "an Abraham Lincoln garden

variety middle-of-the-road Republican." ABC-TV put it more simply: at the core, it said, he is a patriot. And how suddenly refreshing that word sounds in the year 1968.

It was inevitable that Everett's sideline career in show business would create union problems.

The American Federation of Television and Radio Artists, generally known as AFTRA, politely asked Everett to join up and pay the initiation fee and dues.

Just as politely, Everett declined.

The union had been after him to become a member because of his paid performances on such television programs as the Johnny Carson and Red Skelton shows, and *Hollywood Palace*. And particularly after his popular record, *Gallant Men*, came out, they began putting more pressure on him.

"Why should I be compelled to join a union just to give people the benefit of the Lord's Prayer?" he asked.

And he remained adamant in his refusal to join AFTRA.

It was well known that my husband had long been an opponent of compulsory union membership. After all he had not led those two filibusters and fought that long hard battle against repeal of the 14-B bill for nothing. He could not reverse his stand.

He felt so strongly on the matter that he would have given up his little fling in show business rather than be compelled to join a union. The Senate floor was his favorite stage anyway.

There was a small flurry when he was invited again to be a guest on the Red Skelton Show, and this time AFTRA went so far as to send a representative from the Miami local to our home in DeBary, where we were at the time, to give Everett an application to join.

He took the form but he never filled it out.

He also told the TV representative from the Red Skelton Show that if he appeared it would only be under the condition that he did not have to join AFTRA.

Red Skelton was one of my husband's favorite entertainers. They had become good friends. I did not know that he was also a fine musician and a prolific composer until he composed a piece especially for my husband, called the *Everett McKinley Dirksen*

March. It had its première performance, played by the Pasadena City College Band, when Everett appeared as Grand Marshal of the New Year's Day Rose Bowl Parade.

Any time Red Skelton wanted Everett on his show, he would have been more than happy to oblige. But even for him he would not join AFTRA. Suddenly, for some reason, the union people stopped bothering him and Everett went on the show. It was some time later we learned that Senator George Murphy, a long-time member, had quietly paid Everett's dues!

One small postscript on *Gallant Men:* while Everett was hospitalized with pneumonia and unable to sleep, he wrote a children's book also called *Gallant Men,* as a companion to his album. It was aimed for children from eight to twelve years of age, and it tells the story of heroic Americans from the Pilgrim Father, William Bradford, to astronaut John Glenn. Thus the Grammy-winning Senator from Illinois also became a children's author, even if not a narrator of nursery rhymes. It is a lovely, patriotic little book and of far more significance, to my way of thinking, than would have been the senator's recording of *Winnie the Pooh* and *Peter Rabbit.*

No mention of Everett's show business career would be complete without some notice of his weekly TV show with House Minority Leader Charles Halleck from Indiana. In 1962, Everett and Congressman Halleck started holding weekly news conferences to talk to the press about the Republican party's views during the Democratic administration. Everyone began calling it the *Ev and Charlie Show* but it was not making too much of a splash until President Kennedy called attention to it during a speech he made at the Gridiron Club dinner in Washington. Then it seemed that suddenly everyone was watching it on television and talking about it. It became very popular but Everett also regarded it as an important contact with the public, and a way of keeping the people informed—informally—of the "happenings" on Capitol Hill.

In January 1965, the *Ev and Charlie Show* became the *Ev and Jerry Show,* when Gerald R. Ford from Michigan was voted the new House Minority Leader. And without interruption, the

Monday morning press conferences from the Capitol continued
to be televised.

When Everett won his Grammy for *Gallant Men*, he said then,
regarding his show business career, "I started out in life with
theatrical aspirations. I regard this as another channel of expression. I'm willing to do more records if we can find the right
scripts. But I do have a limited amount of time, you know. I don't
want my legislative work to suffer."

And no matter how great he was on records or on television,
I still think his best performances were given on the political
stage. That was his world, and I know that long after people will
have forgotten his *Gallant Men*, they will remember my husband,
the *Senator*.

Chapter 17

His Last Campaign

Nowhere was my husband's flair for showmanship demonstrated more dramatically than on the political stage of the Republican National Convention in Miami Beach in August of 1968.

This was the year the GOP forces were split among Governors Ronald Reagan of California and Nelson A. Rockefeller of New York, and Richard M. Nixon, who had been on hiatus from politics for six years, since his defeat for Governor of California in 1962.

Both Governors Reagan and Rockefeller had approached Everett and asked him to nominate them for President. Everett's loyalty, of course, was to Nixon. But this time he was not making a nominating speech for anyone.

He was starring in a far more important and prestigious role in the political spotlight as Chairman of the Republican National Convention Platform Committee.

He was happy and proud to be chairman of this committee, which plans and produces the issues for the party in presidential election years. Everyone knows the chairmanship is a post of great prestige, but it is also one of a prodigious amount of hard work. And in a sense it is a rather thankless task because all too often the party platform is soon forgotten in the heat of the campaign.

Many wondered why Everett would want the job. He was seventy-two years old. Some of the press had speculated that he accepted the position because he realized that this would be his last chance to be platform chairman. I am sure this thought never entered his mind.

Although as it turned out, this was to be his last convention and his last campaign.

He accepted the position of Chairman of the Platform Committee because it was another challenge, because he wanted a Republican President in the White House, and because he felt that he could draft a platform that would have meaning in the coming campaign rather than being discarded. The "feel" was there for a Republican victory in '68, he said, and not only had he committed himself to back Nixon but this time he seemed convinced that Nixon was going to win the nomination—and that he, better than any of the other aspirants, would stick to the party platform issues in his campaign.

Meanwhile, however, there was the job of working out all those issues and planks of the party platform within the 100-man committee, which included many of the states' governors as well as members of Congress. And drafting a platform that would be acceptable to all concerned was certainly one of the greatest challenges of his career.

His position might be compared with that of an orchestra leader conducting a 100-piece orchestra, but with a few of them not wanting to follow the conductor's lead and creating a sour note or two.

However, with Everett wielding the baton—in the shape of his golden oilcan which is "mightier than the sword" if I may mix my metaphors—he was able to do the impossible and achieve harmony between the three discordant factions of the party, the conservatives, moderates, and liberals. In fact, someone referred to him as the "Toscanini of the political world" for his role in that 1968 convention, and I think it is a very apt description.

I was with him during all those long hours in committee and subcommittee meetings in Miami Beach, and so I had a fairly good behind-the-scenes view of what goes on in those smoke-filled rooms of political machinations and manipulations at a national convention.

As chairman of the committee, Everett was given a large suite at the Fontainebleau Hotel so that he could hold meetings there, early in the morning or late at night, when regular convention business was over. Usually his assistant chairmen or subcommittee chairmen would drift up to our suite about eleven o'clock at night to hash over the day's proceedings and to do more work on fashioning the language of the party platform. These informal sessions always went on until two or three or four o'clock in the morning, and I stayed up with them to see to it that they didn't go hungry. I kept the coffeepot going for them and always made sure there were plenty of cold cuts and crackers for them to nibble on, and of course I was fascinated at listening in on their discussions. Sometimes I would go and nap a bit in the other room, but never for long, because I didn't want to miss anything.

During the daytime also I attended many of their meetings, especially those of the subcommittees who were working on different portions of the platform. And I attended all the full committee meetings when I was allowed to do so—meaning those that were not behind closed doors.

I believe this convention gave me a better insight into Everett's genius at soothing opposing factions through the art of persuasion than on any other occasion.

The Platform Committee is always a large, unwieldy group which needs a strong positive person to take command. There are representatives from each state and with many diverse opinions over what should take precedence in the party platform. Bitter controversy and open floor fights over some platform planks have disrupted many conventions of both parties.

The major battles within the GOP ranks in 1968 were waged over two issues—the war in Vietnam, and crime and disorder at home.

Everett spent many hours with all the platform representatives, listening to all their ideas, and in my opinion working miracles in the fine art of compromise to arrive at the finished product, a platform acceptable to all and upon which all candidates could stand with comfort.

The setting, of course, was an ideal one for the exercise of those arts symbolized by a golden oilcan on his desk, and I watched him use quantities of "oilcan" diplomacy soothing the injured feelings of governors and others in high places.

But there was something that impressed me even more than his "oilcan" skills as I sat in on his meetings with all these men and women, and that was his astounding storehouse of knowledge. Of course I was always very much aware of this. You cannot live with a man like Everett Dirksen all those years and not be aware of it. His was indeed a great intellect. I knew it. I lived with it every day. I never ceased to marvel at it.

And yet here I was in 1968 thinking so many times to myself, as if for the first time, "My husband is really a brilliant man. He is coordinating everyone's thinking."

I'm sure it was again the setting, an ideal one not only for him to exercise all those arts for which he was known, but for me to observe him in comparison with the other men. He was so far ahead of them in his thinking because he could dip into his storehouse of knowledge accumulated from forty years of practical experience, thousands of legislative battles, and almost total recall of the pages of American history and related world events over the centuries.

He was so knowledgeable about so many things, and I am certain that it was this more than anything else which amazed the committee members, gained their respect, and closed the ranks on issues of controversy.

So many times a committee member would come to me and tell me how awed he was with Everett's background knowledge of certain events or issues. Others would tell me how fair he was in taking the time to listen to everyone's ideas. I still see or hear from some of those who were members of that 100-man platform committee of 1968, and they never fail to tell me what a privilege it was to have been able to work with Everett.

Everyone talks about what a laborious and difficult and thankless job it is to be chairman of a party platform committee, and I suppose it would have been quite a hard task for most people, but because of Everett's great fund of knowledge in so many areas, it was not really such a difficult job for him. He thoroughly enjoyed it. And so did I!

The party platform is always presented the day before the nominations and balloting for President.

And the senator was in great form that day.

He staged a virtuoso performance that not only rescued the

convention from apathy but again made him a hero with the headline writers, who hailed him as "the Grand Old Party's grand old orator, master showman" and so on, and generally credited him with enlivening the otherwise dull convention proceedings and stealing the show with his wit and oratory.

Up to then the convention had been rather a drone of lackluster speeches. (One reporter described them as "pussyfooting palaver.")

When Everett stepped up to the rostrum, the house burst into thunderous applause. It went on and on until he boomed into the microphone, "Quiet!"

Those who were expecting him to do the unexpected were not disappointed. When the demonstration died down, he stood there quietly for a second, his tousled silver locks glittering in the glare of the spotlights, and then looking out into the sea of faces, he solemnly intoned, "I accept the nomination."

This brought down the house. It was the first joke to emanate from the prosaic proceedings, and the delegates loved it. There was another loud ovation, more cheering and shouting. Never have I experienced a more delightful, exhilarating sense of release and relief at a convention. It was a marvelous accolade to my husband. But the cheering went on and on.

Again he thundered into the microphone, "Quiet!"

And still there was no quiet.

Then he held up for all to see a folder a foot thick containing the full texts of all the committee co-chairmen's speeches and outlines of platform planks.

"I'll make a deal with you," he told the audience. "If you'll be quiet for forty-five minutes, you won't have to listen to these. I'll throw them anywhere you want me to throw them."

There was a roar of approval and Everett hurled the packet into the audience to peals of laughter and applause.

Once he started his own speech, however, there was no more joking. His rich, resonant tones soon reduced his vast audience to attentive silence. He had them in the palm of his hand. It was obvious to everyone that the Senator from Illinois at seventy-two years of age still had the magic art of spellbinding in the old-fashioned style of one of his great idols, William Jennings Bryan.

And it certainly should have been obvious to all of those who had criticized him for "playing footsies," as some called it, with President Johnson, just where he stood on the matter of the Democrats' political slogan, "The Great Society."

"Great Society indeed! Never has an undeclared war embroiled America so long, never the casualty toll so great, never the outcome so remote . . . Never has the nation been so mired in debt, never its budget so bloated . . . Never have our cities writhed in such jeopardy and fear . . . Never promises so lavish, performance so dismal . . .

"This ballyhooed 'Great Society'—the fancy of an English socialist six decades ago—is not a new deal, no, not even a fair deal; it's just a straight-out misdeal. Humor it longer, and it will destroy what the Founding Fathers wrought . . .

"Clearly, my friends, the hour is late and our problems legion. It is America's hour of need.

"And that need—so urgent, so undeniable—is to depose this fumbling Democratic party, to depose its inept leadership—that party and those leaders oh, so long in promise, oh so short in performance. An outraged, heartbroken, shocked America joins us in this injunction to the Great Society—a sentiment voiced by Oliver Cromwell three centuries ago:

" 'You have sat too long here for any good you have been doing. Depart, I say, and let us have done with you. In the name of God, go!' . . ."

No one could call that "pussyfooting!"

After his introductory speech came the formal presentation of the GOP platform planks. But instead of the usual long-winded speeches, Everett's seven assistant chairmen delivered five-minute condensations of their sections. And the platform was accepted by acclamation!

It all looked so easy, so simple. But I knew the work and patience and persuasion and skills that had gone into it. I think it can truly be said that my husband was a master craftsman in his calling.

I consider his performance at the 1968 convention an important contribution to his party. In my opinion it was his "finest hour" on the convention stage, despite that more publicized one at the 1952 convention in Chicago where he "stole the show" by accusing Governor Dewey of taking us "down the road to defeat."

Flashback . . .

Everyone knows the outcome of the convention's balloting and the November election. I have only a short personal postscript to add for Pat Nixon. It is by way of apology for something I'm sure she would never have known about unless she reads this. I was so happy for her when her husband won the presidential nomination. I remember so well watching her and her two daughters, Julie and Tricia, as they came to the convention platform with Mr. Nixon, and how they beamed during his address.

But the event had a special meaning for me because it recalled a little unhappy circumstance of that *other* convention—1952 again.

When General Eisenhower won the nomination, Nixon of course was his running mate, and Mrs. Nixon, therefore, soon to be a Vice-President's wife instead of a senator's wife.

At that time, I did not know Mrs. Nixon very well. We had met, of course, through our Senate Ladies group, but she was much younger than I and very busy with her children who were just growing up.

And it must be remembered that Everett went to that convention as the leader of the Taft troops—and we lost.

When we flew back to Washington, Mrs. Nixon happened to be on the same plane with us, but her husband was not. I assume he had remained in Chicago with General Eisenhower and other Republican leaders. But I don't know because I didn't ask her. In fact I did not say anything to her. Oh, I'm sure we probably smiled and spoke in passing on the plane, but that was all. Everett and I were so wrapped up in ourselves and in our disappointment and hurt for Bob and Martha Taft, that I didn't even think to go over and talk with Mrs. Nixon.

It wasn't until much later that my conscience began to bother me. In looking back I remembered that she seemed so lonely on that long plane ride home. She was probably flying back to Washington to take care of her children while her husband stayed behind with his political chores, and it would have been a gracious gesture if I had gone over to sit with her for a while or say a few words to her. Come to think of it, I hadn't even congratulated her for her husband's nomination. I really considered that rather rude of me.

Later I came to know Mrs. Nixon better and to admire her greatly. We saw more of the Nixons while he was Vice-President, and I found Mrs. Nixon to be a warm and friendly person, and completely devoted to her husband.

In fact, I decided, we were somewhat alike—always thinking of our husbands first, and building our lives around their work, their efforts, their hopes and dreams. And the better I knew her, the more guilty I felt for that little unintentional slight during the plane ride in the summer of '52. I should have made more of an effort to be friendly to her. But I never gathered up the courage to tell her.

After all, I was then relatively new as a Senator's wife and by the time I might have found the courage she was already a Vice-President's wife. In Washington protocol is everything.

But in Miami Beach in the summer of '68, I did my best to atone for my little negligence.

"Never has an undeclared war embroiled America so long, never the casualty toll so great, never the outcome so remote."

In his acceptance speech in Miami Beach, Mr. Nixon promised to work to end the war in Vietnam, to negotiate with communism not through weakness but through strength, to take power from Washington and return it to cities and states, and end hate and terror in the streets.

The war issue, of course, was—and still is, as I write this—the most important one. I have been asked so many times how Everett really felt about the undeclared war in Vietnam, whether he really approved of President Johnson's escalation of the war or only supported it because Johnson was President and Commander-in-Chief, whether he really felt that both President Kennedy and President Johnson were "war lovers," as has been implied, whether he would approve of President Nixon's policy of pulling more and more troops out after promising to work to end the war in Vietnam.

Let me say at the outset that I prefer not to address myself on this very complex subject except for a few generalizations, and these only because otherwise I probably would be accused by some of deliberately evading the issue for devious reasons.

First of all, my husband was a peace-loving man who had seen enough of war in World War I. Secondly, I know that his career in office, from the Roosevelt administration on through the Kennedy and Johnson years, came at those times when he had to decide whether to support his Commander-in-Chief on that gravest of all issues—war.

I remember the first time he came home and said to me, with a sorrowful look on his face, "I may have helped to vote this country into war." That was during the Roosevelt administration, when he and Senator Vandenberg, once labeled as "isolationists," helped persuade Congress to give the President permission to declare war.

His earlier feeling was that we should stay out of war, but once he realized we were already involved, by degrees, and would eventually be forced into the war, he was then anxious to get Congress to support the President and his administration.

This same attitude prevailed with the Vietnam conflict. Everett was sympathetic with the effort which the Commander-in-Chief made as he faced the many difficult and monumental decisions to help find satisfactory solutions. He worked harmoniously with the entire Cabinet and helped carry the burden of trying to explain and make comprehensible for the public the reasons behind the President's decisions on the war in Vietnam.

Basically, Everett was opposed to war but he believed there were things worth fighting for, including freedom from the encroachments of Soviet-Communist tyranny.

He had backed both President Kennedy and President Johnson when they shipped more troops to Vietnam and escalated the war. He felt that since we were there, we should go in and get it over with as soon as possible, so it would not just drag on and on, slowly killing more and more of our boys. To him, this was a case where the ends justified the means, much as it hurt him.

How often, oh, so many times I heard him repeat that one line of the poet John Donne: "Every man's death diminishes me because I am involved in mankind."

And so many times I heard him refer to President Woodrow Wilson's speech to Congress at the time of World War I, when

the galleries were filled with men in tuxedos and ladies in long
dresses and glittering jewels, and after the President concluded
his speech, everyone stood up in a body, shouting their assent
and support of his war declaration.

But after it was all over and during the drive back to the White
House, President Wilson said to a friend who was with him,
"Well, they applauded my speech but that speech means death to
young men all over the world."

My husband had much the same feeling about war.

Because he held a high position in government he felt a deep
sense of responsibility for the death of every boy in Vietnam as
he had in World War II. Perhaps it would be more accurate to
say that every man's death "diminished" him a little, whether at
Flanders Field, Normandy Beach, or Vietnam.

He received many letters from wives and mothers of men
serving in Vietnam, as he had during World War II, asking for
his help in obtaining a discharge for a son or a husband. He
would always write to the boy first and ask him if there was any
particular reason why he wished a release from war duty. More
often than not the boy would write back, sometimes very in-
dignantly, and ask the senator not to pay any attention to that
letter from his mother or his wife, saying that he was perfectly
willing to do his share in the war effort until the conflict was
over, no matter what hardships he might have to suffer.

It saddened him to think of our boys fighting over there in
the jungles, not knowing the North Vietnamese from the South
Vietnamese, not knowing if they were surrounded by friends or
enemies.

But at the same time he felt that we were committed to helping
the South Vietnamese in their fight against communism, and he
agreed with General MacArthur who once said, "There is no
substitute for victory." Victory in Vietnam meant when the
Viet Cong laid down their arms. That is why he supported
President Johnson's policy in Vietnam. It didn't bother him a bit
to be called "hawkish" in this respect. As to the question of
pulling troops out, he always asked, "What are you going to tell
the mothers and fathers and the wives and families who have
boys buried over there?"

He did not feel that we should pull out of Vietnam, without

honor, without having accomplished anything, leaving a job half done.

This is the way he *did* feel.

I do not know how he would feel today. I think he would feel terribly frustrated at the situation. It seems incredible to me and I'm sure it would seem so to him that the undeclared war in Vietnam has gone on for so long, nearly fifteen years now as I write this. President Nixon inherited it from President Johnson who inherited it from President Kennedy who inherited it from President Eisenhower. Each of these Presidents has had to deal with the situation in his own way. And I know that each of them had my husband's heartfelt sympathy on the difficult decisions they had to make, as well as his support when they needed it.

I can say one thing for certain—Everett definitely would not agree with the implications in the Pentagon Papers that either Kennedy or Johnson deliberately deceived the American public regarding the build-up of the war, or deliberately withheld bombing plans or other military "secrets" from the press and public. I know he felt there were some things which the government should keep private, which the layman does not need to know because they involve fine points of foreign diplomacy, the delicate relationships between countries and governments. After all, medical and psychiatric files are not open to the press and the public. Business corporations do not reveal all their operations. Why should not the government have the right to keep some things top secret?

Of course he did not approve of either President Kennedy's or President Johnson's foreign policy in its entirety. He was critical of President Kennedy's policy of "co-existence with communism," and of President Johnson's vacillation over Vietnam. ("One month the administration says the war in South Vietnam can be successfully concluded by the end of 1965 and a few months later Secretary of Defense Robert S. McNamara tells us we are withdrawing from South Vietnam by the end of 1965, regardless of the outcome.")

But as I have said, Everett tried to look at the good side in everyone, and if the President's actions sometimes dismayed him he was more inclined always to say that he had been "ill-advised."

I am positive that Everett most emphatically would not agree with the implications that President Kennedy and President Johnson deliberately tried to get us embroiled in the war. Nor would he have felt this about President Eisenhower. Quite the opposite. Everett always felt that especially when a man was elected as head of our government, he became *more* devoted to the idea of peace, not less. And those three Presidents especially knew war well. They most assuredly would not have involved their country in another conflict unless there was no way out.

I am not sure how Everett would feel about President Nixon's policy of gradually pulling more and more troops out of Vietnam, in light of his 1968 campaign promise to work to end the war. I think my husband would feel a great sense of frustration and sadness because we are still not accomplishing a conclusion in Vietnam. And I think if he were here now, he would be quite put out with the inaction on the part of those involved in the Paris peace talks.

Rapport With Youth

If my husband were here now I can assure you he would also deal harshly with draft card burners and anti-Vietnam demonstrators. Everett loved young people and had a great rapport with them. He sympathized strongly with those students who want so desperately to change the world. But he did not approve of their protest and violence against situations which they had not studied enough to understand.

He blamed our educational system for the way some young people are behaving. He felt that our schools are not teaching students proper attitudes nor motivating them toward good citizenship and patriotic ideals. He often remarked that too many of our young people are devoid of a sense of history. If they had been taught basic patriotic ideals and a sense of history, he said, they would not be burning draft cards to protest United States' involvement in Vietnam.

But do not think for one second that he regarded a few "bad apples" as typical. On the contrary, he had great faith in the goodness and decency of our young people, and in their courage to cope with the complex problems of their times.

One of our most moving experiences at the 1968 convention in

Miami Beach was our meeting with some thirty or so boys who were members of actor Hugh O'Brian's Youth Foundation. We had heard and read about Mr. O'Brian's wonderful projects with his Youth Foundation, which he had created to stimulate leadership in young people and to inspire them to high goals. Each year, one high school junior from each state is chosen to participate in the Foundation's annual seminar, which in 1968 was called, "Our Democratic Process in Action." Half of the boys attended the Democratic Convention and the other half were brought to Miami to see what the Republicans were doing.

When Hugh O'Brian asked Everett if he had time to talk to the boys he of course said yes, although I certainly did not see how he was going to find the time between all those committee meetings. But he did.

However, he was too busy to prepare a speech, so he just spoke to them spontaneously. I'll never forget the sight of those boys, all in special uniforms provided by the Foundation, sitting around on the floor of the living room of our suite. Nor will I forget the look on their young faces as they listened while Everett talked to them. It was one of the most beautiful and inspiring talks I ever heard him give, so moving, in fact, that I had to retire to the bedroom to hide my tears. Hugh O'Brian came to me later and said that every one of those teen-age boys had told him they would never forget what the senator said to them that day. And neither shall I . . .

On the lighter side, there was Everett's great popularity with young people who were his "fans." The busloads of school children who came to Washington on spring vacations always mobbed him for autographs. He was never too busy or too tired to sign his name. He actually enjoyed this contact with the youngsters. He was like a Pied Piper with them. I cannot think of another politician who was asked for his autograph as often as Everett was, and I believe no one will dispute me if I say that he was asked for his autograph more than the rest of the entire congressional membership together.

I remember once when he came home and told me about a pretty little fifteen-year-old girl who was touring the U. S. Senate with her high school class, and when she met Everett she wailed, "Why can't *you* be President?"

"I told her," he said seriously, "the people in their wisdom choose our leaders according to our Constitutional procedure."

As we traveled about the country campaigning, parents would often come up to me and tell me how their children felt that a trip to Washington would not be complete unless they saw Senator Dirksen.

Of course, after his album, *Gallant Men,* came out, he became even more popular with the young set. In fact, a popularity poll of outstanding Americans was taken among fifty teen-age contestants (representing each state) in the "America's Junior Miss" pageant held in Mobile, Alabama, in 1967, and Everett came in fourth, exceeded only by Jackie Kennedy, President Johnson, and comedian Bob Hope.

Some people said Everett placed high on the list because of his hit record but when one of the girls was asked why she voted for Senator Dirksen, she replied that it was because of his "perceptive mind." Another said, "It is his ability to keep a sense of humor in the worst situation."

How right she was!

I have one letter from a little thirteen-year-old girl named Shawn which I especially cherish because it reaffirms my faith and hope that my husband's work was not in vain, that he did indeed instill some of his beliefs in some of the children who wrote to him.

I have never met Shawn. But I answered one of her letters after Everett was gone, and then she began writing to me. Here is an excerpt from one:

Dear Mrs. Dirksen,

Your letter came at a perfect time. We are having our end-of-semester tests and your letter cheered me up . . . Fall is here. The leaves are beautiful . . . Mom says in a way it makes her sad, for Fall means Winter is on the way. My Dad and I like winter and cold weather but Mom says the only good thing is the log fires she loves and now she can't even enjoy them, knowing she is adding to the pollution.

That reminds me! My parents say the world has always been

*troubled and dangerous, from caveman days to Egypt's enslave-
ment of the civilized world, then Greece's, Rome's, and so on, but
now it is SCARY! When I read about the "Black Panthers" and
others, and the sniping of policemen, the bombings, and newspapers calling police "pigs" and explaining how to make bombs
—well, it scares me half to death. Dad says this is what the so-
called revolutionaries mean to do—to scare the people and
frighten the police and lawmakers, even the President.*

*You know what Senator Dirksen would do and tell others to do.
Would you tell me what one thirteen-year-old girl can do? What
my family, my friends, my church can do to help our country, to
keep it strong and brave?*

*Why doesn't the F.B.I. stop the "Panthers" and others who
want to destroy America? Why are they allowed to print bomb
instructions and papers calling police names? I don't understand
it! I still remember reading "The Man Without a Country,"
about the man who was sentenced to spend his life on a ship,
never to return to America because, just once and in anger he
cursed his country.*

*I felt sorry for him then, knowing how sorry he was as soon
as it was out of his mouth, but now I think anyone who curses
their country, its laws, its police and destroys its flag does not
deserve to be protected by its Constitution. They should be
treated as any other traitor and put in prison or deported.*

*I know how Senator Dirksen felt about these things. I do
worry so. What do you think he would say is the best thing to do
or the best way to help? . . .*

The senator would have been proud of that letter from Shawn.

Chapter 18

Memories . . . Memories

The new year, 1969, dawned bright with hope. Life had been good to us since Everett first stepped down from that baker's truck back in Pekin.

He had successfully finished his last re-election campaign, won his fourth term in the Senate, and this time the man he backed for President won also.

The Republicans were in the White House again, and the Dirksens were jubilant.

We had celebrated our forty-first wedding anniversary on Christmas Eve in DeBary, Florida, and then flew back to Washington for the inaugural ceremonies.

Everett's five-foot logs were blazing in the hearthside at Heart's Desire as we sat planning his annual birthday party with Ben Regan. Ben, our long-time close friend from Chicago, had moved to New York and spent a great deal of time in Washington. He was well known in political circles and he had started the custom —which soon became a tradition—of hosting a big birthday party for Everett each year.

Everett's birthday parties were not only famous but they were always more fun than most of the other parties we attended during the year.

The President and Vice-President were always invited, and they usually came, as well as Cabinet members, congressional leaders, and our friends in the various government agencies.

We were very fortunate to have Ben hosting the parties for us because protocol is a way of life in Washington and you may not like it but you have to live with it. Everett's birthday parties became more or less a social status symbol. Everyone clamored for invitations and Ben took the brunt of handling the guest list so that anyone not invited could not put the blame on us.

Everett's birthday was January 4. The party was usually held soon after that date, making it one of the first big parties of the year in Washington. Traditionally it was held in the Chinese Room of the Mayflower Hotel.

But in our elation over the Republican victory we decided to have his birthday party at Heart's Desire. After all, it was a beautiful setting, the weather was lovely, we could set up tables outside as well as inside, and that is what we did.

The President and Mrs. Nixon came, Vice-President and Mrs. Agnew, most members of the Cabinet, and leaders of both the House and Senate. I suppose there were about one hundred guests. We had a catered sit-down dinner, and then everyone gathered around the fireplace or on the patio for informal party fun and merriment.

Everyone, of course, was in quite good spirits.

And Everett, naturally, couldn't wait to sing *Danny Boy*. I remember it as though it were yesterday. He called me over to the organ to play for him, and he stood there with his arm around my shoulder as we sang together. He was never in better form, or better voice.

Soon the others joined us in singing songs by popular request. It was all very informal and great fun.

What else do I remember about it?

I remember, oh, so well, President Nixon's words when he stood and drank a toast to my husband's seventy-third birthday.

"Now that we're in the White House," he said, "I promise you, Everett, that we're going to have your next birthday party at 1600 Pennsylvania Avenue."

I am glad we had his last birthday party at Heart's Desire.

Texas Barbecue at the White House . . .

Life in Washington can become an endless round of parties if you want it to. Everett had more fun than anyone at his own birthday parties but otherwise he was not one for much socializing so we had to be very selective about accepting invitations.

There were a few parties, though, besides our own, which stand out in my memory. One was President and Mrs. Johnson's Texas barbecue on the roof of the White House! The invitation said "Informal Dress," with the "informal" underlined, since most White House parties are at least black tie.

One does not wear blue jeans to the White House. But when we arrived we found that the President really did mean *informal*. He was dressed in Western-type pants, a wild shirt, high-heeled cowboy boots and a big Texas hat. Mrs. Johnson and the girls wore Western cotton dresses—the kind they would wear to a Texas barbecue on a ranch.

The barbecue was held on the roof of the Executive Wing of the White House, which is on the same level as the State Dining Room. We first had to pass through the State Dining Room, its tables bedecked with red and white checked tablecloths, then through an alcove and out onto the roof where we were greeted by a spectacle I won't soon forget.

Big, wide planks had been laid down for a flooring, and all around the open-ended roof were long groaning tables filled with food, and open fire pits with great chunks of imported steer meat from Texas roasting on moving spits.

It was one of those help-yourself affairs. We took our plates from the tables, helped ourselves to beans and salad, and then proceeded to the fire pits where a line of chefs, also LBJ's Texas imports, were tending the meat spits.

Many of the ladies who couldn't bring themselves *not* to wear long dresses at the White House had a bit of a problem with their skirts catching on those planks. Fortunately, I had decided on a simple short cocktail dress which was quite informal compared to the long gowns I usually wore.

We carried our plates into the State Dining Room, and found places wherever we could at the tables. There were no place cards, and the assortment of silverware—some of it formal with gold handles, some quite plain, some "everyday" cutlery, and none of it matching—was really something to behold.

The ghosts of past Presidents must have shivered in their

graves at this awesome breach of protocol but a good time was had by all.

The highlight of the evening came when the balmy night air was blasted with skrieking fire sirens, and we looked down to see a caravan of red fire engines and throngs of people running toward the White House, some of them shouting "Fire! Fire!" They had seen the flames and smoke up there on the roof, and even after the President assured them it was only a barbecue, some of the firemen and the crowd lingered on, obviously waiting for the catastrophe which never happened.

I'm sure the Fire Commissioner must have come close to having a heart attack that night, but when the President decides to throw a barbecue, you cannot very well tell him not to.

Jackie's Splurge . . .

The most beautiful party I remember was Jackie Kennedy's much publicized dinner reception and concert on the lawn of Mount Vernon in honor of the President of Pakistan, Mohammed Ayub Khan in July of 1961. It created a great sensation because it was the first party to be held at Mount Vernon in years and the First Lady was criticized in the press for the amount of money she must have spent on the event. I do not know how much it cost but I'm sure it had to be in the thousands.

The guests were transported down the Potomac to Mount Vernon on four yachts. (During Jackie's elaborate preparations for the party, her new nickname around the White House was "Cleopatra on her Barge.") The presidential party arrived aboard the presidential yacht *Honey Fitz*.

Special green tents bedecked with hanging baskets of flowers had been set up on the lawn, and Jackie had engaged the National Symphony Orchestra and some strolling trios to provide music for the occasion. Colored spotlights played on the vast expanse of lawn all the way down to the Potomac, and with the majesty of Mount Vernon, the home itself, silhouetted against the sky, it really was a breathtaking setting for a party. I feel privileged to have been among those invited. It was quite an experience!

Educational . . .

You can collect some rather fascinating morsels of information at Washington parties if you listen carefully. I spent one evening listening to the French Ambassador, Hervé Alphand, explain how you can drink all the champagne you want with no aftereffects. The senator was the ranking guest at a dinner party the ambassador and his wife Nicole gave at the French Embassy. As the wife of the ranking guest, I was seated at the ambassador's right.

The Alphands, who were good friends of ours, served all the proper wines, but their favorite was champagne. Everett never cared much for champagne. He would just as soon toast a visiting dignitary with a glass of water. But the ambassador loved it and he knew he had a captive audience in his non-champagne-drinking dinner guest from Pekin, Illinois. I was all ears.

He asked a servant to bring him a champagne swizzle stick, which is made of wood and looks somewhat like a skewer with a little ball at one end. The ambassador put the ball-like part down into the glass. He held the stick upright and then twirled it between the palms of his hands until all the bubbles were out of the champagne. He assured me that if I would do this, I could drink any amount of champagne I wanted and never feel it the next day. But I must admit I was not enough of a doubting Thomas to try it.

Protocol . . .

As you may have deduced by now, protocol is all important in Washington. No one is ever introduced by his title, only by name. This is fine if you happen to be a walking encyclopedia of everyone in government. But our government is a massive catacomb of departments, agencies, bureaus, and branches—executive, legislative, judicial. My husband served so many years in Washington that you might think we should have known everyone. But we did not.

If you are sitting across the table from someone whose place card you can't see, it is considered a breach of etiquette to introduce yourself, expecting him or her to do likewise, as is done outside of political circles. Or if you are sitting next to someone whose place card you can see and it says John Smith but you can't place the name or the face, you never ask leading questions such as, "Which branch of the government are you in, Mr. Smith?" because you're supposed to know. If you don't, he might be offended.

And I must tell you that not everyone's face at a Washington party is as recognizable as an Everett Dirksen or a Mike Mansfield.

I finally learned at least how to tell the rank of importance in guests at a dinner party. It all depends on how far away they are sitting from the salt! The host and hostess and guest of honor are always at the top of the Double-L shaped table, and the salt at the opposite ends, at the bottom of the table, so to speak.

The guests are seated according to rank, in descending order, from the top, next to the host and hostess—ambassadors, Cabinet members, senators, congressmen, and so on right down to the salt. But sometimes it happens that those sitting closest to the salt, perhaps from some minor government agency, turn out to be the most scintillating dinner conversationalists—if only you knew who they were!

For me it was frustrating. Had I been Alice Longworth, with her position and age, I think on many occasion I might have ignored this protocol business and just asked John Smith what his job was.

At my own parties I always tried to make it easier for others who may have felt as I did. I introduced everyone both by name and by title, as for example, "This is Mary Brooks, Director of the Mint."

They could take it from there.

I remember one rather amusing occasion when I deliberately broke protocol because a First Lady had forgotten hers. Mrs. Harry Truman, then wife of the President, was the honored guest at an afternoon party of the Congressional Wives Club. Of course she had been a member while her husband was a senator and she knew most of the wives personally. She was quite friendly with some of them and she was enjoying herself so thoroughly at the party that she stayed and stayed. And stayed.

The ladies knew they could not leave before the First Lady made her departure. They were quite aware of the protocol

but some were worried because they had children who had
to be picked up from school. Finally a few of them came up
to me, because I was one of the co-chairmen in planning the
party, and asked what we should do. They *had* to leave the
party. And Bess Truman showed no signs of wanting to go.

I gradually eased myself away from the others and onto the
sidelines, and at an opportune moment when Mrs. Truman
couldn't see me, I went sneaking out the back door. I knew
that if the frantic ladies saw me leave, they would probably
follow suit because they were relying on me to let them know
if it would be all right to break protocol, just this once. Fortunately, there were enough other ladies at the party and Bess
Truman was having such a good time that I doubt whether she
ever even noticed the absence of a few guests.

I hope I do not offend any of the First Ladies I have known
by saying that my favorite was, and always will be, Mamie
Eisenhower. We saw each other at parties and political functions,
but our real friendship started when the General and Everett
were spending time at Walter Reed Hospital. The VIP rooms
are all together in one section, and we would often be waiting
together while the doctors examined our husbands. This gave
us a special bond which deepened into friendship with the
passing years. Memories, Memories!

I treasure the memory of an unexpected visit from Madame
Chiang Kai-shek which also did not fit the pattern of Washington
protocol. Everett knew Generalissimo Chiang Kai-shek rather
well. Not only had he been a strong supporter of increased military appropriations for the general, but during his visits overseas
he sometimes stopped over in Taiwan where the general and
his wife would entertain him. On occasion, when she came to
Washington, the Chinese Embassy would call to invite us over
for some function or other, and we would renew our acquaint-
ances.

But out of the clear blue sky one day, Madame Chiang Kai-
shek's nephew called to say that she was in Washington and
would like very much to come and pay her respects to us in
Virginia and see our home in the country.

Of course I was thrilled. She was coming the next day at teatime. Everett arranged to come home to be her host. She arrived in a limousine from the Chinese Embassy and she had not been out of the car for more than a few minutes before Everett was touring her around his gardens and showing off his marigolds and his birdhouses.

She was fascinated. And she was charming also. When I went into the kitchen to prepare the teatime snack, she came with me, bringing me a gift of some cans of shredded meat. I opened one of them, and you can imagine my surprise when Madame Chiang Kai-shek proceeded to take over my kitchen, making delicate little shredded meat finger sandwiches and a delicious Chinese tea.

I often think how much fuller and richer my life was with him, all the pleasures I would have missed and the people I would never have met had I not been the wife of Senator Dirksen.

PART IV

SUI GENERIS . . . ONE OF A KIND

SUI GENERIS

(Of his, her, or its own kind; in a
class by itself; unique; peculiar.)
Webster's.

*We shall always remember Everett Dirksen in the terms he used to
describe his beloved marigolds: Hardy, vivid, exuberant, colorful, and
uniquely American.*

From a Eulogy by the President of the
United States, Richard M. Nixon
(In the rotunda of the Capitol,
September 9, 1969)

Excerpts from Other Eulogies . . .
*Ev Dirksen was as American as apple pie and watermelon and mari-
golds.*
*He was unique, made of the stuff which will leave an indelible mark
upon our Nation's highest legislative body. The name of Everett
McKinley Dirksen is indeed assured an honored niche in the history
of America, for he walked long and tall on the center stage of public
life . . . An incomparable man has left us . . . Aloha . . .*

Senator Hiram L. Fong of Hawaii

. . . he will be thought of as the epitome of a very unique American political tradition—and we are unlikely to see his like again . . .

Senator Jacob K. Javits of New York

He was the Mr. Republican of an era . . . His uniqueness is the stuff of legends, and he leaves here a permanent imprint and an enduring echo.

Senate Majority Leader
Mike Mansfield of Montana

There was only one like Ev Dirksen. He served his country and his world well. His death ends an era and improverishes all of us.

From the Orlando (Florida) *Sentinel,*
September 9, 1969

. . . Above all, he was a unique individual—an original in an era that discourages originality.

Senator Charles H. Percy of Illinois

Chapter 19

The Golden Box

I believe that the most popular image of Everett Dirksen is as a political orator.

Someone once wrote that it was my husband's sense of the theater which made him unique and Dirksen the orator whom the country knows best.

He most surely was *sui generis*, one of a kind, unique, and very special to me.

Perhaps this is why I feel that it was far more than his sense of the theater which made him unique, and why I hope that he will be remembered for something more than his oratory.

I think that sometimes his theatrics and oratory obscured his more important achievements.

But in a sense perhaps his political and oratorical career became one, for certainly it was his persuasive rhetoric that influenced his colleagues and even Presidents on important legislative matters.

In any case, since his voice was his trademark and his rhetoric the tool with which he chiseled his career, I suppose it would be remiss not to include here a widow's intimate views of her husband as an orator, for whatever they may be worth in the over-all evaluation of Dirksen the man for the history books.

I do this with great reluctance for the simple reason that I feel so inadequate in contrast to my husband's way with words. What he could do with the English language was simply not to be believed unless you heard it or read it.

I sometimes suspected him of carrying on a little love affair with the English language. He would hang onto his vowels as long as possible and often flagrantly divided words into syllables, I think, to make them last longer.

He had a genuine love of rhetoric. He believed that words have color and music and rhythm if they are properly put together. He could make them sound like a Mozart minuet or a Wagnerian dirge. He used to tell me that certain words are brightly colored, like the red, white, and blue of the flag; some are pastels, and others are the multicolored hues of a sunset or rainbow. To him all words were alive, like people. In a sense, they were living, breathing little people-words that fluttered out of his typewriter or off his tongue, much as his little birds fluttered out of their gourd nests. With his magic touch he could make words take wing like his birds, or come alive like the flowers in his gardens.

He seemed to have complete mastery of the English language and an astounding ability to coin a colorful phrase or a word when he needed it. He used adjectives I didn't even know existed, and if he could not find them in the dictionary, he made up his own.

A perfect example is to be found in his last speech for the Prayer Amendment (see Chapter 15), in which he refers to "white lilies apsending themselves." "Apsending" is neither a typographical error nor a misspelled word. My husband coined the word as an adjective from the word "apse," which is defined as the projecting part of a building, especially of a church, usually semicircular in plan, as an arch.

When Everett said that the white lilies were "apsending" themselves (and that *is* the correct spelling), he meant that they were curving over, as in an arch, and if you read the rest of the sentence in the full text, you will know why he invented the word and how precisely it expresses what he meant to say.

It is well known that he referred to the Bible and Lincoln more frequently than to any other literary sources, but he often interpreted them with his own unique Dirksenisms.

Who else but Everett, for instance, could translate the Biblical reference, "God created man in the Garden of Eden" in the following fashion:

*Then came the only creature that was created with intelligence,
a soul, a personality, the prospect of divinity. There he was, this
lonely creature. He had a beautiful home, if a garden can be
called a home. God made it without the aid of the Housing
Administration. They were not even around then. God decided
that Adam needed a companion. He put Adam to sleep and
took from him a rib and made for him a consort whom he
called Eve. Eve was only a side issue then. She's the whole
thing now.*

He had a rich, deep, sonorous voice, although it was not
always described as such by the political pundits, who preferred
the sound of their own words. They liked to call him "Oleaginous
Ev," or "the Wizard of Ooze," or the senator "who marinates
his tonsils in honey."

The senator, to tell the truth, really marinated his tonsils
in Pond's cold cream.

I am sure this will come as a surprise to many, as it did to
me, and I am sure he will forgive me for revealing his secret
now.

But throughout his lifetime people never ceased asking, *how*
did he do it? How did he acquire that marvelous golden voice
box of his, and how did he keep it in such good working order?
For he was known for his vocal stamina, as well as the style
and content of his oratory.

When Wendell Willkie lost his voice while campaigning against
Roosevelt in 1940, it was Everett who came to his rescue and
substituted for him.

President Kennedy lost his voice on several occasions and
turned to Everett for help. My husband probably only told
him to speak from his diaphragm and not tighten his throat
muscles. I am certain he did not tell him that he lubricated
his golden voice box daily with Pond's cold cream.

But how well I remember that little jar of inexpensive cold
cream on his washbasin each morning. He would poke his finger
into the jar, pop it in his mouth, wobble the cream around
with an audible *basso profundo* gargle that sounded like something out of a bazooka, and then swallow it. I remember how
surprised I was the first time I saw my husband do this, and

when I asked him about it, he chuckled and said, "It keeps my pipes lubricated."

He also informed me that this was the way the famous soprano, Galli-Curci, kept her beautiful singing voice in top condition.

When I asked him how it tasted, he replied, "Not bad." I was never curious enough to try it myself, but I always strongly suspected that the cold cream also had a medicinal effect, because Everett never had laryngitis or a sore throat.

Even when he had head colds they never had any effect on his voice.

It was also his regular practice to gargle with a mouth wash first thing in the morning, but I think that was more for personal cleanliness than for lubricating his "pipes."

This daily ritual of "marinating his tonsils" in cold cream, of course, was only one contributing factor to his vocal projection and skill as an orator. It must be remembered that he prodigiously practiced this art most of his life, beginning in his early boyhood when he was afflicted with "bigworditis" and spent a great deal of time preaching to Bossy, the cow.

Although it is not generally known, during the early years of our marriage he often took the pulpit at church to deliver the Sunday sermon. He enjoyed preaching. If he had chosen to become a minister I am sure he would have been one of the best. But he was perfectly satisfied with the podium of the United States Senate.

He undoubtedly was born with a beautiful voice but he also worked to cultivate it, both physically and intellectually. He was blessed with an inquisitive mind, a gifted tongue, and an ambition to be somebody. And all of that helped.

His "golden pipes," as he sometimes called them, were used for singing, preaching, debating, and high-flung oratory. He always said, "The voice is like an organ and must be suited to the occasion, the subject, and the audience. Sometimes all stops are out, and sometimes, for contrast, it must be soft and modulated."

The Oilcan Is Mightier Than the Sword

One of Everett's favorite expressions with which he was often identified was "The oilcan is mightier than the sword."

He believed in the art of persuasion rather than bombast.

He never raised his voice in anger. He never used it for petty haranguing. He never used it vindictively or in bitterness.

He was always courtly and courteous, sometimes cajoling, if he had to be.

He once said, "Public opinion is varied, and manifestly, the purpose and art of public speech is to persuade and alter opinions of those who may be in disagreement."

He was manifestly successful at this, and never more so than at his last convention in 1968.

He opposed some of President Nixon's choices for high office. But he did it in such a persuasive way that he was never accused of being disloyal to his President or his party. And President Nixon either withdrew the nominations or never actually made them.

Everett often quoted Aristotle's definition of rhetoric as "the faculty of discovering all the possible means of persuasion in any subject."

I know it sounds dull but we had no arguments at our house because my husband always used his extraordinary powers of persuasion to bring me around to his way of thinking on practically everything—from where to send our daughter to school to which end of the garden to plant the petunias.

He never became really angry. Or if he did, he didn't show it. He did not believe in temperament, or in raising one's voice in anger. During his years in public service he must have felt infuriated many times, but he was always able to contain his temper and express himself in beautiful language that sometimes made his opponents cringe. He never brought to our home any of the heat of an argument on the Senate floor and he would have no part of domestic squabbles at home.

He believed that anger and arguments were a display of weakness.

You couldn't even work up a good old-fashioned spat with Everett. The spats just fizzled out. You can't have much of an argument if it's all one-sided. He would always listen to me very carefully. And I like to think that once in a while he reconsidered some of the things he might have planned because of what I said, but he would never argue a point.

I know we had our little disagreements, but we always talked them out, he always won, and I always knew he was right.

Now, looking back over our years together, I really cannot remember any serious arguments that we ever had. If we did have any, they were lost in the serenity of a love and faith in each other that transcended pettiness.

. . . With a Golden Thesaurus in His Mouth . . .

Of all those labels the press pinned on my husband—"Liberace of the Senate," "marinated tonsils," "honey-coated tongue," and so on—the one that often amused us was "he was born with a golden thesaurus in his mouth."

I am sorry that I cannot remember which political writer deserves the credit for this distinctive sum-up of my husband. It is really a delightful *bon mot.*

But Everett was *not* born with a "golden thesaurus in his mouth." That is somebody's fancy way of putting it.

The plain truth is that my husband happened to be a very well-read man.

And he had a retentive memory. Once anything was photographed on his mind it was never erased.

His "golden thesaurus" came from this golden treasure chest in his head.

As Everett himself said, "It is a case of reading one's self full and developing a background which is always on tap, particularly when a speech is of an extemporaneous nature."

But it was more than that.

Everett embroidered upon that golden treasure chest in his head with his own wit and humor, his flair for creative writing and theatrics.

One of his most oft-quoted speech samplers is this one on Ireland and Freedom:

Good old Ireland! I have tried to hold up the flag for Ireland. I introduced a resolution to try to memorialize the whole wide world, if that could be done, to compel Great Britain to give to Ireland her undivided freedom. That is the way I feel. I take my freedom straight. I am like little Johnny. His teacher asked him, "How do you spell straight?" He said, "S-T-R-A-I-G-H-T." The teacher then asked, "What does it mean?" He said, "Without ginger ale." That is the way I take my freedom, I take it without ginger ale. I take it straight. So I am for the Irish people, who want their united freedom.

And I especially like this one which is an excerpt from a speech he made just before a Senate adjournment:

The moving finger writes, and the fortuities of politics will probably result in a change of some faces when we return in January . . . Old faces go and new faces come, but somehow, like Tennyson's brook, the free Republic continues to go on with vitality, vigor and an energized faith, as it moves to newer heights and newer achievements for its people in the great moral climate of freedom . . . So au revoir. We shall see you on the home diamond somewhere; and when it is all over, all the healing waters will somehow close over our dissidence, and we shall go forward as a solid phalanx once more.

This was Everett at his bigworditis best, mixing simile and poetry, Bible and baseball, to express his homespun philosophy in colorful and descriptive language.

Nor were his words ever empty words. Everett Dirksen, the orator, never orated just to hear the sound of his own voice, although he may have liked it as much as anyone else. He always had something to say. Everyone on Capitol Hill knew that the senator did his homework. That was why they all turned out to hear him when he spoke on the Senate floor. No matter what they might be doing—in committee work or in their offices with constituents—if they heard that Everett Dirksen was going to speak, they would drop everything to go and hear him.

For behind that golden tongued oratory, which they loved, was an intellect that they thoroughly respected.

During his years in public service, Everett worked on many bills. He always studied them carefully until he knew them as well as he knew the Bible. Other senators and congressmen knew that if they went to hear Everett speak on a certain bill pending, they could learn more about it in ten minutes than they could in wading through a whole stack of government printing on the subject. His colleagues in Congress frequently leaned on Everett's "golden thesaurus" to condense, capsule, or summarize the meat of a bill for them, and they leaned on his golden treasure chest of homework to guide them in making decisions. Of course they did not always agree with him and they voted against him on many occasions, but they did go there to listen and to learn.

Stage Play . . .

Acting was always so much a part of Everett's character, whether he was playing the Prince to my Princess back in Pekin or holding forth on the Senate floor.

He had a few attention-getting devices which were very effective. One, often reported in the press, was the way he wielded his glass of water, as a prop. He always had a glass of water on the rostrum, supposedly to wet his throat. But he used it as a prop in a very dramatic way, to heighten suspense. He would raise the glass toward his lips and still keep talking before taking the first sip. Everyone knew about this famous, typically Dirksenesque bit of stage play, but no matter how often they had seen it, the trick still worked. When they saw the glass going up toward Everett's mouth, they could not take their eyes off it. My husband used that glass the way a conductor uses a baton—slowly, quickly, raising and lowering it, until everyone in the audience had their gaze fixed upon it. Sometimes he played this game for ten or fifteen minutes before he took a drink. And sometimes he returned the glass to the rostrum without even touching it.

His sense of theater was always with him. He played with words the way a cat plays with a mouse. He would let a phrase come out slowly, then chase it with something loud and clear, all the while using gestures and poses to make his point. He loved putting words together in an involved, elegant way to describe the simplest of things.

I remember once I mentioned to him that perhaps he should not use so many four- and five-syllable words because people might not understand them. And I remember exactly what he said to me: "Look, Toots, it's good to use those words. An audience does not want to be talked down to, and even if they don't have the education to understand every word, at least they have pride and they want to try to understand."

I think that is one reason he was such a popular speaker. He never talked down to his audience.

Even though he spoke a simple, homespun, folksy philosophy, he always embellished it with a theatrical flamboyancy and the choicest of words.

He had a genuine love of the English language and a huge respect for it. I never heard him use profanity around the house. He may have used a swear word when he was with men friends—just to be a "good fellow"—but I never heard him say so much as a "damn." Some of the offensive four-letter words in vogue today would have given him great concern.

Everett often chided me when I vented some small frustration with so much as a "darn," or such. I didn't think it was too bad a word, but he would always say, "You should control your emotions, and it won't be necessary to express yourself that way."

He always felt there was a better word for it than those used in profanity. His theory was that the English language has so many beautiful words to select from that it is degrading to use cheap little words to express yourself. He used to say "I must use beautiful words. I never know when I might have to eat them."

Many have remarked that the senator looked and acted the way a senator should.

His appearance became almost as much a trademark as his voice. Especially his tousled hair and dark-framed glasses (without glass) and stylish ties.

At first he was inclined to be a little vexed because his curly hair was so unmanageable. But when he found that people liked his mussed-up look, he went along with it, even cultivated it sometimes, especially after television came in. If his hair wasn't rumpled-up enough for his public image, he would muss it some more by running his big hands through it. And sometimes he practiced his lip movements and facial gestures in front of the mirror to achieve the proper effect. If people expected him to look and act like an aging Shakespearean actor he did not want to disappoint them.

He was often called a "ham." Someone even called him the biggest ham in the Senate. Of course he was a ham, when the occasion called for it. He never got the theater out of his blood. But this does not mean he was ever insincere in his beliefs.

It was probably the ham in him, for example, that got the attention of a restless audience who had just finished dinner and a few cocktails. Everett had a habit of just standing there quietly at the rostrum, and gazing out solemnly at such an audience without saying a word. Sometimes he might wait a whole minute. The audience would finally notice, and then they would quiet down of their own accord. And once quieted, you could have heard a pin drop. I do not know of anyone who ever had more quiet audiences than Everett.

He had almost a psychic rapport with his audiences.

He once answered a question on public speaking by saying, "There is not too much I can say about the techniques of public speaking; however, one thing I can say is that behind it there are more than thirty years of constant and unremitting effort to become thoroughly familiar with the psychology of audiences, friendly, indifferent, or hostile . . ."

He preferred a hostile audience to an indifferent one. "If it is hostile, you can cope with it. Of course, this comes in part with experience. You must have poise. You must have sea legs. Some men are afraid. You can never be afraid. But if you know your subject, and if you can assess the audience, and if you understand the occasion, you can always gain command. You must expect to do so. But of course there are other things. I always hope people will enjoy what I have to say. But I'd think I'd really failed if I didn't enjoy it more."

That is my husband at his best—always the twinkle in his eye, the ability to smile at himself, the wit to know the difference between a smile and a sneer. Who could sum up Senator Everett McKinley Dirksen any better than Everett Dirksen? And who would enjoy it more?

His greatest stage was the floor of the Senate on Capitol

Hill. It was there that he played his best roles and assumed his most dramatic poses because that was his toughest audience.

It was there that the delightful ham in him found its greatest fulfillment.

He once shamelessly admitted:

"I have been able to bring a blush to my face, the blush of rage, as I brandished my clenched fist and thrust my face within six inches of the face of another senator during debate on the floor. I was able to relax instantly and smile to show it was sham. My colleagues seemed to think it was the funniest thing they had ever seen—I looked around and felt they were all near death from apoplexy."

That was Everett at his *sui generis* best.

Chapter 20

The Bag of Pills

We all have our little quirks. One of Everett's was his penchant for pills. The windowsill above our breakfast table was a small pharmacy containing the newest and latest in pills and vitamins, all shapes, sizes, and colors. Especially colors. Everett could get as excited over a new colored pill as a boy with a new toy.

He was always trying the latest in vitamins. He always carried bottles of pills in his briefcase, and was always pleased to try any new pill anyone might offer him.

He considered his pill-taking more a preventive than a cure. But if he had any aches and pains, he believed there was a pill somewhere to cure them—though he did not need the aches and pains to enjoy pills.

So far as I know, his pill-taking never really prevented any illnesses. On the contrary, my husband was afflicted with a rather phenomenal assortment of ailments that had him in and out of hospitals numerous times. Undaunted, he always took his own pills to the hospital with him and was most indignant when the doctors and nurses tried to take them away from him.

After he had been in and out of Walter Reed Hospital several times, the nurses finally realized that he was a much better patient if he were permitted to take his own "health" pills, so they allowed him to keep his supply with him.

This special eccentricity was not so well known in other hospitals. I remember once when he had to be rushed to

Passavant Hospital in Chicago with a terrible pain in his back, which later was revealed to be a chipped vertebra of the spine. His campaign manager, Harold Rainville, was with us. We stayed with him as long as we were permitted, then had left his room and were halfway down the corridor toward the elevator when one of the interns called us back.

I was concerned that something serious had happened. In a way it had. One of the hospital's top specialists, Dr. John Laadt, stood there holding out Everett's bag of pills toward us.

"May I inquire what these are for?" he asked.

"Those are his pills," I replied.

"Oh?" said Dr. Laadt, with raised eyebrow. "So the patient brings his own pills to the hospital?"

"Well, he's got pills you probably haven't even heard of yet," Mr. Rainville explained, "and you might run out of his favorites."

In the end, Everett himself settled the matter when he learned that Dr. Laadt was about to confiscate his pill bag. His back may have pained him but this pained him more. "Keep your cotton-pickin' hands off my pills," he said, and he meant it. Fortunately, John Laadt was a staunch Republican with a sense of humor, and an avid admirer of Everett's. That was the beginning of a warm friendship between them.

Everett had once used that same phrase to the eye surgeon who was about to operate, "Keep your cotton-pickin' hands off my eyes." I mention this again because I believe it was that long bout with his eyes that turned him into a pill-taker. At least I do not remember his being so preoccupied with pills before then, although he was always conscious of the necessity to stay in good health if he were to stay in politics.

Everett always worked at taking care of himself and in a way it paid off. For in spite of the ravages of time and many illnesses, as a campaigner he could still hold his own against men half his age.

He developed a genuine interest in pharmacology and was very insistent that the correct pharmaceutical name be on each bottle of pills, thus adding another compartment to that "golden thesaurus" in his head.

If anyone should ask, he would be delighted to tell you that a Coricidin Nasal Mist, for example, was a decongestant anti-

histaminic containing so many *cc*'s and *mg*'s of chlorphenira-
mine, gluconate, and phenylephrine hydrochloride. If you think
I can remember all of that, you're wrong. I copied it off the
bottle. I was never a pill-taker or nose sprayer myself. But
Everett could roll off those pharmaceutical words as easily as
he could quote Shakespeare, Lincoln, or the Bible.

Any time a new pill or vitamin or throat lozenge came on
the market, he was one of the first to try it.

I remember the time he heard a television commercial about a
new brand of pink-striped toothpaste and he couldn't wait to
try it. I think we probably had the first tube of pink-striped
toothpaste in our area, because I had to go from drugstore to
drugstore until I found one that had the new brand in stock.

At one time I even made out pill charts for him, showing
which pills to take when and for what throughout the day. I
went to a lot of trouble to try to be helpful. But then I found
out he was not paying any attention to the charts, and in fact
was too busy even to be bothered taking his pills during the
day—unless I was there to pop them in his mouth for him. He
usually just took his handful of pills in the morning, then
became so absorbed in his work that he forgot about them
unless he happened to look in his briefcase. I am sure there
were times (when I wasn't there) that he opened his briefcase
and saw his pills and was reminded to take them. But knowing
Everett, I'm sure he just swallowed another handful, without
rhyme or reason, without taking the time to look at my pill
chart. So I stopped making them. Anyhow, I think he was basically more interested in adding to his pharmaceutical bigworditis
than adding years to his life.

Everett's illnesses (in spite of his pill cures and preventive
precautions) and his little sojourns in and out of hospitals were
always fully reported in the press. There is little I can add to
them here, except to say that he overcame most of them because
he was a great fighter and God was on his side.

Nothing, of course, will ever compare to that first dreadful
time when we thought he was losing his sight.

But in his last years it did seem that he struggled with a
startling variety of physical ailments, including a hairline crack

in the vertebra (apparently damaged during a violent fit of coughing and which necessitated his lashing himself up in a corsetlike affair with a steel spinal brace), a duodenal ulcer, another undiagnosed stomach ailment, a broken hip, and of course his chronic emphysema, which was so bad that he sometimes could not sleep. At one time he had pneumonia on top of his emphysema.

Even when he was not feeling too well, he never lost his vitality, his restless energy and love of life. I love that line someone once wrote about him: "Dirksen endures his physical difficulties with a rakish gallantry."

Everett had a theory about any physical handicap—that it was only a momentary disturbance and should never interfere with what he wanted to accomplish.

Of course his emphysema was not momentary but he overcame it in his mind. It would have helped him physically to give up smoking.

The closest we ever came to having an argument was about his smoking.

I would fuss at him and he would try to give it up and I would think, Oh, we have it licked. Then the next morning he would light up another cigarette. He finally got so he wouldn't light a cigarette until after he had his cup of coffee. Sometimes he would cut his cigarettes to four a day for nearly a week.

Many times when he was struggling so for breath, he would light a cigarette to calm his nerves, and I would fuss at him again. I regret now that I did, because he really did try hard. He was strong enough to do almost anything else but he was not strong enough to stop smoking. For some strange reason, the doctors kept telling *me* that Everett should stop smoking, but they never told *him* that he *had to stop* and he never did.

Everett always went to Walter Reed Hospital for periodic checkups, but in later years, he was in and out of the hospital so much that it practically became our second home.

As if the illnesses themselves weren't enough, he also was prone to freak accidents. I had gone to Tennessee to visit Joy and her family on Mother's Day of 1966, and the morning after I arrived, I received a phone call from Washington with the news that Everett was in Walter Reed Hospital with a broken hip—from falling off the bed. I said that was impossible because our bed was only six inches off the floor and we had a heavy padded rug under it.

But it was true all right. Everett had taken advantage of my absence to go to the hospital for a checkup and a little treatment for his emphysema. He had a habit at night of sitting on the edge of the bed for about ten minutes, to say his prayers and to meditate. On this particular night, he was sitting on the edge of his hospital bed, probably after having been given a sedative, and he dozed and fell off the bed.

Mamie Eisenhower told me when I arrived there that she heard the thud from the adjoining room, where she was with the General, who was also in the hospital for treatment. In fact, Everett had been with Mamie and General Eisenhower earlier in the evening, and had not been back in his own room very long when the accident occurred.

Soon after I received the news in Tennessee, the telephone rang again. It was President Johnson, calling from Texas. He had just heard about Everett's broken hip and offered to pick me up in his plane in Knoxville on his way back to Washington. I hurried to the airport and found the Johnsons had been delayed but they had sent another presidential jet for me. We landed at Andrews Field where President Johnson and Lady Bird were waiting and we were picked up by his helicopter. We landed for only a few seconds on the White House lawn. The Johnsons got out and then we were off again to Walter Reed Hospital, where the helicopter swooped down on a beautiful little bit of green grass no bigger than a postage stamp. I was there with my husband within only a few hours of that early-morning call, and I shall always be grateful to President Johnson for making that possible.

I stayed at Walter Reed with my husband the entire time he was there. He was operated on right away to "put in the nails and pins" as he called it, and he was so determined to get well fast that he was out of bed and in a wheelchair in no time at all. He enjoyed visiting with the boys in the Vietnam ward. He would take them flowers and fruit which his many friends had sent him.

He was back on the Senate floor—on crutches, of course—in only two weeks, which astounded everyone including the Washington press corps who are not easily astounded. His return from the hospital this time was the most widely publicized of all his infirmities, I suppose because the whole affair lent itself to more colorful coverage. First, not many people fall off a bed and break a hip after they're already in a hospital. And not many manage to recover so quickly, especially if they're seventy years of age. He was an inspiration to many people with handicaps. The press really had a field day describing Everett and his condition—"the beloved old scalawag hobbled onto the Senate floor on crutches. He was held together by eleven pins and a screw," or as others put it—"nailed together like an old house." He delighted them when he talked about his scar and said, "Thirty-two stitches—that's pretty good for an amateur."

He delighted them even more when he stalked onto the Senate floor and livened things up by launching right into an attack on a bill that was being considered—and pounding and pointing his crutches for emphasis.

In time he was able to put the crutches aside and use only a cane. He used it like a baton. And what a collection of canes he acquired! People would see pictures of Everett in the newspapers hobbling along with a cane, which would inspire them to send one of theirs which they thought was better.

Everett's remarkable sense of humor is nowhere better displayed than in a letter to our friends, Dr. and Mrs. Ralph Kunstadter, a short time before his surgery to remove the plate and pins from his hip.

Dear Marge and Doc:

. . . Things are moving along nicely and they are fattening me up for the knife. Sounds like slaughter, doesn't it, but really the surgeons are quite satisfied. The coming out party takes place on Wednesday, October 26. Really that will be a great day. I will save the spikes for my favorite railroad. They may want to use them to nail down rails on those heavy cross ties.

> *Best wishes,*
> (signed) *Everett*
> *Everett McKinley Dirksen*

There is an epilogue to the broken-hip episode. In retrospect it seems like a minor miracle that Everett did not end up back in the hospital with another broken hip.

He had only recently recovered from his "coming out" surgery to remove the plate and pins from his hip, and we were celebrating my birthday with a little dinner party at our home in Virginia.

Our good friend Lee Naegel was with us, and we were about to sit down to dinner when I absent-mindedly asked Everett to reach over and pull the lamp so it would be centered over the table. We had one of those hanging lamps in our dining room— the kind that moves along a traverse rod so that it can hang low over the table or up and away to the side of the room.

I should have known better than to ask Everett to move it. For anyone else it would have been a simple little twist of the wrist. But not for him. He proceeded to step up on a dining room chair and give a strong yank. The lamp moved so easily and quickly that he was knocked off balance and fell. And of course he fell on his bad hip.

Back to the hospital he went! Fortunately, the only damage was a bruise, and they let him come home in a wheelchair. I don't remember what happened to my birthday dinner but I did remember never to ask him to move that lamp again.

Chapter 21

Man of Many Talents

My husband happened to be one of the most artistically creative men I ever met, a fact that was generally overshadowed by his far more important role as a senator.

At one time he even designed my hats for me. That was back in the days when women were wearing lots of hats. I remember one especially that he designed. It was my V-for-Victory hat for the war years, when that particular sign was being displayed everywhere. He first designed the hat frame out of wire, with a V in front, and I covered it with fabric and flowers and wore it several years. He got such enjoyment out of seeing *his* hat on my head when we were out together.

He also designed our Christmas cards every year until he became too busy. He would first draw or sketch his own design, then take it to the print shop to have it made into a Christmas card. They were all his own creations. There is one I especially remember. We sent it just after he was first elected to Congress. It was an outline of the State of Illinois, with some cities indicated, and in the Pekin location there was a Christmas tree.

He also composed all the verses for our cards.

He must have inherited some of his artistic talents and his love of beauty from his father, who painted those fancy curlicues and stripes on the buggy wheels for the Pekin Wagon Company.

He not only loved all the growing things in his gardens, but he loved to "program" them just so, and some of his results were quite spectacular.

He took into account the color, height, and shape of the plants and shrubs he was working with and formed of his flowering friends a panorama as carefully planned as a painting.

His birdhouses also were miniature masterpieces of architecture, fashioned from his gourds and boxes in varying shapes, sizes, and colors that blended into their surroundings.

Just as his use of words oftentimes made pure poetry out of mundane subject matter, so he could create those lovely birdhouses from scraps.

Do Clothes Make the Man? . . .

Everett was no fashion plate but he certainly had a talent for attracting attention to his tousled appearance, which became almost as much a trademark as his voice. He simply didn't like to be bothered shopping for clothes, wore his suits until they were threadbare, and his ties until they were so frayed that I had to sneak them out of the closet and dispose of them. He was reluctant ever to throw anything away, yet he never noticed when a cufflink was missing. He collected flashy cufflinks and ties.

His usual rumpled look had nothing to do with money or cleanliness. He was very meticulous about the latter, and changed his shirts two or three times a day if he thought about it, and he would have Violet press a suit almost every morning, not realizing that this was hard on the material. But he had a gangly build, and did not wear clothes well. Even though he started out in the morning looking fresh and neat, he always managed to get himself disarranged during the day.

His attentive secretary, Glee Gomien, was a great help in keeping him from looking too shabby. Every now and then I received a call informing me, "The senator is looking seedy again. We think he looks handsome but people are beginning to comment on it. Maybe we'd better do something?"

That always meant it was time for me to put in an SOS call to Ben Gingiss in Chicago and ask him to make up some new things for Everett as soon as possible.

Ben was in the tux-rental business and he and Everett had

become good friends after Joy's wedding, when the father of the bride had worn a rented Ben Gingiss formal cutaway. Ben did not usually make custom suits, but he seemed not to mind making them for Everett.

My husband once told Ben he wanted him to make up a morning coat and striped trousers as a gift for President Eisenhower. "I'm sure the President would be glad to look as good as Senator Dirksen," said Everett. He was joking, of course. It was meant as a compliment to Ben Gingiss for his fine tailoring. Everyone knew that Eisenhower had the meticulous look of an army general, even in his civilian clothes.

Everett's first experience with a rented tux made nationwide headlines. It happened in 1933, back in the days before tux-rental places were as common as they are today and when it was generally assumed that if you were a congressman in Washington you owned a tuxedo. Everett had never owned a tuxedo and could not afford to buy one. President and Mrs. Roosevelt had invited all the newly elected members of Congress to a White House reception. Everett knew that he had to wear formal dress of some kind, so he simply rented a tuxedo instead of buying one.

The word spread, and a news photographer came up to his hotel room to take pictures of him while he was dressing. I was not with him at the time. I was in Pekin.

I must say I was somewhat shocked to see all those pictures of my husband putting on his first formal clothes. The wire services had picked up the pictures and story and spread them in newspapers all over the country, with captions about the new Congressman from Illinois "tying his own tie" and wearing a *rented* tuxedo to his first formal affair in the White House.

This did not ruffle Everett. He went right on renting a tux until he could afford to buy one.

When he was running for his second term in the Senate in 1956, some of his campaign aides became concerned about the heavy bags under his eyes, the result of a rigorous diet to lose weight. It was suggested that the senator be operated on and have the loose skin under his eyes removed for the sake of his "public image," especially the one on television. The senator flatly refused to have a "facelift," so his aides presented him with

a pair of heavy horn-rimmed glasses—with no glass in them—
and urged him to wear them when he was on the air.

He did. Inevitably, the press started to question him about
wearing glasses while on television when he did not use them at
any other time. Was he having trouble with his eyes again?

Everett merely looked at the reporters, took the glasses out of
his pocket, casually stuck his finger though the eyepiece, and said,
"Oh, these are just to make me look good. No glass, see? The staff
wanted me to hide the bags under my eyes and the heavy rims
do that." He had a talent for telling it like it was.

A Man of Simple Tastes

In his early years in Washington, my husband either walked to
work or rode the streetcar. And that always amazed the Capitol
Hill office workers to see the Congressman from Illinois getting
off a streetcar. The going rate those days was ten cents by
streetcar and twenty cents by taxi from his hotel.

After he became a senator, a number of Chicago friends and
businessmen got together and bought him a new car, I suppose
because they figured he needed one and would not buy one
for himself. But they made the mistake of buying a Cadillac
with all the trimmings, including a telephone. It did not come
complete with a chauffeur. That was my job.

Although the car was really much too big and fancy for us,
Everett did not want to offend his friends by asking them to
exchange it for something simpler. But he did have the phone
taken out the next day.

We were never too comfortable in that car, and it was only
after he merited a Cadillac limousine with a chauffeur that he felt
at ease in a Cadillac. This was in 1959, after he was elected
Senate Minority Leader. The chauffeured Cadillac went with the
job. This one, too, had a telephone but Everett had it removed
because it interfered with his reading and thinking on the way
to his office.

Before he did, though, he telephoned Democrat Lyndon
Johnson, then Senate Majority Leader, just to show him that he
rated some of the same privileges.

"Hello, Lyndon," he said. "This is Everett. I'm calling you
from my limousine with my new phone."

The story goes that there was a split-second pause before Lyndon replied, "Just a minute, Everett. My other phone is ringing."

I do not know how true the story is. I was not there. But Everett never denied it and he always chuckled when he heard it.

He had to get accustomed to having a chauffeur, also, but that was not too difficult because fortunately the one he had was a gem. His name was Wilbur Walker and he was so devoted to the senator he was like a one-man dog. Quite possessive of him also. I remember asking him to do some errands for me once and he said, "Did the senator say I should?"

I have mentioned elsewhere my husband's simple tastes in food at home but I must add that his tastes were sometimes a little too simple for his campaign manager, Harold Rainville, who was with him in restaurants a great deal. Harold swears he could and did eat anything on the menu. He told me of the time on a hot midsummer day in Chicago when he almost lost his appetite because Everett ordered pig's knuckles and sauerkraut for lunch.

He told me also, with some amusement, of the sly way Everett managed to get rid of him in the early-morning hours when he did not want him around. Rainey usually arose at dawn to accompany Everett to the airport when he was ready to fly back to Washington from Chicago. And Everett preferred not having his well-meaning campaign manager around so early in the morning. It wasn't that he didn't like Harold. He did, very much. He was quite fond of him, in fact, and apart from their political activities, they had become good friends.

But Everett usually liked to have those early-morning hours to himself. He had noticed Rainey's aversion to the greasy Bratwurst sandwiches he often ordered for lunch. So he took to ordering them for breakfast at O'Hare Airport. And Rainey stopped taking him to the plane . . .

The Kissing Senator . . .

I sometimes found it amusing that my baker boy from Pekin who was once too shy to ask a girl for a date should become known as "the kissing Senator from Illinois."

He was especially generous with his kisses for all those members of the many Republican women's organizations that supported him and campaigned for him and helped him win each time.

Photographers were forever shooting pictures of Everett besieged by women clamoring for his kisses. The press always played up "the kissing senator," especially at campaign time. It was good copy.

So many people have asked, how did I feel about my husband going around kissing all those women?

I did not mind. He always had enough left over for me!

And I still cherish a precious little memory of how his kissing talent (for political purposes only!) really began.

It was my wonderful little old Grandmother Carver back in Pekin who started it all. She used to be Everett's most devoted audience from the very beginning of his American Legion speech-making days in Tazewell County. We would bundle her up in the back seat of the car and take her with us to many of his speeches, and she would sit there in the audience listening with true adoration.

I remember how excited she was during his first campaigns for Congress, how disappointed she was when he lost, but then how overjoyed when he won the next time.

While Everett was speaking from the platform, he always noticed how Grandmother Carver sat there, so rapt and attentive. When he finished speaking he always went over and gently kissed her on the cheek.

Sometimes he noticed other little old ladies in the audience looking a bit envious, so he would go over and kiss them also.

And that is how it all started. He soon felt right at home with women audiences, and through the years he developed his kissing technique to the point where he had the ladies waiting in line for his kisses. I even heard some of them say after he kissed them that they would never wash that spot again. I am sure he enjoyed it as much as they did.

While "the kissing senator" perhaps won some votes with his kisses, on a more serious level a great deal of Everett's success in his campaigns can be contributed to those loyal, hard-working women's organizations that are the backbone of any political campaign. In addition to the regular party organizations, special credit must be given to an extra-special battalion of ladies in Chicago who blanketed every ward and precinct in the city with the hardest-working teams of vote-getters I ever saw.

Everett and I both were well aware and most appreciative of the job done by these volunteer workers and their outstanding women leaders, such as Marjorie Kunstadter, Joan Regenstein, Grace MacCaughtry, and our dear friend, Marie Suthers, a great woman in her own right who was appointed to Chicago's Board of Election Commissioners.

There were so many others. I wish there were room here to name them all. They played a very important role in helping my husband win all his campaigns, and for that the "kissing Senator" and I were always grateful.

The Senator's Bar . . .

Everett's doctor had prescribed that he have a drink at the end of the day to relax. He kept a well-stocked bar in an old cabinet in a small room just behind his large office. Friends called it his "medicine cabinet."

The Back Room, as it was always known, became the most popular after-hours meeting spot on Capitol Hill. There are some who would argue that the Back Room was as famous as the senator's passion for marigolds. At least the press did their bit to build it up, as they did the "kissing senator's" image.

Everett had a special talent for getting along with the press, personally, no matter which side of the political fence they were on. He never barred anyone from press conferences and never ignored or evaded newsmen's questions. He answered them frankly and honestly and they respected him for it. (This didn't keep them from criticizing him when they felt so inclined.)

He was usually willing to give them "off the record" material for their own background information, not for publication. But he was very firm about this. When a reporter broke a confidence, he was never told anything off the record again.

A favorite picture with photo editors was the one of Everett in the position he usually assumed at his press conferences, sitting up on a table with his legs crossed under him in lotus-like style, blowing smoke rings and "holding court" with the press.

His newspaper friends, of course, were among his most frequent visitors in the senator's back-room bar. But they were by no means the only important ones.

I remember one occasion especially, after Lyndon Johnson had become President, when I stopped by Everett's office at the end of the day to drive home with him—as I often did when I was in the city. He was in the back office with Senator Mike Mansfield and two or three others, winding up the affairs of the day.

At one point in their discussion, Senator Mansfield decided to telephone the President to clear up a question on a certain piece of legislation. When he finished, Everett took over the phone and casually invited the President to come over and join the group. The rest of the family was away in Texas at the time.

The President accepted Everett's invitation, and shortly thereafter a very famous dog, "Him," entered the back office through the foyer, leading the President by "his" leash.

Glee Gomien and I took over as dog-sitters in the outer office until the back-room summit conference was over.

The Senator's Sui Potpourri . . .

What else can I say about the Senator from Illinois that has not already been said?

—That he always sent me a dozen red roses for Mother's Day, but he sometimes forgot my birthday.

—That he always remembered our anniversary because it was on Christmas Eve.

—That in his enthusiasm for bringing me gifts he sometimes spoiled the "surprise" by giving them to me as soon as he bought them because he couldn't wait for Christmas.

—That he was not superstitious but he collected good luck charms, including a genuine Illinois jack-rabbit's foot which he always carried in his pocket with his loose change.

—That he had a bit of an ego and kept voluminous scrapbooks of all the stories printed about him.

—That in spite of his rumpled look, he liked an uncluttered desk and each book in its proper place in his bookcases. He might forget birthdays but he could quote long passages from many books by memory, including sometimes even the page number.

—That he eschewed the social graces and never really learned to dance, but never outgrew his little clowning habit of kicking off his shoes and twirling about on tiptoe with his finger on his head.

—That he could, as the poet said, "walk with Kings nor lose the common touch."

Yes, my husband was a very special kind of person. I can well understand why it took David Burpee twenty years to develop the Dirksen marigold which he named for my husband. It is a one-of-a-kind marigold, because there will never be another like it. Or him.

And there it is now in our garden, reminding me not with sadness, but with joy that I was able to share his life with him.

EPILOGUE

DANNY BOY

But when ye come,
and all the flow'rs are dying,
If I am dead, as dead I well may be,
Ye'll come and find
the place where I am lying,
And kneel and say an Ave there for me;
And I shall hear,
though soft you tread above me.
And all my grave will warmer, sweeter be,
For you will bend
And tell me that you love me,
And I shall sleep in peace until you come to me!

(Second Verse)

Chapter 22

He Drops the Torch

Except for the handiwork of the Great Designer, nothing in this world is created and nothing is destroyed . . .

The gaily colored leaves fall so gently to earth in this autumn season not to be destroyed but to be embraced by nature for future use. The falling leaves are a reminder that winter will soon be here to embrace the earth in wintry sleep. Comes the inevitable caress of spring, also from the hand of the Great Designer, to bring life and color, fragrance and beauty to the eager earth.

It is the Resurrection of spring. It is an answer to the ageless question of Job, "If a man die, shall he live again?" Surely he shall, as surely as day follows night, as surely as the stars follow their courses, as surely as the crest of every wave brings its trough . . .

These were my husband's words and his beliefs. They are from the text of a eulogy he delivered (October 20, 1965) during a memorial service for Robert Humphreys, a former newspaperman and staff member of the Senate-House Republican Leadership Conference, who died at age of sixty on October 15, 1965.

And here are his words which I wish to preserve from an address he made at a testimonial dinner in his honor, in September of 1961 in his home town of Pekin, Illinois.

After long absences from home enforced by the duties of office in Washington, there always comes back to me some lines from that poem which I learned long ago, 'Breathes there a man with soul so dead, who never to himself has said, this is my own, my native land.' This is my own, my native land, my native city, where the family taproot went deep many generations ago, and it will ever be so, no matter what tasks life may assign to me.

All the major decisions in my life have been made here. The determination to go to college even though I had no funds when high school days were over; the decision to marry, if she would have me, the girl who had been my constant inspiration; my first venture into the field of public service when I became a candidate for the City Council; the decision to run for Congress and find public service at the national level; the decision to run again for Congress despite lack of success in 1930 resolved every doubt as to what course I wanted to pursue in life; the recurring decisions made every two years when I became a candidate for re-election to Congress; the agonizing decision to retire after an eye malady threatened my vision; the decision to seek a seat in the Senate despite the fact that those who counselled this course stated at one and the same time that it would be impossible to win; the decision to seek a second term in the Senate—these, all these decisions were made here in my home town . . .

The inspiration which I received here from a saintly mother, a devoted family, steadfast friends, the constant faith of teachers who taught me, the inspiration I found here in church, and the atmosphere of a quiet and well ordered community were the forces which helped to fashion those decisions, and for these I shall be always and eternally grateful . . .

Those words were spoken on a warm September day in 1961, and eight years later, almost to the day, it was another warm September sun that bathed the countryside when Everett Dirksen's body was given to the good earth near his beloved birthplace in Pekin, Illinois.

When I stepped off the plane which carried Everett's body back to Illinois for burial, after it had lain in state in the

Rotunda of the Capitol Building in Washington, the prairie-
clean clear air with its sweet smell of autumn opened floodgates of
memories.

But the memory of that long, slow procession from the Peoria
Airport to the cemetery on the outskirts of Pekin is one I shall
carry with me all my years.

It was his last trip home. He would have loved it. He would
have been proud of his beloved Land of Lincoln, for never have
I seen a more beautiful and moving tribute to anyone than from
those thousands of people lining the streets and roadsides in
silence and reverence—and proudly holding up American flags as
the body of Everett Dirksen passed by.

I shall never forget it.

There were hundreds of little children who stood beside the
roads and on the streets, and all of them holding in their
hands an American flag. As we passed they would hold their
flags up high in tribute to my husband. And I saw literally
hundreds of fathers and mothers who also held the American
flag. They held it with pride and without embarrassment.

I remember when we passed the Limestone High School in
Pekin. There must have been seven hundred or so students in
the schoolyard, but they were not moving about or talking. They
were standing in a solid line in complete silence, quiet and
reverent as the body of Senator Dirksen passed.

I remember that everywhere I looked the American flag was
raised high—in front of private homes, stores, and business offices.

I know that this was done out of respect for Everett Dirksen
but I also believe that in doing it those thousands of Americans
in the Land of Lincoln were thinking of Everett Dirksen as
the symbol of an America which is still very much alive, a
symbol of what's right with America, a symbol of the values
that many Americans still cherish.

Sometimes a death reminds us that the heartbeat of America
continues to live, and that it is worth fighting for and dying
for.

Sometimes a death reminds us that there are still millions
of people in this country who are good decent citizens and
who believe very much in what Everett Dirksen believed.

Yes, he was taking his last trip home, in the slowly moving big black funeral car ahead of mine, but as I looked out the window upon that sea of solemn faces in the golden sunshine and saw all their American flags fluttering in the breeze, I was comforted.

He had dropped the torch. But it was not extinguished. All these people who loved him and believed in him as I did would carry on his work. He had planted his seeds in the minds of American youth and I knew they would take root and flourish no less than the seeds in his gardens. I knew this when I saw all those children and young people with their American flags raised in tribute to my husband.

He had served his country well.

And I hope I may be forgiven for saying that on a very sad September day in 1969, my home state of Illinois seemed for a little while to be every bit as much the Land of Dirksen as it was the Land of Lincoln.

How do I spend my days without him?

I manage to keep busy. President Nixon has appointed me to his Committee on Aging which is a very interesting project and I enjoy working on it. Also I am on a women's committee for the Plaza beautification of a new 80-story Standard Oil of Indiana building being constructed on the lake front in Chicago. This is a committee of nine women and we are designing an outdoor cafe on the Plaza as well as the interior of the first floor of the building. Lady Bird Johnson and Clare Boothe Luce are also on the committee with me.

I am also on the Board of Directors of the Canaveral Florida Area Heart Association.

Then there is my work on the Board of Directors of the First National Bank in my little adopted home town of DeBary, Florida. I am very proud to have been appointed to the board because I think there are very few women who hold such a position. The president of the bank, Mr. Samuel Faron, is known for being farsighted, and I think he persuaded the Board that it would be a good idea to have a woman's point of view on the kind of services the bank should offer.

When I went to the first board meeting, the president apologized to me quietly outside the office before we went in and told me that the men were accustomed to meeting alone and they might use a little rough language now and then. And of course during the meeting, one of the directors got a little carried away and used a word for which he asked my pardon. So perhaps I am a bit of a handicap to the men where vocabulary is concerned, but otherwise I think we have all enjoyed being together.

I give little speeches here and there, trying to incorporate and carry on my husband's beliefs as much as possible.

My main concern and biggest project, though, is to work toward the completion of the Everett McKinley Dirksen Research Center, which is to be a part of the new Pekin Library. This was another one of Everett's dreams, to have a wing of the Pekin Library devoted to a collection of his works, and not for the mere purpose of perpetuating his ego.

Everett felt that not enough factual material was available for students covering the Roosevelt to Nixon years. In his opinion these were years that completely changed America, years in which some glorious achievements were realized but also years when the people's morale and pride and incentive have been greatly taxed.

My husband received a great many letters from young people who wanted to write themes or college theses on the political affairs of those years from 1930 to 1970 and who complained that they could not find enough source material from which to work.

Some of the most dramatic and drastic changes in our government took place during that period. Everett's collected papers would be invaluable as a study guide for students. They include all the outlines of his speeches and all the scripts for his radio and television programs, as well as the mountains of legislative paperwork that went into his forty years of political life and public service.

I am sure that students would find them both interesting and helpful in understanding the history of their country—as well as understanding Senator Everett Dirksen, the man. He was pre-eminent in his field and a legend in his time. Many looked on him as not only a senator but an institution, and surely the collected works of a man whose political career spanned four decades and six Presidents should be preserved.

Everett felt that his carefully kept papers could make a contribution to future generations. I, along with many devoted friends, am determined to see that this dream is realized. This is my way of carrying on the torch that he dropped, so that others may carry it on for him also.

One special event that would have pleased him so much was a benefit dinner held in Washington in February of 1970 to raise funds for the Dirksen Memorial Library. I was proud that so many people turned out for the affair and so grateful to the celebrities who donated their time to help raise $80,000 for the project. Danny Thomas was the master of ceremonies. Dinah Shore sang and so did Frank Sinatra. I must admit there was a small lump in my throat when Mr. Sinatra sang "Danny Boy" and dedicated it to Everett.

I did not know until my collaborator, Norma Lee Browning, told me that Frank Sinatra, Jr. was a great admirer of the senator and considered him one of the most inspiring of our political leaders for his influence on young people.

President Nixon was not able to attend the benefit dinner but he wrote me the following letter:

THE WHITE HOUSE
Washington

February 26, 1970

Dear Louella:

My very best wishes go to all of those who attend the Everett McKinley Dirksen Memorial Library and Congressional Research Center dinner. It is fitting that a center housing an important part of the story of our time should be named after one who contributed so much to that story. In life, Everett Dirksen was a man of great oratorical eloquence; now, the record of his life and times will speak with a different eloquence to scholars and students from all over the world.

This memorial has my wholehearted support. Senator Dirksen's thirty-five years in Congress—sixteen in the House, nineteen in the Senate—saw tremendous changes in our nation and the world.

*I am gratified to know that future generations will have a chance
to study those changes as they were recorded by Senator Dirksen
and other congressional leaders. His memorable voice is now
stilled, but his great heart will live on through his words and inspire generations to come with the patriotism that was his pride
and his power.*

With warm personal regards,

Sincerely,

Dick (signed)

How do I spend my days?

I water his marigolds and feed his birds and I pick foot-long
cucumbers from his garden.

Each morning I go out and raise the American flag on the
big white flagpole that is planted in the center of the Dirksen
Marigold garden, and each evening I go out and lower it again,
and fold it and bring it into the house.

I have a new companion now, an enormous St. Bernard dog
born on the Fourth of July. So I named her Betsy Ross. Everett
would have liked that. My winter months are spent at our
home "Contentment" in DeBary, which Everett also loved. Betsy
Ross goes along with me and dear friends make it a happy
southern holiday. In early spring Betsy and I come back to
"Heart's Desire" and we revel in the glories of nature, from
the early bulbs through the summer marigold. We can and
freeze fruits and vegetables and have a glorious time.

I still receive a great deal of mail from friends and fans of
Everett's and I try to answer all of it. Today's mail brought
several copies of an interesting letter in the "Voice of the
People" section of the Chicago *Tribune* of Thursday, July 15,
1971, nearly two years after his death.

EV'S MARIGOLDS

PINCKNEYVILLE, ILL.—*I want to make a public, posthumous
apology to the late Sen. Everett M. Dirksen. I used to ridicule
his constant homage to the marigold, and I always wondered
how he could honestly like the stinky, stiff and graceless things.*

That was because I had never met a marigold in person or lived near one.

Now, every time I walk by the marigolds in my garden I ask their forgiveness and Sen. Dirksen's, too. They are the prettiest, perkiest and most colorful flowers in my garden. In addition, they have a nice long flowering season down here in far Southern Illinois and usually last 'til late September.

I laughed when Sen. Dirksen nominated the marigold as our national flower. Now I wish he could be here to lead the campaign and that I could join him in it.

Virginia L. Marmaduke

Everett would have been delighted with that letter. Also it would please him so much to know that they're renaming the road in front of our Heart's Desire, and calling it Marigold Lane.

I look out at the weeping willow trees we planted together on the front lawn of Heart's Desire more than fifteen years ago. They were tiny saplings then. Today they are great round green canopies of soft, sun-dappled beauty. And I remember how sometimes, after we took the flag down, he would just stand there for a few minutes, meditating under the weeping willow trees.

I chase a squirrel away from a bird-feeder on the river side of the house, and my eyes fall on that little gray marker that brings back more memories—of how he often stood there beside it, hands clasped, head bowed in quiet communion with those words:

The kiss of the sun for pardon,
The song of the birds for mirth,
One is nearer God's heart in a garden
Than anywhere else on earth.

My husband did believe that if a man die, he shall live again. He sometimes called it a Divine Plan, sometimes a "living plan." He believed that God never completely destroys a man or a flower or a bird or a tree; that whatever the body might be— the stem of a flower or leaves from a tree or a human being— after death it goes back into the good earth and is absorbed by nature.

How many times I heard him say, "God made this earth out of the firmament and he would not just go off and neglect it. He would want to see that it bloomed and was nurtured. And that's why he sends the sunshine and the rain and why we have a change of seasons. It's all part of a plan, a Divine Plan."

And that is why I cannot look on his death with sadness, for he is still here, all around me.

That is why I can look back on our life together with eloquent satisfaction.

My husband loved life. It seemed to love him also. He was awed by the beauty of the flower and the spoken word. He could cultivate them as no other man could. His flowers continue to grow. His words still echo.